To Val and S,

Great friends.

Laugh Harder;

Love Longer!

1/18

The Almost Wet Your Pants Book of Humor

R. BRUCE BAUM, ED.D., CLL

authorHOUSE®

AuthorHouse™
1663 Liberty Drive, Suite 200
Bloomington, IN 47403
www.authorhouse.com
Phone: 1-800-839-8640

First published by AuthorHouse   3/11/2010

ISBN: 978-1-4389-3973-5 (sc)

Printed in the United States of America
Bloomington, Indiana

This book is printed on acid-free paper.

Contents

DEDICATION

This book is dedicated, in loving memory, to my parents, Elias ('Wick') and Lenora Baum.

IN MEMORY...

This book is also dedicated to the memory of Bob Greene: a respected leader for many years in the Creative Problem Solving Institute, a loving husband and father, a civic leader, a great friend and a very funny guy.

ACKNOWLEDGEMENTS

There are many people who have influenced me prior to preparing the manuscript for this book as well as during the process of writing. First, I want to thank Loretta Francis for her love, patience and understanding. In addition, I wish to express sincere thanks to:

My children Ari and Leah Baum with love, hope and faith in their respective futures.

My former wife Wendy Gabel Baum who remains a consistent source of support.

Domiche Lovings for her acceptance and tolerance.

My brother Howard and his wife Shelly for their efforts to stay connected.

Friends and colleagues who I miss dearly: Mary Murdock, Ruth Noller, Maryanne Pflug, Richard 'Dick' Towne, Jim Kreider, Andy Pacioni and Bob Greene.

Friends and colleagues in the Humor and Health Association (HA HA) of Western New York: Tena Garas, Nels Cremean, Sue Spindler, Paul Chudy, Craig and Dawn Werner, Mary Dahl, and Nancy Burstein

Long-time poker buddies: George Schena, David Pomerantz, David Landrey, Paul Lexner, and Jack Myers.

My friend, colleague and business mentor Bill Grieshober (A.K.A. "The Wizard")

Colleagues in the Exceptional Education Department and at Buffalo State College including Horace ('Hank') Mann, Sarita Samora, Dean Ronald Rochon, Provost Dennis Ponton and President Muriel Howard, Roger Firestien, Gerard Puccio, Jo Yudess, Mike Fox, John Cabra and Cindy Argona.

Friends, colleagues and associates including Linda and Warren Gleckel, Tony and Rachel Lewis, Sir Gerald and Patsy Gorman, Kobus Neethling, and friends in the South African creativity community, John Frederick, John Moffat, Kathleen Thomas, Dimis Michaelides (my magic mentor), Kanes Rajah, Norm Bakos, William Sturner, Eileen Hothow, Suzanne Chamberlain, Christina Coyle, Christina Masucci, Joe Spahn, Joe Miguez Kristen Petersen, Renee Paser-Paul and Marguerite Battaglia.

Fellow members of Buffalo Sunrise Rotary group.

Leaders and members my line dancing classes.

Friends and Colleagues in the Gene Gordon Ring #12 of the International Brotherhood of Magicians.
The many leaders of the Creative Problem Solving Institute, especially Sid and Bea Parnes, Eileen Doyle, Alan Black, Andre DeZanger, Tim Hurson, Bill Olsen, Amy Basic, Rosemary Rein and Dawn DePasquale.

INTRODUCTION

For People Who Do Not Read Introductions

Enjoy the humor!

For People Who Read Introductions

Actually, it's been great fun writing this book, as I had the opportunity to review a lot of humor and select items that I found particularly funny. Some of its old, some new, a lot borrowed… all just for you. The book is arranged in categories, so if you if you are looking for a particular type of humor, you can review the 'Contents' page which might help you locate what you want.

I tried diligently to provide sources of humor whenever I knew them or could identify them. If you know the source of items for which credit is not properly provided, please let me know so I can make changes in any subsequent editions. Contact information is available at the end of the book.

As a humorist, I want to provide additional sources of humor and laughter for those readers who might be interested. Several organizations come to mind, and there are many others you should be able to find as well:

- Association for Applied and Therapeutic Humor - www.aath.org
- World Laughter Tour - www.worldlaughtertour.com
- The Humor Project - www.humorproject.com
- International Society for Humor Studies - http://www.hnu.edu/ishs/
- HumorCreativity.Com - www.humorcreativity.com (our website)
- The Red Hat Society - www.redhatsociety.com

There are also many organizations for clowns, magicians and lay people that relate directly or indirectly to humor. This book also refers frequently to Chris White who directs Top Five and Top Ten Lists on a daily or frequent basis. I have subscribed to the Humor Digest for years and have found it a helpful source of a variety of types of humor (HUMOR@LISTSERV.UGA.EDU).

I am hopeful you will enjoy the book... feedback, both positive and constructive, is always appreciated.

R. Bruce Baum

Aging and the Elderly Humor

WHO DID THE SHOOTING?

An 80 year-old man goes to his doctor for his quarterly check-up. The doctor asks him how he is feeling.

The man says, "Things are great. In fact, I've never felt better. I've got a 20 year-old bride and she's pregnant with my child. What do you think about <u>that</u>?"

The doctor is quiet for a moment, and then says, "I have an older friend, a lot like you. He's an avid hunter. Never misses a season. One day he set off into the woods to pick up some game. He was in a hurry and accidentally picked up his walking cane instead of his gun. As he neared a lake he came across a very large deer standing at the water's edge."

"He realized he'd left his gun at home and so couldn't shoot the magnificent creature," says the doctor, "but out of habit he raised his cane, aimed it at the animal as if it was his favorite hunting rifle and yelled, 'Bang! Bang! Bang!'" Miraculously, three shots rang out and the deer fell over dead. Now, What do you think about that?"

The old guy says, "If you ask me, I'd say somebody else pumped a couple of rounds into that deer."

The doctor says, "My point precisely!"

AGING - SOME THOUGHTS

- I started out with nothing, and I still have most of it.
- My wild oats have turned into prunes and All Bran.
- I finally got my head together; now my body is falling apart.
- Funny, I don't remember being absent minded.
- All reports are in; life is now officially unfair.
- If all is not lost, where is it?
- It is easier to get older than it is to get wiser.
- Some days you're the dog; some days you're the hydrant.
- I wish the buck stopped here; I sure could use a few.
- Kids in the back seat cause accidents.
- Accidents in the back seat cause kids.
- It's hard to make a comeback when you haven't been anywhere.
- Only time the world beats a path to your door is when you're in the bathroom.
- If God wanted me to touch my toes, he would have put them on my knees.
- When I'm finally holding all the cards, why does everyone decide to play chess?
- It's not hard to meet expenses - they're everywhere.
- The only difference between a rut and a grave is the depth.
- These days, I spend a lot of time thinking about the hereafter...I go somewhere to get something and then wonder what I'm here after.
- Unable to remember if I have mailed this to you or not.

THE THREE SISTERS

Three sisters ages 92, 94 and 96 live in a house together. One night the 96 year old draws a bath. She puts her foot in and pauses. She yells to the other sisters, "Was I getting in or out of the bath?" The 94 year old yells back, "I don't know. I'll come up and see." She starts up the stairs and pauses. "Was I going up the stairs or down?" The 92 year old is sitting at the kitchen table having tea listening to her sisters. She shakes her head and says, "I sure hope I never get that forgetful, knocking on wood." She then yells, "I'll come up and help both of you as soon as I see who's at the door."

I CAN HEAR JUST FINE!

Three retirees, each with a hearing loss, were playing golf one fine March day. One remarked to the other, "Windy, isn't it?" "No," the second man replied, "it's Thursday." And the third man chimed in, "So am I. Let's go have a beer."

THE 80 YEAR OLD COUPLE

An 80-year-old couple was having problems remembering things, so they decided to go to their doctor to get checked out to make sure nothing was wrong with them.

When they arrived at the doctor's office they explained to the doctor about the problems they were having with their memory. After checking the couple out, the doctor tells them that they were physically okay but might want to start writing things down and making notes to help them remember things. The couple thanked the doctor and left.

Later that night while watching TV, the old man got up from his chair and his wife asks, "Where are you going?" He replies, "To the kitchen."

She asks, "Will you get me a bowl of ice cream?" He replies, "Sure."

She then asks him, "Don't you think you should write it down so you can remember it?"

He says, "No, I can remember that."

She then says, "Well I also would like some strawberries on top. You had better write that down cause I know you'll forget that."

He says, "I can remember that you want a bowl of ice cream with strawberries."

She replies, "Well I also would like whip cream on top. I know you will forget that so you better write it down."

With irritation in his voice, he says, "I don't need to write that down. I can remember that." He then fumes into the kitchen.

After about 20 minutes he returns from the kitchen and hands her a plate of bacon and eggs.

She stares at the plate for a moment and says, "You forgot my toast."

CREATIVE THINKING IN THE ELDERLY

An elderly man in Alabama had owned a large farm for several years. He had a beautiful large pond at the back of the property next to the road, and he'd fixed it up real nice with picnic tables, horseshoe pits, and he'd planted some nice flowers and fruit trees next to the pond.

One evening the old farmer decided to go down to the pond to look it over, as he hadn't been down there for a while. He grabbed a five-gallon bucket to bring back some fruit.

As he neared the pond, he heard splashing and female voices shouting and laughing with glee. As he came closer he saw that 5 young women had parked their car at the side of the road, climbed the fence and were skinny-dipping in his pond. He made the women aware of his presence and they all went hurriedly splashing to the deep end.

One of the women shouted to him, "We're naked and we're not coming out until you leave!" The old man frowned and yelled back, "I didn't come down here to watch you ladies swim naked or make you get out of the pond."

Holding the bucket up he said, "I'm just here to feed the alligator."

SUPERSEX

A little old lady was running up and down the halls in a nursing home. As she walked, she would flip up the hem of her nightgown and say, "Supersex!" She walked up to an elderly man in a wheelchair. Flipping her gown at him, she said, "Supersex!" He sat silently for a moment or two and finally answered, "I'll take the soup."

GRANDMA'S IDEA

A young man goes to visit his grandparents.

When he arrives he notices his granddad sitting on the porch in a rocking chair, wearing a shirt but nothing from the waist down.

"Grandpa, what are you doing?" he says, "Your thing is just hanging out for everybody to see!"

The old man looks off into the distance without answering.

"Grandpa, why you sitting out here without your drawers?" he asks again.

The old man slowly looks up and says, "Weelll....last week I sat here without no shirt, and I got a stiff neck. This was your grandma's idea."

OLD FRIENDS

Two elderly ladies had been friends for many decades. Over the years, they had shared all kinds of activities and adventures. Lately, their activities had been limited to meeting a few times a week to play cards.

One day, they were playing cards when one looked at the other and said, "Now don't get mad at me. I know we've been friends for a long time, but I just can't think of your name! I've thought and thought, but I can't remember it. Please tell me what your name is." Her friend glared at her. For at least three minutes she just stared and glared at her. Finally she said, "How soon do you need to know?"

WHAT IS A GRANDMOTHER?
(RECEIVED THROUGH TOPFIVE © CHRIS WHITE)

Written by 3rd graders at, St. Andrews School, Wash, D.C.:

A grandmother is a lady who has no little children of her own. She likes other people's.

A grandfather is a man grandmother.

Grandmothers don't have to do anything except be there.

They are old, so they shouldn't play hard or run.

It is enough if they drive us to the market and have lots of dimes ready.

When they take us for walks, they slow down past things like pretty leaves and caterpillars.

They never say "hurry up."

Usually grandmothers are fat, but not too fat to tie your shoes, they wear glasses and funny underwear.

They can take their teeth out.

Grandmothers don't have to be smart, they only have to answer questions like, "Why isn't God married?" and "How come dogs chase cats?"

When they read to us, they don't skip lines or mind if we ask for the same story over again.

Everybody should try to have a grandmother, especially if you don't have a TV, because they are the only grown-ups who have time.

SENIOR DRIVING

As a senior citizen was driving down the freeway, his cell phone rang. Answering, he heard his wife's voice urgently warning him, "Herman, I just heard on the news that there's a car going the wrong way on Interstate 77. Please be careful!"

"Hell," said Herman, "It's not just one car. There's hundreds of them!"

WHO'S DRIVING?

Two elderly women were out driving in a large car, both could barely see over the dashboard. As they were cruising along, they came to an intersection. The stoplight was red, but they just went on through. The woman in the passenger seat thought to herself "I must be losing it. I could have sworn we just went through a red light." After a few more minutes, they came to another intersection and the light was red again. Again, they went right through. The woman in the passenger seat was almost sure that the light had been red but was really concerned that she was losing it. She was getting nervous. At the next intersection, sure enough, the light was red and they went on through.

So, she turned to the other woman and said, "Mildred, do you know that we just ran through three red lights in a row? You could have killed us both!" Mildred turned to her and said, "Crap, am I driving?"

MYSTERY THIEF!

An elderly Floridian called 911 on her cell phone to report that someone had broken into her car.. She was hysterical as she explained her situation to the dispatcher: "They've stolen the stereo, the steering wheel, the brake pedal and even the accelerator!" she cried. The dispatcher said, "Stay calm. An officer is on the way."

A few minutes later, the officer radios in. "Disregard.", He says. "She got in the back-seat by mistake."

WEDDING PREPARATIONS

Gene, age 89, and Lillian, age 78, are all excited about their decision to get married. They go for a stroll to discuss the wedding and on the way they pass a large and busy drugstore. Gene suggests they go in.

Gene addresses the man behind the counter: "Are you the owner?" The pharmacist answers, "Yes."

Gene: "We're about to get married. Do you sell heart medication?"

Pharmacist: "Of course we do."

Gene: "How about medicine for circulation?"

Pharmacist: "All kinds."

Gene: "Medicine for rheumatism?"

Pharmacist: "Definitely."

Gene: "How about Viagra?"

Pharmacist: "Of course."

Gene: "Medicine for memory problems, arthritis, jaundice?"

Pharmacist: "Yes, a large variety. The works."

Gene: "What about vitamins, sleeping pills, Geritol, antidotes for Parkinson's disease?"

Pharmacist: "Absolutely."

Gene: "You sell wheelchairs and walkers?"

Pharmacist: "All speeds and sizes."

Gene: "We'd like to register here for our wedding gifts, please."

OLD IS WHEN...

"OLD" IS WHEN:

...Your sweetie says, "Let's go upstairs and make love, "and you answer, "Pick one, I can't do both!"

...Your friends compliment you on your new alligator shoes and you're barefoot.

...Going bra-less pulls all the wrinkles out of your face.

...You don't care where your spouse goes, just as long as you don't have to go along.

..."Getting a little action" means I don't need to take any fiber today.

..."Getting lucky" means you find your car in the parking lot.

...An "all-nighter" means not getting up to pee.

RETIREMENT AT WAL-MART
(SHARED BY ELISE LAMBERT)

After I retired, my wife insisted that I accompany her on her trips to Wal-Mart. Unfortunately, like most men, I found shopping boring and preferred to get in and get out. Equally unfortunately, my wife is like most women - she loved to browse. Yesterday my dear wife received the following letter from the local Wal-Mart.

Dear Mrs. Samsel,

Over the past six months, your husband has been causing quite a commotion in our store. We cannot tolerate this behavior and have been forced to ban both of you from the store. Our complaints against Mr. Samsel are listed below and are documented by our video surveillance cameras.

June 15: Took 24 boxes of condoms and randomly put them in people's carts when they weren't looking.

July 2: Set all the alarm clocks in Housewares to go off at 5-minute intervals.

July 7: Made a trail of tomato juice on the floor leading to the women's restroom.

July 19: Walked up to an employee and told her in an official voice, 'Code 3 in Housewares. Get on it right away.'

August 4: Went to the Service Desk and tried to put a bag of M&M's on layaway.

August 14: Moved a 'CAUTION - WET FLOOR' sign to a carpeted area.

August 15: Set up a tent in the camping department and told other shoppers he'd invite them in if they would bring pillows and blankets from the bedding department.

August 23: When a clerk asked if they could help him he began crying and screamed, 'Why can't you people just leave me alone?'

September 4: Looked right into the security camera and used it as a mirror while he picked his nose.

September 10: While handling guns in the hunting department, he asked the clerk where the antidepressants were.

October 3: Darted around the store suspiciously while loudly humming the ' Mission Impossible' theme.

October 6: In the auto department, he practiced his 'Madonna look' by using different sizes of funnels.

October 18: Hid in a clothing rack and when people browsed through, yelled 'Pick Me! Pick Me!'

October 21: When an announcement came over the loud speaker, he assumed a fetal position and screamed 'Oh no! It's those voices again!'

October 23: Went into a fitting room, shut the door, waited awhile, and then yelled very loudly, 'Hey! There's no toilet paper in here!'

SENILITY

An elderly man went to his doctor and said "Doc, I think I'm getting senile. Several times lately, I have forgotten to zip up."

"That's not senility," replied the doctor. "Senility is when you forget to zip down."

HE COULD FLY

One night, an 87-year-old woman came home from bingo to find her 92-year-old husband in bed with another woman. She became violent and ended up pushing him off the balcony of their 20th floor apartment, killing him instantly.

Brought before the court, on the charge of murder, she was asked if she had anything to say in her own defense.

"Your Honor," she began coolly, "I figured that at 92, if he could make love, he could fly."

DRIED ARRANGEMENT

Two old men were sitting on a park bench outside the local town hall where a flower show was in progress. One leaned over the other and said, "Cripes! Life is boring. We never have any fun these days. For two bucks, I'd take my clothes off and streak through the flower show!"

You're on!" said the other old fellow, holding up two dollars. As fast as he could, the first old man fumbled his way out of his clothes and completely naked, streaked through the front door of the town hall.

Waiting outside, his friend heard a huge commotion inside the hall, followed by loud applause. The naked old man burst out through the door and cheering could be heard in the background..

"How did it go?" asked his friend.

"Great!" he said, "I won first prize for a dried arrangement."

STAMINA SECRET

Two old guys, one 80 and one 87, were sitting on their usual park bench one morning.

The 87 year old had just finished his morning jog and wasn't even short of breath.

The 80 year old was amazed at his friend's stamina and asked him what he did to have so much energy

The 87 year old said 'Well, I eat Jewish rye bread every day. It keeps your energy level high and you'll have great stamina with the ladies.'

So, on the way home, the 80 year old stops at the bakery. As he was looking around, the lady asked if he needed any help. He said, 'Do you have any Jewish rye bread?'

She said, 'Yes, there's a whole shelf of it. Would you like some?'

He said, 'I want 5 loaves.

She said, 'My goodness, 5 loaves...by the time you get to the 5th loaf, it'll be hard'

He replied, 'I can't believe it! Everybody in the world knows about this stuff but me!'

IMPORTANT QUESTION

How old would you be if you didn't know how old you were?

MOE AND SAM

Two ninety year old men, Moe and Sam, have been friends all their lives. It turns out that Sam is dying, so Moe comes to visit him.

"Sam," says Moe, "You know how we have both loved baseball all our lives. Sam, you have to do me one favor. When you go, somehow you have to let me know if there's baseball in Heaven."

Sam looks up at Moe from his deathbed and says, "Moe, you've been my friend many years. This favor I'll do for you." And with that, Sam passes on.

It is midnight a couple nights later. Moe is sound asleep when a distant voice calls out to him, "Moe....Moe...." "Who is it?" says Moe sitting up suddenly. "Who is it?"

"Moe, it's Sam."

Come on. You're not Sam. Sam died."

"I'm telling you," insists the voice. "It's me, Sam!"

"Sam? Is that you? Where are you?"

"I'm in Heaven," says Sam, "and I've got to tell you, I've got some good news and some bad news."

"Tell me the good news first," says Moe.

"The good news," says Sam "is that there **is** baseball in Heaven."

"Really?" says Moe, "That's wonderful! What's the bad news?"

"You're pitching Tuesday!

LOOKING FOR WIVES

Two old guys are pushing their carts around Wal-Mart when they collide. The first old guy says to the second guy, "Sorry about that I'm looking for my wife, and I guess I wasn't paying attention to where I was going."

The second old guy says, "That's OK. It's a coincidence. I'm looking for my wife, too. I can't find her and I'm getting a little desperate."

What does she look like?"

The second old guy says: "Well, she is 27 years old, tall, with red hair, blue eyes, long legs, big bust, and is wearing short shorts. What does your wife look like?"

To which the first old guy says, "It doesn't really matter, let's look for your wife."

RETIREMENT: FREQUENTLY ASKED QUESTIONS

Question: When is a retiree's bedtime?
Answer: Three hours after he falls asleep on the couch.

Question: How many retirees does it take to change a light bulb?
Answer: Only one, but it might take all day.

Question: What's the biggest gripe of retirees?
Answer: There is not enough time to get everything done.

Question: What is the common term for someone who enjoys work and refuses to retire?
Answer: NUTS!

Question: Why does a retiree often say he doesn't miss work, but misses the people he used to work with?
Answer: He is too polite to tell the whole truth

Question: How many days in a week?
Answer: 6 Saturdays, 1 Sunday.

Question: Why don't retirees mind being called seniors?

Answer: The term comes with a 10% percent discount.

Question: Among retirees what is considered formal attire?
Answer: Tied shoes.

Question: Why do retirees count pennies?
Answer: They are the only ones who have the time.

Question: Why are retirees so slow to clean out the basement, attic or garage?
Answer: They know that as soon as they do, one of their adult kids will want to store stuff there.

Question: What do retirees call a long lunch?
Answer: Normal.

Question: What is the best way to describe retirement?
Answer: The never ending Coffee Break.

Question: What's the biggest advantage of going back to school as a retiree?
Answer: If you cut classes, no one calls your parents.

Question: What do you do all week?
Answer: Monday to Friday nothing, Saturday and Sunday I rest.

IT'S A CRIME

The eighty-nine year old man was caught trying to molest a forty-five year old woman. He was charged with 'assault with a dead weapon.'

GUESSING GAME

A little old lady in a nursing home raises her fist and says, "Whoever can guess what's in my hand can have sex with me tonight."
A little old man in the back of the room yells, "An elephant."
She says, "Close enough."

HARD OF HEARING

An elderly gentleman of 85 feared his wife was getting hard of hearing. So one day he called her doctor to make an appointment to have her hearing checked.

The Doctor made an appointment for a hearing test in two weeks, and told the man there was a simple informal test he could do in the meanwhile to give him some idea of the state of her problem.

'Here's what you do,' said the doctor, "start out about 40 feet away from her, and speak in a normal conversational speaking tone to see if she hears you. If not, go to 30 feet, then 20 feet, and so on until you get a response."

That evening, the wife is in the kitchen cooking dinner, and he's in the living room. He says to himself, "I'm about 40 feet away, let's see what happens."

Then in a normal tone he asks, 'Honey, what's for supper?" No response.

So the husband moved to the other end of the room, about 30 feet from his wife and repeats, "Honey, what's for supper?" Still no response.

Next he moves into the dining room where he is about 20 feet from his wife and asks, "Honey, what's for supper?"

Again he gets no response so he walks up to the kitchen door, only 10 feet away. "Honey, what's for supper?"

Again there is no response, so he walks right up behind her. "Honey, what's for supper?"

"Damn it, Earl, for the fifth time, CHICKEN!"

GRANDMA'S OFF HER ROCKER

In the dim and distant past
When life's tempo wasn't so fast,
Grandma used to rock and knit,
Crochet, cook and baby sit.
When the kids were in a jam,
They could always call on Gram.
But today she's in the gym

Exercising to keep slim.
She's checking the web or surfing the net,
Sending some e-mail or placing a bet.
Nothing seems to stop or block her,
Now that Grandma's off her rocker.

SENILITY

The nice thing about being senile is you can hide your own Easter eggs.

GRANDPARENT ANECDOTES

She was in the bathroom, putting on her makeup, under the watchful eyes of her young granddaughter as she'd done many times before.

After she applied her lipstick and started to leave, the little one said,

'But Gramma, you forgot to kiss the toilet paper good-bye!'

My granddaughter's Grade 2 class was asked to write about their personal heroes. Her father was extremely flattered to find out that she had chosen him.

"Why did you pick me?" he asked her.

"Because I couldn't spell Arnold Schwarzenegger," she replied.

My young grandson called the other day to wish me Happy Birthday.

He asked me how old I was, and I told him, '62.'

He was quiet for a moment, and then he asked, 'Did you start at 1?'

After putting her grandchildren to bed, a grandmother changed into old slacks and a droopy blouse and proceeded to wash her hair.

As she heard the children getting more and more rambunctious, her patience grew thin.

Finally, she threw a towel around her head and stormed into their room, putting them back to bed with stern warnings.

As she left the room, she heard the three-year-old say with a trembling voice, **'Who was that!?'**

A grandmother was telling her little granddaughter what her own childhood was like:

'We used to skate outside on a pond. I had a swing made from a tire; it hung from a tree in our front yard. We rode our pony. We picked wild raspberries in the woods.'

The little girl was wide-eyed, taking this all in.

At last she said, 'I sure wish I'd gotten to know you sooner!'

My grandson was visiting one day when he asked, 'Grandma, do you know how you and God are alike?'

I mentally polished my halo while I asked, 'No, how is we alike?'

'You're both old,' he replied.

A little girl was diligently pounding away on her grandfather's word processor.

She told him she was writing a story. 'What's it about?' he asked

'I don't know,' she replied. 'I can't read.'

I didn't know if my granddaughter had learned her colors yet, so I decided to test her.

I would point out something and ask what color it was.

She would tell me and was always correct. It was fun for me, so I continued.

At last she headed for the door, saying sagely,

'Grandma, I think you should try to figure out some of these yourself!'

When my grandson Billy and I entered our vacation cabin, we kept the lights off until we were inside to keep from attracting pesky insects.

Still, a few fireflies followed us in. Noticing them before I did, Billy whispered,

'It's no use, Grandpa. The mosquitoes are coming after us with flashlights.'

When my grandson asked me how old I was, I teasingly replied, 'I'm not sure.'

'Look in your underwear, Grandpa,' he advised. 'Mine says I'm four to six.'

A second grader came home from school and said to her grandmother,

'Grandma, guess what? We learned how to make babies today.'

The grandmother, more than a little surprised, tried to keep her cool.

'That's interesting,' she said, 'how do you make babies?'

'It's simple,' replied the girl. 'You just change 'y' to 'i' and add 'es'.'

THE FLORIDA ADVANTAGE

I've had two bypass surgeries, a hip replacement and new knees. I've fought prostate cancer and diabetes. I'm half blind, can't hear anything quieter than a jet engine, take 40 different medications that make me dizzy, winded, and subject to blackouts. I have bouts with dementia. I have poor circulation; hardly feel my hands and feet anymore. I can't remember if I'm 85 or 92. I have lost all my friends. But thank God, I still have my Florida driver's license.

TOP TEN PARTY GAMES FOR SENIORS

10. Sag! You're it!

9. Pin the toupee on the bald guy.

8. 20 questions shouted in your good ear.

7. Kick the bucket.

6. Red rover red rover, the nurse says bend over.

5. Doc doc goose.

4. Simon says something incoherent.

3. Musical recliners.

2. Spin the bottle of Mylanta.

1. Hide and go pee.

REMEMBER WHEN

Then: Killer Weed
Now: Weed Killer

Then: Hoping for a BMW
Now: Hoping for a BM

Then: Getting out to a new, hip joint
Now: Getting a new hip joint

Then: Getting your head stoned
Now: Getting your headstone

Then: Long hair
Now: Longing for hair

Then: Acid rock
Now: Acid reflux

Then: Worrying about no one coming to your party
Now: Worrying about no one coming to your funeral

Then: The perfect high
Now: The perfect high-yield mutual fund

Then: Elvis in the army
Now: Elvis in a UFO

Then: KEG
Now: EKG

Then: You're growing pot
Now: Your growing pot

Then: Whatever...
Now: Depends

THE WEDDING NIGHT

At 85 years of age, Morris marries LouAnne, a lovely 25-year-old. Because her new husband is so old, LouAnne decides that on their wedding night, she and Morris are to have separate bedrooms. The newlywed is concerned that her new husband may overexert himself if they spend the entire night together. After the wedding festivities, LouAnne prepares herself for bed, and for the expected "knock" on the door. Sure enough, the knock comes, the door opens, and there is her 85-year-old groom, ready for action. They unite as one. All goes well, whereupon Morris takes leave of LouAnne, and she prepares to go to sleep.

After a few minutes, LouAnne hears another knock on her bedroom door. It's Morris! And he's again ready for more action. Somewhat surprised, LouAnne consents to further coupling. When the newlyweds are done, Morris kisses LouAnne, bids her a fond goodnight, and leaves.

LouAnne is set to go to sleep again. However, after a few short minutes, there is another knock at her door, and there he is again... Morris, as fresh as a 25-year-old and ready for a bit more action. And again they enjoy one another. As Morris is once again set to leave, the young bride says to him, "I am thoroughly impressed that at your age, honey, you can perform as you have. I've been with guys less than a third your age who were only good once! You're a great lover, Morris."

Morris, somewhat embarrassed, turns to LouAnne and says, "You mean I was here already?"

IN CHURCH

An elderly couple was attending church services, about halfway through the wife leans over and says to her husband, "I just passed some gas, but luckily it was silent. What do you think I should do?"

He replies "Put a new battery in your hearing aid."

SUPER GRANNY - A TRUE STORY

An elderly Florida lady did her shopping, and upon returning to her car, found four males in the act of leaving with her vehicle. She dropped her shopping bags and drew her handgun, proceeding to scream at the top of her voice, "I have a gun, and I know how to use it! Get out of the car!" The four men didn't wait for a second invitation. They got out and ran like mad. The lady, somewhat shaken, then proceeded to load her shopping bags into the back of the car and get into the driver's seat. She was so shaken that she could not get her key into the ignition. She tried and tried, and then it dawned on her why.

A few minutes later she found her own car parked four or five spaces farther down! She loaded her bags into the car and then drove to the police station. The sergeant to whom she told the story nearly tore himself in two with laughter. He pointed to the other end of the counter, where four pale men were reporting a car jacking by a mad, elderly woman described as white, less than five feet tall, glasses, curly white hair and carrying a large handgun.

No charges were filed.

STAYING IN SHAPE

For those people getting along in years, here is a little secret for building your arm and shoulder muscles. You might want to adopt this three days a week.

Begin by standing straight, with a 5-pound potato sack in each hand. Extend your arms straight out from your sides and hold them there as long as you can. Try to reach a full minute.

Relax.

After a few weeks, move up to 10-pound potato sacks, and then 50-pound potato sacks, and eventually try to get to where you can lift a 100-pound potato sack in each hand and hold your arms straight out for more than a full minute.

After you feel confident at that level, start putting one or two potatoes in the sacks.

SONGS FOR SENIORS

Herman's Hermits--"Mrs. Brown You've Got a Lovely Walker"
The Rolling Stones--"You Can't Always Pee When You Want"
Paul Simon--"Fifty Ways to Lose Your Liver"
Carly Simon--"You're So Varicose Vein"
The Bee Gees--"How Can You Mend a Broken Hip?"
Roberta Flack--"The First Time Ever I Forgot Your Face"
The Temptations--"Papa's Got a Kidney Stone"
Nancy Sinatra--"These Boots Are Made To Give Me Arthritis"
ABBA--"Denture Queen"
Leo Sayer--"You Make Me Feel Like Napping"
Commodores--"Once, Twice, Three Trips to the Bathroom"
Procol Harem--"A Whiter Shade of Hair"
The Beatles--"I Get By with a Little Help From Depends"
Credence Clearwater Revival--"Bad Prune a-Rising"
Marvin Gaye--"I Heard It Through the Grape Nuts"
The Who--"Talkin' 'Bout My Medication"

NEW HEARING AID

A man was telling his neighbor, "I just bought a new hearing aid. It cost me four thousand dollars, but its state of the art. It's perfect."

"Really," answered the neighbor. "What kind is it?"

"Twelve thirty."

DOING WHAT THE DOCTOR SAID

Morris, an 82 year-old man, went to the doctor to get a physical.

A few days later the doctor saw Morris walking down the street with an attractive woman on his arm.

A couple of days later the doctor spoke to Morris and said, "You're really doing great, aren't you?"

Morris replied, "Just doing what you said, Doc: 'Get a hot mamma and be cheerful.' "

The doctor said, "I didn't say that. I said, 'You've got a heart murmur. Be careful.'"

THE LOVING HUSBAND

An elderly gent was invited to his old friends' home for dinner one evening. He was impressed by the way his buddy preceded every request to his wife with endearing terms-Honey, My Love, Darling, Sweetheart, Pumpkin, etc... The couple had been married almost 60 years, and clearly they were still very much in love. While the wife was in the kitchen, the man leaned over and said to his host, "I think it's wonderful that, after all these years, you still call your wife those loving pet names."

The old man hung his head. "I have to tell you the truth," he said, "About two years ago I forgot her name."

THE NURSING HOME

One evening a family brings their frail, elderly mother to a nursing home and leaves her, hoping she will be well cared for. The next morning, the nurses bathed her, fed her a tasty breakfast, and set her in a chair at a window overlooking a lovely flower garden. She seemed OK, but after a while she slowly started to lean over sideways in her chair. Two attentive nurses immediately rushed up to catch her and straightened her up.

Again she seemed OK, but after a while she started to tilt to the other side. The nurses rushed back and once more brought her back upright. This went on several times during the morning. Later the family arrived to see how the old woman is adjusting to her new home.

"So Ma how is it here? Are they treating you all right?" they ask.

"It's pretty nice." she replies. "Except they won't let you fart."

SENIOR BLESSINGS

A group of seniors were sitting around talking about all their ailments. "My arms have gotten so weak I can hardly lift this cup of coffee," said one. "Yes, I know," said another. "My cataracts are so bad; I can't even see my coffee."

"I couldn't even mark an "X" at election time, my hands are so crippled," volunteered a third.

"What? Speak up! What? I can't hear you!"

"I can't turn my head because of the arthritis in my neck," said a fourth, to which several nodded weakly in agreement.

"My blood pressure pills make me so dizzy!" exclaimed another.

"I forget where I am, and where I'm going," said another.

"I guess that's the price we pay for getting old," winced an old man as he slowly shook his head.

The others nodded in agreement.

"Well, count your Blessings," said a woman cheerfully "and thank God we can all still drive"

A QUESTION OF MEDICATION

A distraught senior citizen phoned her doctor's office. "Is it true," she wanted to know, "that the medication you prescribed has to be taken for the rest of my life?" "Yes, I'm afraid so," the doctor told her.

There was a moment of silence before the senior lady replied, "I'm wondering, then, just how serious is my condition because this prescription is marked 'NO REFILLS'."

HIGH SCHOOL REUNION

A friend recently went to her high school reunion and said that her former classmates became so overweight, gray and wrinkled that they could hardly recognize her.

THE SPERM BANK

The 87 year old man goes to the Sperm Bank to donate. As he is completing the paperwork, the nurse says, "It is rare that we get a man of your age donating here at the Sperm Bank." He says, "It is something I always wanted to do, and thank you for accepting my application." She gives him a jar and asks him to go to the restroom down the hall. She gets busy and then remembers the elderly gentleman. She knocks on the restroom door and he says she can open the door. He says, "First I tried the left hand, and that didn't do anything. Then I tried the right hand and that didn't help. Then I ran it under cold water with no effect and then under hot water with the same result. Now I was just banging it against the sink here, and you know I still can't get this cap off this jar."

A WELL-PLANNED LIFE

Two women met for the first time since graduating from high school. One asked the other, "You were always so organized in school, did you manage to live a well planned life?" "Yes," said her friend. "My first marriage was to a millionaire; my second marriage was to an actor; my third marriage was to a preacher; and now I'm married to an undertaker."

Her friend asked, "What do those marriages have to do with a well planned life?"

She replied, "One for the money, two for the show, three to get ready, and four to go."

THE ELDERLY COUPLE

An eighty-three year old woman finished her annual physical examination, whereupon her doctor said, "You are in fine shape for your age, but tell me, do you still have intercourse?"

"Just a minute; I'll have to ask my husband," she said.

She went out to the reception room and said, "Morris, do we still have intercourse?"

Morris answered impatiently, "If I told you once, I told you a thousand times. We have Blue Cross."

THE WORST AGE (shared by Tony Lewis)

Sixty is the worst age to be," said the 60-year-old man. "You always feel like you have to pee and most of the time you stand there and nothing comes out."

"Ah, that's nothing," said the 70-year-old. "When you're seventy, you don't have a bowel movement any more. You take laxatives, eat bran, sit on the toilet all day and nothing' comes out!"

"Actually," said the 80-year -old, "Eighty is the worst age of all."

"Do you have trouble peeing, too?" asked the 60-year old.

"No, I pee every morning at 6:00. I pee like a racehorse on a flat rock; no problem at all."

"So, do you have a problem with your bowel movements?"

"No, I have one every morning at 6:30."

Exasperated, the 60-year-old said, "You pee every morning at 6:00 and crap every morning at 6:30. So what's so bad about being 80?"

"I don't wake up until 7:00."

EULOGIES

After dying in a car crash, three friends go to Heaven for orientation. They are all asked the same question: "When you are in your casket, and friends and family are mourning over you, what would you like to hear them say about you?"

The first guy immediately responds, "I would like to hear them say that I was one of the great doctors of my time, and a great family man."

The second guy says, "I would like to hear that I was a wonderful husband and school teacher who made a huge difference in the lives of our children of tomorrow."

The last guy thinks a minute and replies, "I'd like to hear them say... LOOK, HE'S MOVING!!!"

LOWER SEX DRIVE

A 97 year old man goes into his doctor's office and says, "Doc, I want my sex drive lowered." "Sir", replied the doctor, "You're 97. Don't you think your sex drive is all in your head?" "You're damned right it is!" replied the old man. "That's why I want it lowered!"

SENIOR PRAYER

God, grant me the senility
To forget the people
I never liked anyway,
The good fortune
To run into the ones I do,
And the eyesight to tell the difference.

BABY BOOMER TRIVIA QUIZ

1. "Hey kids, what time is it?" _____ _____ _____ ___
2. What do M&M's do? _____ ___ _____ _____, _____ ___ ___
3. What helps build strong bodies 12 ways? _____ _____
   _.
4. Long before he was Mohammed Ali, we knew him as ___ _____
   _
5. "Brylcream: ___ _____ _____ _____ _____ _____"
6. Bob Dylan advised us never to trust anyone _____ ____.
7. From early rock 'n roll, finish this line: "Oh, I wonder, wonder, wonder, wonder who; _____ _____ ____ _____ ___ _____?"
8. Meanwhile, back home in Metropolis, Superman fights a never-ending battle for truth, justice, and _____ _____ _____.
9. "I found my thrill, _____ _____ _____."
10. "Good night, David." "_____ _____,_____."

BABY BOOMER TRIVIA QUIZ - ANSWERS

1. "It's Howdy Doody Time!"
2. "Melt in your mouth, not in your hand."
3. Wonder Breakd
4. Casius Clay
5. "A little dab will do you."
6. Over 30.
7. "Who wrote the book of love."
8. "the American Way."
9. "On Blueberry Hill."
10. "Good night, Chet."

Animal Humor

LITTLE NANCY

Little Nancy was in the garden filling a hole when her neighbor peered over the fence. Interested in what the cheeky-faced youngster was up to, he politely asked, "What are you up to there, Nancy?" "My goldfish died," replied Nancy tearfully without looking up, "and I've just buried him." The neighbor was concerned. "That's an awfully big hole for a goldfish, isn't it?" Nancy patted down the last heap of earth then replied, "That's because he's inside your damn cat."

TOP TEN REASONS WHY DOGS ARE BETTER PETS THAN CATS (© CHRIS WHITE)

1. Dogs will tilt their heads and try to understand every word you say. Cats will ignore you and take a nap.
2. Cats look silly on a leash.
3. When you come home from work, your dog will be happy and lick your face. Cats will still be mad at you for leaving in the first place.

4. Dogs will give you unconditional love until the day they die. Cats will make you pay for every mistake you've ever made since the day you were born.

5. A dog knows when you're sad, and he will try to comfort you. Cats don't care how you feel, as long as you remember where the can opener is.

6. Dogs will bring you your slippers. Cats will drop a dead mouse in your slippers.

7. When you take them for a ride, dogs will sit on the seat next to you. Cats have to have their own private basket, or they won't go at all.

8. Dogs will come when you call them, and they will be happy. Cats will have someone take a message and get back to you.

9. Dogs will play fetch with you all day long. The only things cats will play with all day long are small rodents or bugs, preferably ones that look like they're in pain.

10. Dogs will wake you up if the house is on fire. Cats will quietly sneak out the back door.

BUDDY

An out-of-towner drove his car into a ditch in a desolated area. Luckily, a local farmer came to help with his big strong horse named Buddy. He hitched Buddy up to the car and yelled, "Pull, Nellie, pull!"

Buddy didn't move. Then the farmer hollered, "Pull, Buster, pull!" Buddy didn't respond.

Once more the farmer commanded, "Pull, Coco, pull!" Nothing happened. Then the farmer nonchalantly said, "Pull, Buddy, pull!" And the horse easily dragged the car out of the ditch. The motorist was most appreciative and very curious. He asked the farmer why he called his horse by the wrong name three times. The farmer said, "Oh, Buddy is blind and if he thought he was the only one pulling, he wouldn't even try!"

HOW TO BATHE THE CAT

1. Thoroughly clean toilet.
2. Lift both lids and add shampoo.

3. Find and soothe cat as you carry him to bathroom.
4. In one swift move, place cat in toilet, close both lids, and stand on top...so cat cannot escape.
5. The cat will self agitate and produce ample suds. (Ignore ruckus from inside toilet, cat is enjoying this).
6. Flush toilet 3 or 4 times. This provides power rinse, which is quite effective. Cat is too big to go anywhere.
7. Have someone open outside door, stand as far from toilet as possible, and quickly lift both lids.
8. Clean cat will rocket out of the toilet and outdoors, where he will air dry. Cat will return when hungry.

Sincerely,
The Dog

THE HAMSTER EMERGENCY

If you have raised kids (or been one), and gone through the pet syndrome including toilet-flush burials for dead goldfish, the story below will have great meaning for you.

Overview: I had to take my son's hamster to the vet. Here's what happened:

Just after dinner one night, my son came up to tell me there was "something wrong" with one of the two hamsters he holds prisoner in his room. "He's just lying there looking sick," he told me. "I'm serious, Dad. Can you help?"

I put my best hamster-healer statement on my face and followed him into his bedroom. One of the little rodents was indeed lying on his back, looking stressed. I immediately knew what to do. "Honey," I called, "come look at the hamster!"

Oh, my gosh," my wife diagnosed after a minute. "She's having babies."

"What?" my son demanded. "But their names are Bert and Ernie, Mom!" I was equally outraged. "Hey, how can that be? I thought we said we didn't want them to reproduce" I accused my wife. "Well, what do you want me to do, post a sign in their cage?" she inquired. (I actually think she said this sarcastically!) "No, but you were supposed to get two boys!" I reminded her, (in my most loving, calm, sweet voice, while gritting my teeth together). "Yeah, Bert and Ernie!" my son agreed.

Well, it's just a little hard to tell on some guys, ya know," she informed me. (Again with the sarcasm, ya think?) By now the rest of the family had gathered to see what was going on. I shrugged, deciding to make the best of it. "Kids, this is going to be a wondrous experience, I announced. "We're about to witness the miracle of birth." "Oh, Gross!", they shrieked. "Well, isn't that just great!; what are we going to do with a litter of tiny little hamster babies?" my wife wanted to know. (I really do think she was being snotty here, too, don't you?)

We peered at the patient. After much struggling, what looked like a tiny foot would appear briefly, vanishing a scant second later. "We don't appear to be making much progress," I noted. Its breech," my wife whispered, horrified. "Do something, Dad!" my son urged.

"Okay, okay." Squeamishly, I reached in and grabbed the foot when it next appeared, giving it a gingerly tug. It disappeared. I tried several more times with the same results. Should I call 911?" my eldest daughter wanted to know. "Maybe they could talk us through the trauma." (You see a pattern here with the females in my house?)

"Let's get Ernie to the vet," I said grimly. We drove to the vet with my son holding the cage in his lap. Breathe, Ernie, breathe," he urged

"I don't think hamsters do Lamaze," his mother noted to him. (Women can be so cruel to their own young. I mean what she does to me is one thing, but this boy is of her womb, for God's sake.)

The vet took Ernie back to the examining room and peered at the little animal through a magnifying glass. "What do you think, Doc, a c-section?" I suggested scientifically. "Oh, very interesting," he murmured. "Mr. and Mrs. Cameron, may I speak to you privately for a moment?" I gulped, nodding for my son to step outside.

"Is Ernie going to be okay?" my wife asked. "Oh, perfectly," the vet assured us. "This hamster is not in labor. In fact, that isn't ever going to happen...Ernie is a boy." "What!?"

"You see, Ernie is a young male. And occasionally, as they come into maturity, like most male species, they um.... er.... masturbate. Just the way he did, lying on his back." He blushed, glancing at my wife. "Well, you know what I'm saying, Mr. Cameron." We were silent, absorbing this. "So Ernie's just...just...Excited?" my wife offered. "Exactly," the vet replied, relieved that we understood.

More silence.

Then my vicious, cruel wife started to giggle. And giggle. And then even laugh loudly. "What's so funny?" I demanded, knowing, but not believing that the woman I married would commit the upcoming affront to my flawless manliness. Tears were now running down her face. "It's just...that...I'm picturing you pulling on its...its...teeny little...." she gasped for more air to bellow in laughter once more. "That's enough," I warned.

We thanked the Veterinarian and hurriedly bundled the hamster and our son back into the car. He was glad everything was going to be okay. "I know Ernie's really thankful for what you've done, Dad," he told me.

"Oh, you have NO idea," my wife agreed, collapsing with laughter.

2 - Hamsters - 10 bucks...

1 - Cage - 20 bucks

Trip to the Vet ...30 bucks...

Images of your hubby pulling on the hamster's weenie ......
PRICELESS

JOINT VENTURE

Did you hear about the veterinarian and the taxidermist who went into business together?

Their slogan was, "Either way you get your pet back."

MAN'S BEST FRIEND

A dog is truly a man's best friend.

If you don't believe it, just try this experiment.

Put your dog and your wife in the trunk of the car for an hour.

When you open the trunk, you'll see who is really happy to see you.

TEXAS TALKING DOG

One day out in the Texas panhandle, a guy sees a sign in front of a house: "Talking Dog for Sale." He rings the bell and the owner tells him the dog is in the backyard. The guy goes into the backyard and sees a black Lab just sitting there. "You talk?" he asks. "Yep," the Lab replies.

They guy is amazed and says, "So, what's your story?"

The Lab looks up and says, "Well, I discovered this gift when I was pretty young and I wanted to help the government, so I told the CIA about my gift. In no time they had me jetting from country to country, sitting in rooms with spies and world leaders; because no one figured a dog would be eavesdropping. I was one of their most valuable spies eight years running."

"The jetting around really tired me out, and I knew I wasn't getting any younger and I wanted to settle down. So I signed up for a job at the airport to do some undercover security work, mostly wandering near suspicious characters and listening in. I uncovered some incredible dealings there and was awarded a batch of medals. Then I got married, had a mess of puppies, and now I'm just retired."

The guy can't believe it! He goes back in and asks the owner what he wants for the dog. "Ten dollars." The guy says, "This dog is amazing! Why on earth are you selling him so cheap?"

"He's a big liar. He didn't do any of that stuff."

THE PARROT

A woman went to a pet shop and immediately spotted a large, beautiful parrot. There was a sign on the cage that said $50.00. "Why so little?" she asked the pet store owner.

The owner looked at her and said, "Look, I should tell you first that this bird used to live in a house of prostitution, and sometimes it says some pretty vulgar stuff."

The woman thought about this, but decided she had to have the bird any way. She took it home and hung the bird's cage up in her living room and waited for it to say something. The bird looked around the room, then at her, and said, "New house, new madam."

The woman was a bit shocked at the implication, but then thought "that's really not so bad." When her two teenage daughters returned from school the bird saw them and said, "New house, new madam, new girls." The girls and the woman were a bit offended but then began to laugh about the situation considering how and where the parrot had been raised.

Moments later, the woman's husband Keith came home from work. The bird looked at him and said, "Hi, Keith."

DOCTOR DAVE

Doctor Dave had slept with one of his patients and felt guilty all day long. No matter how much he tried to forget about it, he couldn't. The guilt and sense of betrayal was overwhelming. But every once in a while he'd hear an internal, reassuring voice in his head that said:

"Dave, don't worry about it. You aren't the first medical practitioner to sleep with one of their patients and you won't be the last. And you're single. Just let it go."

But invariably another voice in his head would bring him back to reality, whispering:.. Dave...you're a veterinarian".

LIFE LESSONS

If you can start the day without caffeine or pep pills,
If you can be cheerful, ignoring aches and pains,
If you can resist complaining and boring people with your troubles,
If you can eat the same food everyday and be grateful for it,
If you can understand when loved ones are too busy to give you time,
If you can overlook when people take things out on you when, through no fault of yours, something goes wrong,
If you can take criticism and blame without resentment,
If you can face the world without lies and deceit,
If you can conquer tension without medical help,
If you can relax without alcohol or medicine,
If you can sleep without the aid of drugs,
Then you are probably a cat or a dog.

EXCERPTS FROM A DOG'S DIARY

DAY NUMBER 180

8:00 am - OH BOY! DOG FOOD! MY FAVORITE!
9:30 am - OH BOY! A CAR RIDE! MY FAVORITE!
9:40 am - OH BOY! A WALK! MY FAVORITE!
10:30 am - OH BOY! A CAR RIDE! MY FAVORITE!
11:30 am - OH BOY! DOG FOOD! MY FAVORITE!
12:00 noon - OH BOY! THE KIDS! MY FAVORITE!
1:00 pm OH BOY! THE YARD! MY FAVORITE!
4:00 pm - OH BOY! THE KIDS! MY FAVORITE!
5:00 PM - OH BOY! DOG FOOD! MY FAVORITE!
5:30 PM - OH BOY! MOM! MY FAVORITE!

DAY NUMBER 181

8:00 am - OH BOY! DOG FOOD! MY FAVORITE!
9:30 am - OH BOY! A CAR RIDE! MY FAVORITE!
9:40 am - OH BOY! A WALK! MY FAVORITE!
10:30 am - OH BOY! A CAR RIDE! MY FAVORITE!
11:30 am - OH BOY! DOG FOOD! MY FAVORITE!
12:00 noon - OH BOY! THE KIDS! MY FAVORITE!
1:00 pm OH BOY! THE YARD! MY FAVORITE!
4:00 pm - OH BOY! THE KIDS! MY FAVORITE!
5:00 PM - OH BOY! DOG FOOD! MY FAVORITE!
5:30 PM - OH BOY! MOM! MY FAVORITE!

DAY NUMBER 182

8:00 am - OH BOY! DOG FOOD! MY FAVORITE!
9:30 am - OH BOY! A CAR RIDE! MY FAVORITE!
9:40 am - OH BOY! A WALK! MY FAVORITE!
10:30 am - OH BOY! A CAR RIDE! MY FAVORITE!
11:30 am - OH BOY! DOG FOOD! MY FAVORITE!
12:00 noon - OH BOY! THE KIDS! MY FAVORITE!

1:00 pm OH BOY! THE YARD! MY FAVORITE!

1:30 pm - ooooooo. bath. bummer.

4:00 pm - OH BOY! THE KIDS! MY FAVORITE!

5:00 PM - OH BOY! DOG FOOD! MY FAVORITE!

5:30 PM - OH BOY! MOM! MY FAVORITE!

EXCERPTS FROM A CAT'S DIARY

DAY 752 - My captors continue to taunt me with bizarre little dangling objects. They dine lavishly on fresh meat, while I am forced to eat dry cereal. The only thing that keeps me going is the hope of escape, and the mild satisfaction I get from ruining the occasional piece of furniture. Tomorrow I may eat another houseplant.

DAY 761 - Today my attempt to kill my captors by weaving around their feet while they were walking almost succeeded, must try this at the top of the stairs. In an attempt to disgust and repulse these vile oppressors, I once again induced myself to vomit on their favorite chair... must try this on their bed.

DAY 765 - Decapitated a mouse and brought them the headless body, in attempt to make them aware of what I am capable of, and to try to strike fear into their hearts. They only cooed and condescended about what a good little cat I was...Hmmm. Not working according to plan.

DAY 768 - I am finally aware of how sadistic they are. For no good reason I was chosen for the water torture. This time however it included a burning foamy chemical called "shampoo." What sick minds could invent such a liquid? My only consolation is the piece of thumb still stuck between my teeth.

DAY 771 - There was some sort of gathering of their accomplices. I was placed in solitary throughout the event. However, I could hear the noise and smell the foul odor of the glass tubes they call "beer." More importantly I overheard that my confinement was due to MY power of "allergies." Must learn what this is and how to use it to my advantage.

DAY 774 - I am convinced the other captives are flunkies and maybe snitch. The dog is routinely released and seems more than happy to return. He is obviously a half-wit. The bird on the other hand has got to be an informant, and speaks with them regularly. I am certain he reports my every move. Due to his current placement in the metal room his safety is assured. But I can wait; it is only a matter of time...

HOW TO GIVE A CAT A PILL

1. Grasp cat firmly in your arms. Cradle its head on your elbow, just as if you were giving a baby a bottle. Coo confidently, "That's a nice kitty." Drop the pill in its mouth.
2. Retrieve cat from top of lamp and pill from under sofa.
3. Follow same procedure as in 1, but hold cat's front paws down with left hand and back paws down with elbow of right arm. Poke pill into its mouth with right forefinger.
4. Retrieve cat from under bed. Get new pill from bottle. (resist impulse to get new cat.)
5. Again proceed as in 1, except when you have cat firmly cradled in bottle-feeding position, sit on edge of chair, fold your torso over cat, bring your right hand over your left elbow, open cat's mouth by lifting the upper jaw and pop pill in - quickly! Since your head is down by your knees, you won't be able to see what you are doing. That's just as well.
6. Leave cat hanging on drapes. Leave pill in your hair.
7. If you are a woman, have a good cry. If you are a man, have a good cry.
8. Now pull yourself together. Who's the boss here anyway? Retrieve cat and pill. Assuming position 1, say sternly, "Who's the boss here anyway?" Open cat's mouth, take pill and ....Oooops!
9. This isn't working, is it? Collapse and think. Aha! Those flashing claws are causing the chaos.
10. Crawl to the linen closet. Drag back a large beach towel. Spread towel on floor.
11. Retrieve cat from kitchen counter and pill from potted plant.

AD IN THE ATLANTA JOURNAL - A TRUE STORY

SINGLE BLACK FEMALE seeks male companionship, ethnicity unimportant. I'm a very good looking girl who LOVES to play. I love long walks in the woods, riding in your pickup truck, hunting, camping, and fishing trips, cozy winter nights lying by the fire. Candlelight dinners will have me eating out of your hand. Rub me the right way and watch me respond. I'll be at the front door when you get home from work, wearing only what nature gave me. Kiss me and I'm yours.

Call xxx-xxxx and ask for Daisy.

Over 15,000 men found themselves talking to the local Humane Society about an 8-week-old Labrador retriever.

DOG QUOTATIONS

The reason a dog has so many friends is that he wags his tail instead of his tongue.   *Unknown*

If there are no dogs in Heaven, then when I die I want to go where they went.   *Will Rogers*

Don't accept your dog's admiration as conclusive evidence that you are wonderful. *Ann Landers*

There is no psychiatrist in the world like a puppy licking your face. *Ben Williams*

The average dog is a nicer person than the average person. *Andy Rooney*

We give dogs time we can spare, space we can spare, and love we can spare. And in return, dogs give us their all. It's the best deal man has ever made.   *M. Acklam*

I wonder if other dogs think poodles are members of a weird religious cult? *Rita Rudner*

Anybody who doesn't know what soap tastes like never bathed a dog. *Franklin P. Jones*

If your dog is fat, **you** aren't getting enough exercise! *Unknown*

My dog is worried about the economy because Alpo is up to $3.00 a can. That's almost $21.00 in dog money! *Joe Weinstein*

Ever consider what our dogs must think of us? We come back from a grocery store with the most amazing haul - chicken, pork, half a cow. They must think we're the greatest hunters on earth!
Anne Tyler

You can say any foolish thing to a dog, and the dog will give you a look that says, "My God, you're right! I never would've thought of that!" *Dave Barry*

My goal in life is to be as good of a person as my dog already thinks I am. *Unknown*

GRIZZLY BEAR ALERT

The Alaska Department of Fish and Game recently issued this bulletin:

"In light of the rising frequency of human/grizzly bear conflicts, the Alaska Department of Fish and Game is advising hikers, hunters, and fishermen to take extra precautions and keep alert of bears while in the field.

We advise outdoorsmen to wear noisy little bells on their clothing so as not to startle bears that aren't expecting them. We also advise outdoorsmen to carry pepper spray with them in case of an encounter with a bear.

It is also a good idea to watch out for fresh signs of bear activity. Outdoors-men should recognize the difference between black bear and grizzly bear manure: Black bear manure is smaller and contains lots of berries and squirrel fur. Grizzly bear manure has little bells in it and smells like pepper-spray."

Attorneys and Law Humor

NO PROBLEM

A man went to his lawyer and said "I would like to make a will but I don't know exactly how to go about it." The lawyer says "No problem, just leave it all to me".

The man looks somewhat upset ... "Well I knew you were going to take the biggest slice, but I'd like to leave a little to my children too!"

ATTORNEY QUESTIONS
(THE HUMOR DIGEST FROM TERRY GALAN - GALANTE@MCMAIL.CIS.MCMASTER.CA)

Some of the following were reported in the *Massachusetts Bar Association Lawyers' Journal.* They are questions actually asked of witnesses by attorneys during trials and, in certain cases, the responses given by witnesses:

1. "Now doctor, isn't it true that when a person dies in his sleep, he doesn't know about it until the next morning?"

2. "The youngest son, the twenty-year old, how old is he?"

3. "Were you present when your picture was taken?"

4. Q: "Doctor, before you performed the autopsy, did you check for a pulse?"
A: "No."
Q: "Did you check for blood pressure?"
A: "No."
Q: "Did you check for breathing?"
A: "No."
Q: "So, then it is possible that the patient was alive when you began the autopsy?"
A: "No."
Q: "How can you be so sure, Doctor?"
A: "Because his brain was sitting on my desk in a jar."
Q: "But could the patient have still been alive nevertheless?"
A: "It is possible that he could have been alive and practicing law somewhere."

5. "Was it you or your younger brother who was killed in the war?"

6. "Did he kill you?"

7. "How far apart were the vehicles at the time of the collision?"

8. "You were there until the time you left, is that true?"

9. "How many times have you committed suicide?"

10. Q: "So the date of conception (of the baby) was August 8th?"
A: "Yes."

Q: "And what were you doing at that time?"

11. Q: "She had three children, right?"
    A: "Yes."
    Q: "How many were boys?"
    A: "None."
    Q: "Were there any girls?"

12. Q: "You say the stairs went down to the basement?"
    A: "Yes."
    Q: "And these stairs, did they go up also?"

13. Q: "Mr. Slatery, you went on a rather elaborate honeymoon, didn't you?"
    A: "I went to Europe, Sir."
    Q: "And you took your new wife?"

14. Q: "How was your first marriage terminated?"
    A: "By death."
    Q: "And by whose death was it terminated?"

15. Q: "Can you describe the individual?"
    A: "He was about medium height and had a beard."
    Q: "Was this a male, or a female?"

16. Q: "Is your appearance here this morning pursuant to a deposition notice which I sent to your attorney?"
    A: "No, this is how I dress when I go to work."

17. Q: "Doctor, how many autopsies have you performed on dead people?"
    A: "All my autopsies are performed on dead people."

18. Q: "All your responses must be oral, OK? What school did you go to?"
    A: "Oral."

19. Q: "Do you recall the time that you examined the body?"
A: "The autopsy started around 8:30 p.m..."
Q: "And Mr. Dennington was dead at the time?"
A: "No, he was sitting on the table wondering why I was doing an autopsy."

20. Q: "You were not shot in the fracas?"
A: "No, I was shot midway between the fracas and the navel."

21. Q: "Are you qualified to give a urine sample?"
A: "I have been since early childhood."

22. Q: This myasthenia gravis, does it affect your memory at all?
A: Yes.
Q: And in what ways does it affect your memory?
A: I forget.
Q: You forget. Can you give us an example of something that you've forgotten?

23. Q: What was the first thing your husband said to you when he woke that morning?
A: He said, "Where am I, Cathy?"
Q: And why did that upset you?
A: My name is Susan.

24. Q: Did you blow your horn or anything?
A: After the accident?
Q: Before the accident.
A: Sure, I played for ten years. I even went to school for it.

25. Q: Do you know if your daughter has ever been involved in voodoo or the occult?
A: We both do.
Q: Voodoo?
A: We do.

Q: You do?
A: Yes, voodoo.

26. Q: Trooper, when you stopped the defendant, were your red and blue lights flashing?
A: Yes.
Q: Did the defendant say anything when she got out of her car?
A: Yes, sir.
Q: What did she say?
A: What disco am I at?

JURY DUTY

A woman had been called for jury duty, but she declined to serve because she did not believe in capital punishment. The judge tried to persuade her to stay: "Madam, this is not a murder case. This is merely a case in which a wife is suing her husband because she gave him $4,000.00 to purchase a new fur coat for her, and he lost it all at the racetrack.

"I'll serve," she said, "I could be wrong about that capital punishment thing."

TOP TEN THINGS THAT SOUND DIRTY IN LAW BUT AREN'T

10. Have you looked through her briefs?
9. He is one hard judge.
8. Counselor, let's do it in chambers.
7. Her attorney withdrew at the last minute.
6. Is it a penal offense?
5. Better leave the handcuffs on.
4. For $200 an hour, she better be good.
3. Can you get him to drop his suit?
2. The judge gave her the stiffest one he could.
1. Think you can get me off?

THE OLDEST PROFESSION

A surgeon, an architect and a lawyer are having a heated barroom discussion concerning which of their professions is actually the oldest profession. The surgeon says: "Surgery is the oldest profession. God took a rib from Adam to create Eve and you can't go back further than that." The architect says: "Hold on! In fact, God was the first architect when he created the world out of chaos in 7 days, and you can't go back any further than that!" The lawyer puffs his cigar and says: "Gentlemen, Gentlemen...who do you think created the chaos?!"

THREE ENVELOPES

An old man was on his death bed. He wanted badly to take all his money with him. He called his priest, his doctor and his lawyer to his bedside. "Here's $30,000 cash to be held by each of you. I trust you to put this in my coffin when I die so I can take all my money with me." At the funeral, each man put an envelope in the coffin. Riding away in a limousine, the priest suddenly broke into tears and confessed that he had only put $20,000 into the envelope because he needed $10,000 for a new baptistery. "Well, since we're confiding in each other," said the doctor, "I only put $10,000 in the envelope because we needed a new X-ray machine at the hospital which cost $20,000." The lawyer was aghast. "I'm shamed of both of you," he exclaimed. "I want it known that when I put my envelope in that coffin, it held my personal check for the full $30,000."

THE COLLISION

A doctor and a lawyer in two cars collided on a country road. The lawyer, seeing that the doctor was a little shaken up, helped him from the car and offered him a drink from his hip flask. The doctor accepted and handed the flask back to the lawyer, who closed it and put it away. "Aren't you going to have a drink yourself?" asked the doctor. "Sure; after the police leave," replied the lawyer.

Bumper Stickers

- Forget world peace; visualize using your turn signal.
- So many cats, so few recipes.
- Save the trees, wipe your butt with an owl.
- Rock is dead. Long live paper and scissors.
- What would Scooby do?
- I am not infantile, you stinky poopyhead.
- People who think they know everything are very irritating to those of us who do.
- My inferiority complex is not as good as yours.
- I plan on living forever - so far, so good.
- I have kleptomania, but when it gets bad, I take something for it.
- To err is human; to blame it on somebody else shows management potential.
- Visualize Whirled Peas
- Beauty is in the eye of the beer holder.
- If you can read this, I've lost the trailer!
- Exaggeration is a billion times worse than understatement.

- The trouble with Sunday drivers is, they don't drive any better during the week.
- If you want the world to beat a path to your door, just try to take a nap on a Saturday afternoon.
- When your dreams turn to dust, it's time to vacuum.
- Is it three or four cars that are allowed to go through an intersection after the light turns red?
- If we do not succeed, we run the risk of failure.
- I'd give my right arm to be ambidextrous!
- I am becoming increasingly worried that there isn't enough anxiety in my life.
- Life is full of uncertainties...or I could be wrong about that?
- Don't treat me any differently than you would the Queen.
- Wrinkled was not one of the things I wanted to be when I grew up!
- Procrastinate now.
- Marriage changes passion. Suddenly you're in bed with a relative.
- A good friend will come and bail you out of jail...but, a true friend will be sitting next to you saying, "Wow...that was fun!"
- Life may not be the party we hoped for, but while we are here we might as well dance.
- My dog can lick anyone!
- I have a degree in Liberal Arts - do you want fries with that?
- I'm out of Estrogen and I've got a gun!
- A journey of a thousand miles begins with a cash advance.
- Quoting one is plagiarism. Quoting many is research.
- No man has ever been shot while doing the dishes.
- Gravity: It's not just a good idea. It's the law.
- Hukt on foniks wrkd fur me!
- Does the name Pavlov ring a bell?
- Stress is when you wake up screaming and you realize you weren't asleep.
- I can't remember if I'm the good twin or the evil one.

- All those who believe in psycho kinesis, raise my hand.
- Chaos, panic, and disorder - my work here is done.
- Is it time for your medication or mine?
- The trouble with the gene pool is that there's no lifeguard.
- I used to be schizophrenic, but we're OK now.
- A day without sunshine is like night.
- First things first, but not necessarily in that order.
- BEER: It's not just for breakfast anymore.
- I R S: We've got what it takes to take what you've got.
- I took an IQ test and the results were negative.
- Consciousness: That annoying time between naps.
- Ever stop to think, and forget to start again?
- What if the hokey pokey is really what it's all about?
- Karaoke bars combine two of the nation's greatest evils — people who shouldn't drink with people who shouldn't sing.
- Honk if you hate peace and quiet.
- Never miss a good opportunity to shut up.
- Time is nature's way of keeping everything from happening all at once.
- Thank God I'm an atheist.
- Never knock on Death's door. Ring the bell and run, he hates that.
- Jesus died for my sins and all I got was this lousy t-shirt.
- I almost had a psychic girlfriend but she left me before we met.
- Support bacteria - they're the only culture some people have.

Children's Humor

THE PHONE CONVERSATION

A boss wondered why one of his most valued employees had not phoned in sick one day. Having an urgent problem with one of the main computers, he dialed the employee's home phone number and was greeted with a child's whisper. "Hello?"

"Is your daddy home?" he asked. "Yes," whispered the small voice.

May I speak with him?" The child whispered, "No."

Surprised and wanting to talk with an adult, the boss asked, "Is your Mommy there?" "Yes."

"May I speak with her?" Again the small voice whispered, "No."

Hoping there was somebody with whom he could leave a message, the boss asked, "Is anybody else there?"

"Yes," whispered the child, "a policeman".

Wondering what the police would be doing at his employee's home, the boss asked, "May I speak with the policeman?" "No, he's busy", whispered the child.

"Busy doing what?"

"Talking to Daddy and Mommy and the Fireman," came the whispered answer.

Growing more worried as he heard a loud noise in the background through the earpiece on the phone, the boss asked, "What is that noise?"

"A helicopter" answered the whispering voice.

"What is going on there?" demanded the boss, now truly apprehensive.

Again, whispering, the child answered, "The search team just landed a helicopter."

Alarmed, concerned and a little frustrated the boss asked, "What are they searching for?"

Still whispering, the young voice replied with a muffled giggle..." ME."

THE COLD DRAFT

Now that the weather is getting cooler, I had to remind my granddaughter, Talia, who's not-quite-four, "Close the door. There's a cold draft coming in." She got a strange look on her face. A little apprehensive, but amazed and curious, she ran to the door and looked this way and that. Then she turned to me, still curious but a little disappointed, and asked, "Where's the cold giraffe?"

A TODDLER'S CREED

If it is on, I must turn it off.

If it is off, I must turn it on.

If it is a liquid, it must be shaken, and then spilled.

If it a solid, it must be crumbled, chewed or smeared.

If it is high, it must be reached.

If it is pointed, it must be run with at top speed.

If it is plugged, it must be unplugged.

If it is not trash, it must be thrown away.

If it is in the trash, it must be removed, inspected, and thrown on the floor.

If it is closed, it must be opened.

If it does not open, it must be screamed at.

If it is full, it will be more interesting emptied.

If it is empty, it will be more interesting full.

If Mommy's hands are full, I must be carried.

If Mommy is in a hurry and wants to carry me, I must walk alone.

If it has buttons, they must be pressed.

If the volume is low, it must go high.

If it doesn't stay on my spoon, it must be dropped on the floor.

If it is not food, it must be tasted.

If it is food, it must not be tasted.

If it is dry, it must be made wet with drool, milk, or toilet water.

AUNT KAREN

The teacher gave her fifth grade class an assignment: Get their parents to tell them a story with a moral at the end.

The next day the kids came back and began to tell their stories. Ashley said, "My father's a farmer and we have a lot of egg laying hens. One time we were taking our eggs to market in a basket on the front seat of the car when we hit a big bump in the road and all the eggs went flying and broke and made a mess."

"What's the moral of the story?" asked the teacher. "Don't put all your eggs in one basket!" "Very good," said the teacher.

Next little Sarah raised her hand and said, "Our family are farmers too. But we raise chickens for the meat market. We had a dozen eggs one time, but when they hatched we only got ten live chicks, and the moral to this story is," don't count your chickens before they're hatched." "That was a fine story Sarah," said the teacher.

"Michael, do you have a story to share?"

"Yes, my daddy told me this story about my Aunt Karen. Aunt Karen was a flight engineer in the Gulf War and her plane got hit. She had to bail out over enemy territory and all she had was a bottle of whiskey, a machine gun and a machete."

"She drank the whiskey on the way down so it wouldn't break and then she landed right in the middle of 100 enemy troops. She killed seventy of them with the machine gun until she ran out of bullets. Then she killed twenty more with the machete until the blade broke. And then she killed the last ten with her bare hands."

"Good heavens," said the horrified teacher, "what kind of moral did your daddy tell you from that horrible story?" "Stay the hell away from Aunt Karen when she's been drinking."

FROM WILLIAM BRABANT
(RECEIVED THROUGH THE HUMOR DIGEST)

My mother was away all weekend at a business conference. During a break, she decided to call home collect. My six-year-old brother picked up the phone and heard a stranger's voice say, "We have a Judith Smith on the line. Will you accept the charges?" Frantic, he dropped the receiver and came charging outside screaming, "Dad! They've got Mom! And they want money!"

NOBODY SLEPT WITH MOMMY

Several years ago, I returned home from a trip just when a storm hit with crashing thunder and severe lightning. As I came into my bedroom about 2 a. m., I found my two children in bed with my wife, apparently scared by the loud storm. I resigned myself to sleep in the guest bedroom that night. The next day, I talked to the children and explained that it was O. K to sleep with Mommy when the storm was bad, but when I was expected home, please don't sleep with Mommy that night.

They said OK.

After my next trip several weeks later, my wife and the children picked me up in the terminal at the appointed time. Since the plane was late, there were hundreds of other folks also waiting for their arriving passengers. As I entered the waiting area my son saw me and came running shouting, "Hi, Dad! I've got some good news!" As I waved back, I said loudly, "What's the good news?" "Nobody slept with Mommy while you were away this time!" Alex shouted. The airport became very quiet, as everyone in the waiting area looked at Alex, then turned to me, and then searched the rest of the area to see if they could figure out exactly who his Mom was.

GOOD AIM

Answering a knock at my door, I found a small boy, about six years old, one I recognized as from a new family that had recently moved in down the street.

Something of his he said had somehow found its way into my garage and he was asking for it back.

I couldn't help but notice several other munchkins about the same age, sort of moping' and shuffling' around on the curb pretending to be disinterested in our negotiations.

Opening the garage door, I noticed two new additions: a base-ball sitting in the middle of the garage floor and a broken window sporting a baseball-sized hole.

"How do you suppose this ball got in here?" I asked the boy. He was a bit hesitant to enter into the open garage more than a foot or two.

But taking one look at the ball, one look at the window, and then one very quick look and assessment at me, the boy blurted out in one big tumble of words, "Wow! I must have thrown it right through that hole!"

CHILDREN'S BOOKS NEVER ACCEPTED FOR PUBLICATION

1. You Are Different and That's Bad
2. The Boy Who Died From Eating All His Vegetables
3. Dad's New Wife Timothy
4. Fun four-letter Words to Know and Share
5. Hammers, Screwdrivers and Scissors: An I-Can-Do-it-Book
6. The Kids' Guide to Hitchhiking
7. Kathy Was So Bad Her Mom Stopped Loving Her
8. Curious George and the High-Voltage Fence
9. All Dogs go to Hell
10. The Little Sissy who Snitched
11. Some Kittens Can Fly

12. That's it; I'm putting You Up for Adoption
13. Grandpa Gets a Casket
14. The Magic World Inside the Abandoned Refrigerator
15. Garfield Gets Feline Leukemia
16. The Pop-Up Book of Human Anatomy
17. Strangers Have the Best Candy
18. Whining, Kicking and Crying to Get your Way
19. You were an Accident
20. Things Rich Kids Have, But You Never Will
21. Pop! Goes the Hamster...And Other Great Microwave Games
22. The Man in the Moon is Actually Satan
23. Your Nightmares are Real
24. Where Would you Like to be Buried?
25. Eggs, Toilet Paper, and Your School
26. Why Can't Mr. Fork and Ms. Electrical Outlet be Friends?
27. Places Where Mommy and Daddy Hide Neat Things
28. Daddy Drinks Because You Cry

TRUE STORY

My wife had just given birth to our son Ari and her sister and family came to visit. Our nephew Corey, who was about four, looked intently at her while she was nursing our son. After a few minutes, he asked, "Is that juice or milk?" She smiled and said, "Milk." Then, looking at the other breast, he asked, "That one too?"

DEAD CAT

A kindergarten pupil told his teacher he'd found a cat. She asked him if it was dead or alive.

"Dead." she was informed. "How do you know the cat was dead?" she asked her pupil.

"Because I pissed in his ear and it didn't move," answered the child innocently.

"You did **WHAT**?!?" the teacher squealed in surprise.

"You know," explained the boy, "I leaned over and went 'pssst' in his ear and he didn't move."

DEEP THOUGHTS
(FROM A NEWSPAPER CONTEST WHERE ENTRANTS AGE 4
TO 15 WERE ASKED TO IMITATE
"DEEP THOUGHTS" BY JACK HANDEY." SUBMITTED TO
THE HUMOR DIGEST BY ERIC MARSHALL
MENTZ - MENTZE@GWIS2.CIRC.GWU.EDU.

- I believe you should live each day as if it is your last, which is why I don't have any clean laundry because, come on, who wants to wash clothes on the last day of their life? - Age 15
- Give me the strength to change the things I can, the grace to accept the things I cannot, and a great big bag of money. - Age 13
- It sure would be nice if we got a day off for the president's birthday, like they do for the queen. Of course, then we would have a lot of people voting for a candidate born on July 3 or December 26, just for the long weekends. - Age 8
- I bet living in a nudist colony takes all the fun out of Halloween.- Age 13
- I often wonder how come John Tesh isn't as popular a singer as some people think he should be. Then, I remember it's because he sucks.- Age 15
- For centuries, people thought the moon was made of green cheese. Then the astronauts found that the moon is really a big hard rock. That's what happens to cheese when you leave it out. - Age 6
- My young brother asked me what happens after we die. I told him we get buried under a bunch of dirt and worms eat our bodies. I guess I should have told him the truth - that most of us go to hell and burn eternally - but I didn't want to upset him. - Age 10
- When I go to heaven, I want to see my grandpa again. But he better have lost the nose hair and the old-man smell. - Age 5

- I once heard the voice of God. It said "Vrrrrmmmmm." Unless it was just a lawn mower. - Age 11
- I like to go down to the dog pound and pretend that I've found my dog. Then I tell them to kill it anyway because I already gave away all of his stuff. Dog people sure don't have a sense of humor. - Age 14
- As you make your way through this hectic world of ours, set aside a few minutes each day. At the end of the year, you'll have a couple of days saved up. - Age 7
- It would be terrible if the Red Cross Bloodmobile got into an accident. No, wait. That would be good because if anyone needed it, the blood would be right there. - Age 5
- Often, when I am reading a good book, I stop and thank my teacher. That is, I used to, until she got an unlisted number. - Age 15

CUSS WORDS

One day, a 10 year old boy, Tom, and his 8 year old brother, John, were in their room playing. Tom said to his brother, "You know, I'm 10 years old now and I think I'm old enough to say a cuss word. I think I'll say 'damn.'" "OK," said John. "I think I'm old enough to cuss too. I think I'll say 'ass.'"

The next morning at the breakfast table, the mom asked, "What would you like for breakfast this morning, Tom?" his mom. Tom replied, "I want some damn bacon and eggs." Shocked, his mother slapped him and he fell to the floor. "Now," she said to John, "What would you like for breakfast?" to which John replied, "You can bet your ass I don't want bacon and eggs!"

HEARTWARMING STORY

This is truly a heartwarming story about the bond formed between a little girl and some construction workers. This makes you want to believe in the goodness of people and that there is hope for the human race.

A young family moved into a house next door to a vacant lot. One day a construction crew turned up to start building a house on the empty lot.

The young family's 5-year-old daughter naturally took an interest in all the activity going on next-door and started talking with the workers.

She hung around and eventually the construction crew, all of them gems-in-the-rough, more or less adopted her as a kind of project mascot. They chatted with her, let her sit with them while they had coffee and lunch breaks, and gave her little jobs to do here and there to make her feel important. At the end of the first week they even presented her with a pay envelope containing a dollar.

The little girl took this home to her mother who said all the appropriate words of admiration and suggested that they take the dollar pay she had received to the bank the next day to start a savings account.

When they got to the bank the teller was equally impressed with the story and asked the little girl how she had come by her very own pay check at such a young age. The little girl proudly replied, "I worked all last week with a crew building a house."

"My goodness gracious," said the teller, "and will you be working on the house again this week, too?"

The little girl replied, "I will if those useless sons-a-bitches at Home Depot ever bring us any drywall that's worth a shit."

SCHOOL HOMEWORK POLICY

Students are requested not to spend more than 90 minutes a night studying. In addition, it is recommended that they budget the allotted time as follows:

15 minutes	Look for the assignment.
11 minutes	Call a friend for the assignment.
23 minutes	Explain to parents why the teacher is mean and does not like children.
8 minutes	Go to the bathroom.
10 minutes	Get a snack.
7 minutes	Check the TV Guide
6 minutes	Tell parents that the teacher never explained the as signment.

10 minutes   Sit at the kitchen table waiting for Mom or Dad to
               do the assignment.

CHILDREN - ANECDOTES

Steven hugged and kissed his Mom goodnight. "I love you so much, that when you die I'm going to bury you outside my bedroom window."

Brittany had an earache and wanted a painkiller. She tried in vain to take the lid off the bottle. Seeing her frustration, her Mom explained it was a childproof cap and she'd have to open it for her. Eyes wide with wonder, the little girl asked: "How does it know it's me?"

It was the end of the day when I parked my police van in front of the station. As I gathered my equipment, my K-9 partner, Jake, was barking, and I saw a little boy staring in at me. "Is that a dog you got back there?" he asked. "It sure is," I replied. Puzzled, the boy looked at me and then towards the back of the van. Finally he said, "What'd he do?"

Anthony and his family lived in the country, and as a result seldom had guests. He was eager to help his mother after his father appeared with two dinner guests from the office. When the dinner was nearly over, Anthony went to the kitchen and proudly carried in the first piece of apple pie, giving it to his father who passed it to a guest. Anthony came in with a second piece of pie and gave it to his father, who again gave it to a guest. This was too much for Anthony, who said, "It's no use, Dad. The pieces are all the same size."

Susan was drinking juice when she got the hiccups. "Please don't give me this juice again," she said, "It makes my teeth cough."

While taking a routine vandalism report at an elementary school, I was interrupted by a little girl about six years old. Looking up and down at my uniform, she asked, "Are you a cop?" "Yes," I answered and continued writing the report. "My mother said if I ever needed help I should ask the police. Is that right?" "Yes, that's right," I told her. "Well, then," she said as she extended her foot toward me, "would you please tie my shoe?"

An acquaintance of mine who is a physician told this story about her then 4 year old daughter. On the way to preschool, the doctor had left her stethoscope on the car seat, and her little girl picked it up and began playing with it. 'Be still, my heart,' thought my friend, my daughter wants to follow in my footsteps!' Then the child spoke into the instrument: "Welcome to McDonald's. May I take your order?"

Darren stepped onto the bathroom scale and asked: "How much do I cost?"

Marc was engrossed in a young couple that were hugging and kissing in a restaurant. Without taking his eyes off them, he asked his dad: "Why is he whispering in her mouth?"

At the beginning of a children's sermon, one girl came up to the altar wearing a beautiful dress. As the children were sitting down around the pastor, he leaned over and said to the girl, "That is a very pretty dress. Is it your Easter Dress?" The girl replied almost directly into the pastor's clip-on mike, "Yes and my Mom says it's a bitch to iron."

Clinton was in his bedroom looking worried. When his Mom asked what was troubling him, he replied, "I don't know what'll happen with this bed when I get married. How will my wife fit in?"

It was one of the worst days of my life: The washing machine broke down, the telephone kept ringing, my head ached, and the mail carrier brought a bill I had no money to pay. Almost to the breaking point, I lifted my one-year-old into his high chair, leaned my head against the tray, and began to cry. Without a word, my son took his pacifier out of his mouth and stuck it in mine.

Tammy was with her mother when they met an elderly, rather wrinkled woman her Mom knew. Tammy looked at her for a while and then asked, "Why doesn't your skin fit your face?"

A certain little girl, when asked her name, would reply, "I'm Mr. Sugarbrown's daughter." Her mother told her this was wrong, she must say, "I'm Jane Sugarbrown." The Vicar spoke to her in Sunday school, and said, "Aren't you Mr. Sugarbrown's daughter?" She replied, "I thought I was, but mother says I'm not."

Seven year old Sarah admitted calmly to her parents that Billy Brown had kissed her after class. "How did that happen?" gasped her mother. "It wasn't easy," admitted the young lady, "but three girls helped me catch him."

One day a little girl was sitting and watching her mother do the dishes at the kitchen sink. She suddenly noticed that her mother had several strands of white hair sticking out in contrast to her brunette hair. She looked at her mother and inquisitively asked, "Why are some of your hairs white, Mom?" Her mother replied, "Well, every time that you do something wrong and make me cry or unhappy, one of my hairs turns white." The little girl thought about this for a while and then said, "Momma, how come **all** of grandma's hairs are white?"

A 3-year-old went with his dad to see a litter of kittens. On returning home, he breathlessly informed his mother that there were two boy kittens and two girl kittens. How did you know?" his mother asked. "Daddy picked them up and looked underneath," he replied. "I think it's printed on the bottom."

A little girl asked her mother, "Can I go outside and play with the boys?" Her mother replied, "No, you can't play with the boys, they're too rough." The little girl thought about it for a few moments and then said, "If I find a smooth one, can I play with him?"

A friend, who worked away from home all week, always made a special effort with his family on the weekends. Every Sunday morning he would take his 7-year old granddaughter out for a drive in the car for some bonding time. One particular Sunday however, he had a bad cold and really didn't feel like being up at all. Luckily, his wife came to the rescue and said that she would take their granddaughter out. When they returned, the little girl anxiously ran upstairs to see her grandfather.

"Well, did you enjoy your ride with grandma?"

"Oh yes, Papa" the girl replied, "and do you know what? We didn't see a single dumb bastard!"

For weeks, a 6-year old lad kept telling his first-grade teacher about the baby brother or sister that was expected at his house. One day the mother allowed the boy to feel the movements of the unborn child. The 6-year old was obviously impressed, but he made no comment. Furthermore, he stopped telling his teacher about the impending event. The teacher finally sat the boy on her lap and said, "Tommy, whatever became of that baby brother or sister you were expecting at home?" Tommy burst into tears and confessed, "I think Mommy ate it!"

While working for an organization that delivers lunches to elderly shut-ins, I used to take my four-year-old daughter on my afternoon rounds. She was unfailingly intrigued by the various appliances of old age, particularly the canes, walkers and wheelchairs. One day I found her staring at a pair of false teeth soaking in a glass. As I braced myself for the inevitable barrage of questions, she merely turned and whispered, "The tooth fairy will never believe this!"

An exasperated mother, whose son was always getting into mischief, finally asked him, "How do you expect to get into Heaven?" The boy thought it over and said, "Well, I'll run in and out and in an out and keep slamming the door until St. Peter says, "For Heaven's sake, Dylan, come in or stay out!'"

When I was six months pregnant with my third child, my three year old came into the room when I was just getting ready to get into the shower. She said, "Mommy, you are getting fat!" I replied, "Yes, honey, remember Mommy has a baby growing in her tummy." "I know," she replied, but what's growing in your butt?"

One summer evening during a violent thunderstorm a mother was tucking her son into bed. She was about to turn off the light when he asked with a tremor in his voice, "Mommy, will you sleep with me tonight?" The mother smiled and gave him a reassuring hug. "I can't dear," she said. "I have to sleep in the same room with Daddy."

A long silence was broken at last by his shaky little voice: "The big sissy."

THE BARBER SHOP

A little girl goes to the barber shop with her father. She stands next to the barber chair, while her dad gets his hair cut, eating a snack cake. The barber says to her, "Sweetheart, you're gonna get hair on your Twinkie." She says, "Yes, I know, and I'm gonna get boobs too."

Corporate and Business Humor

5-MINUTE MANAGEMENT COURSE

Lesson 1:

A man is getting into the shower just as his wife is finishing up her shower, when the doorbell rings. The wife quickly wraps herself in a towel and runs downstairs. When she opens the door, there stands Bob, the next-door neighbor.

Before she says a word, Bob says, "I'll give you $800 to drop that towel."

After thinking for a moment, the woman drops her towel and stands naked in front of Bob. After a few seconds, Bob hands her $800 and leaves.

The woman wraps back up in the towel and goes back upstairs. When she gets to the bathroom, her husband asks, "Who was that?"

"It was Bob the next door neighbor," she replies.

"Great!" the husband says, "did he say anything about the $800 he owes me?"

Moral of the story :

If you share critical information pertaining to credit and risk with your shareholders in time, you may be in a position to prevent avoidable exposure.

Lesson 2:

A priest offered a Nun a lift. She got in and crossed her legs, forcing her gown to reveal a leg. The priest nearly had an accident. After controlling the car, he stealthily slid his hand up her leg.

The nun said, "Father, remember Psalm 129?" The priest removed his hand. But, changing gears, he let his hand slide up her leg again.

The nun once again said, "Father, remember Psalm 129?"

The priest apologized "Sorry sister but the flesh is weak"

Arriving at the convent, the nun sighed heavily and went on her way.

On his arrival at the church, the priest rushed to look up Psalm 129

It said, "Go forth and seek, further up, you will find glory."

Moral of the story:

If you are not well informed in your job, you might miss a great opportunity.

Lesson 3:

A sales rep, an administration clerk, and the manager are walking to lunch when they find an antique oil lamp. They rub it and a Genie comes out.

The Genie says, "I'll give each of you just one wish."

"Me first! Me first!" says the admin clerk. "I want to be in the Bahamas, driving a speedboat, without a care in the world."

Puff! She's gone.

"Me next! Me next!" says the sales rep. "I want to be in Hawaii, relaxing on the beach with my personal masseuse, an endless supply of Pina Coladas and the love of my life."

Puff! He's gone.

"OK, you're up," the Genie says to the manager.

The manager says, "I want those two back in the office after lunch."

Moral of the story:
Always let your boss have the first say.

Lesson 4

An eagle was sitting on a tree resting, doing nothing. A small rabbit saw the eagle and asked him, "Can I also sit like you and do nothing?"

The eagle answered: "Sure, why not."

So, the rabbit sat on the ground below the eagle and rested. All of a sudden, a fox appeared, jumped on the rabbit and ate it.

Moral of the story:
To be sitting and doing nothing, you must be sitting very, very high up.

Lesson 5

A turkey was chatting with a bull. "I would love to be able to get to the top of that tree," sighed the turkey, "but I haven't got the energy."

"Well, why don't you nibble on some of my droppings?" replied the bull. They're packed with nutrients."

The turkey pecked at a lump of dung, and found it actually gave him enough strength to reach the lowest branch of the tree. The next day, after eating some more dung, he reached the second branch. Finally after a fourth night, the turkey was proudly perched at the top of the tree

He was promptly spotted by a farmer, who shot him out of the tree.

Moral of the story:
BullShit might get you to the top, but it won't keep you there.

Lesson 6

A little bird was flying south for the Winter. It was so cold the bird froze and fell to the ground into a large field. While he was lying there, a cow came by and dropped some dung on him.

As the frozen bird lay there in the pile of cow dung, he began to realize how warm he was. The dung was actually thawing him out! He lay there all warm and happy, and soon began to sing for joy.

A passing cat heard the bird singing and came to investigate. Following the sound, the cat discovered the bird under the pile of cow dung, and promptly dug him out and ate him.

Morals of the story:
(1) *Not everyone who shits on you is your enemy.*
(2) *Not everyone who gets you out of shit is your friend.*
(3) *And when you're in deep shit, it's best to keep your mouth shut!*

UNUSUAL BUT REAL EXCUSE NOTES FROM EMPLOYEES

1. At her sister's wedding, an employee chipped her tooth on a mint julep, bent over to spit it out, hit her head on a keg and was knocked unconscious.
2. While at a circus, a tiger urinated on the employee's ear, causing an ear infection.
3. An employee's dog wasn't feeling well, so the employee tasted the dog's food and then got sick.
4. "Someone put LSD in my salad."
5. An employee's roommate locked all his clothes in a shed for spite.
6. "Stuck on an island – canoe floated away."
7. An employee was upset because his favorite "American Idol" contestant was voted off.
8. "I didn't think I had to come in if I had time in my vacation bank. I thought I could take it whenever I wanted."
9. An employee said he wasn't feeling well and wanted to rest up for the company's holiday party that night.
10. A groundhog bit the employee's car tire, causing it to go flat.

TOP TEN THINGS THAT SOUND DIRTY AT THE OFFICE BUT AREN'T

10. I need to whip it out by 5.
9. Mind if I use your laptop?
8. Just stick it in my box.

7. If I have to lick one more, I'll gag.
6. I want it on my desk, NOW!!!
5. HMMMMMMMM....I think it's out of fluid.
4. My equipment is so old, it takes forever to finish.
3. It's an entry-level position.
2. When do you think you'll be getting off today?
1. It's not fair...I do all the work while he just sits there.

INSANITY IN THE WORKPLACE: A HOW TO GUIDE (FROM TONY BLAHA, HTTP://TBLAHA.50MEGS.COM)

-   Page yourself over the intercom. (Don't disguise your voice.)
-   Find out where your boss shops and buy exactly the same outfits.
-   Always wear them one day after your boss does. (This is especially effective if your boss is a different gender than you are.)
-   Make up nicknames for all your coworkers and refer to them only by these names. "That's a good point, Sparky." "No, I'm sorry. I'm going to have to disagree with you there, Chachi."
-   Send email to the rest of the company telling them what you're doing. For example "If anyone needs me, I'll be in the bathroom."
-   "Highlight" your shoes. Tell people that you haven't lost your shoes since you did this.
-   While sitting at your desk, soak your fingers in "Palmolive."
-   Put up mosquito netting around your cubicle.
-   Put a chair facing a printer, sit there all day and tell people you're waiting for your document.
-   Arrive at a meeting late, say you're sorry, but you didn't have time for lunch, and you're going to be nibbling during the meeting. During the meeting eat 5 entire raw potatoes.
-   Insist that your e-mail address be zena_goddess_of_ fire@companyname.com

- Every time someone asks you to do something, ask them if they want fries with that.
- Send email to yourself engaging yourself in an intelligent debate about the direction of one of your company's products. Forward the mail to a co-worker and ask her to settle the disagreement.
- Encourage your colleagues to join you in a little synchronized chair dancing.
- Put your garbage can on your desk. Label it "IN."
- Determine how many cups of coffee is "too many."
- Develop an unnatural fear of staplers.
- Decorate your office with pictures of Cindy Brady and Danny Partridge. Try to pass them off as your children.
- For a relaxing break, get away from it all with a mask and snorkel in the fish tank. If no one notices, take out your snorkel and see how many you can catch in your mouth.
- Send e-mail messages saying free pizza, free donuts etc...in the lunchroom, when people complain that there was none... Just lean back, pat your stomach, and say, "Oh you've got to be faster than that."
- Put decaf in the coffeemaker for 3 weeks. Once everyone has gotten over their caffeine addictions, switch to espresso.

WRITING A RECOMMENDATION FOR THE FIRED EMPLOYEE:
SUGGESTED PHRASES

The employee who is chronically absent:
"It seems her career was just taking off."
"A person like him is hard to find."
The person with no ambition:
"He couldn't care less about the number of hours he had to put in."
"In my opinion, you would be fortunate to get this person to work for you."
The office alcoholic:
"We generally found him loaded with work to do."
The difficult to get along with:

"I am pleased to say that this candidate is a former colleague of mine."

The incompetent employee:

"I recommend this person with no qualifications whatsoever."

"I can assure you that no person would be better for the job."

"I would urge you to waste no time in making this candidate an offer of employment."

COMPANY SHAKEUP

A large company, feeling it was time for a shakeup, hired a new CEO. This new boss was determined to rid the company of all slackers. On a tour of the facilities, the CEO noticed a guy leaning on a wall.

The room was full of workers and he wanted to let them know that he meant business! He walked up to the guy leaning against the wall and asked, "How much money do you make a week?" A little surprised, the young fellow looked at him and replied, "I make $300 a week. Why?" The CEO then handed the guy $1,200 in cash and screamed, "Here's four weeks' pay, now **get out** and don't come back!"

Feeling pretty good about himself, the CEO looked around the room and asked, "Does anyone want to tell me what that goof-off did here?"

From across the room came a voice, "Delivery guy from Pizza Hut."

THE JOB APPLICATION

Job Application This is an actual job application someone submitted for a fast-food establishment.

APPLICATION FOR EMPLOYMENT

NAME: Greg Bulmash

DESIRED POSITION: Reclining. Ha ha. But seriously, whatever's available. If I was in a position to be picky, I wouldn't be applying here in the first place.

DESIRED SALARY: $185,000 a year plus stock options and a Michael Ovitz style severance package. If that's not possible, make an offer and we can haggle.

EDUCATION: Yes.

LAST POSITION HELD: Target for middle-management hostility.

SALARY: Less than I'm worth.

MOST NOTABLE ACHIEVEMENT: My incredible collection of stolen pens and post-it notes.

REASON FOR LEAVING: It sucked.

HOURS AVAILABLE TO WORK: Any.

PREFERRED HOURS: 1:30-3:30 p.m., Monday, Tuesday, and Thursday.

DO YOU HAVE ANY SPECIAL SKILLS?: Yes, but they're better suited to a more intimate environment.

MAY WE CONTACT YOUR CURRENT EMPLOYER?: If I had one, would I be writing this?

DO YOU HAVE ANY PHYSICAL CONDITIONS THAT WOULD PROHIBIT YOU FROM LIFTING UP TO 50 LBS?: Of what?

DO YOU HAVE A CAR?: I think the more appropriate question here would be "Do you have a car that runs?"

HAVE YOU RECEIVED ANY SPECIAL AWARDS OR RECOGNITION?: I may already be a winner of the Publishers Clearinghouse Sweepstakes.

DO YOU SMOKE?: Only when set on fire.

WHAT WOULD YOU LIKE TO BE DOING IN FIVE YEARS?: Living in Bimini with a fabulously wealthy supermodel who thinks I'm the greatest thing since sliced bread. Actually, I'd like to be doing that now.

DO YOU CERTIFY THAT THE ABOVE IS TRUE AND COMPLETE TO THE BEST OF YOUR KNOWLEDGE?: No, but I dare you to prove otherwise.

SIGN HERE: Scorpio with Libra rising.

MEETING BINGO

For those of you who attend a lot of meetings, this should make those meetings go faster! If you don't attend lots of meetings, consider yourself lucky.

How to play: Simply tick off 5 words heard in one meeting from the following list and shout out BINGO! It's that easy!

Synergy
Proactive, not Reactive
Win-Win Situation
Think Outside the Box
On a Daily Basis
Client-Focused
The Bottom Line
Touch Base
On the Same Page
Strategic Fit
Best Practice
Lessons Learned
Revisit
Game Plan
Hardball
You with me on this?
Go the Extra Mile
Benchmark
The Big Picture
Value-Added
Movers and Shakers
Ball Park
Fast Track
Results-Driven
Brain-Storm
A Done Deal
Empower Employees
You Know What I Mean

Knowledge Base
Mindset
Quality-Driven
Move the Goal Posts

OPPORTUNITY KNOCKS

He's never been very successful. When opportunity knocks, he complains about the noise.

THE COPIER IS OUT OF ORDER

NO	We cannot fix it.
YES	We have called the service company.
YES	The repair person will be here today.
NO	We do not know how long it will take.
NO	We do not know what caused it.
NO	We do not know who broke it.
YES	We are keeping it.
NO	We do not know what you are going to do.
YES	We know what to do with it.

THE FAILURE

My friends all told me I'd never be anything but a failure at this business, so I finally decided to take action and do something about it – I went out and made some new friends.

MANAGEMENT TRAINING

A guy in a Brookes Brothers suit, Hermes tie and Gucci loafers walks into a cafe with a shotgun in one hand and a bucket of horse manure in the other. He says to the waiter, "I'd like a cup of coffee".

The waiter says, "Sure, coming right up." He gets the guy a tall mug of coffee and the man drinks it down in one gulp, picks up the bucket of crap, throws it into the air, blasts it with the shotgun and walks out.

The next morning the guy returns. He has his shotgun in one hand and a bucket of horse manure in the other. He walks up to the counter and says to the waiter, "Cuppa joe."

The waiter says, "Whoa, buddy, we're still cleaning up the mess from the last time you were here. What the heck was that all about, anyway?"

The man smiles and proudly says, "I'm in management training. I come in, drink coffee, shoot the shit and disappear for the rest of the day."

MEETINGS

Are You Lonely?
Tired of Working On Your Own?
Do You Hate Making Decisions?
Hold a Meeting!
You Can:

- See People
- Show Charts
- Feel Important
- Point With A Pointer
- Have Others Act Like They Are Listening To You
- Impress Your Colleagues
- Say Catchy Phrases
- Eat Donuts
- Arrange more Meetings

All On Company Time
Meetings: The Practical Alternative to Work!

BEST EXCUSES IF YOU GET CAUGHT SLEEPING IN YOUR CUBICLE:

1. "It's okay...I'm still billing the client."
2. "They told me at the blood bank this might happen."
3. "This is just a 15 minute power-nap like they raved about in the last time management course you sent me to."

4. "I was working smarter, not harder."
5. "Whew! Guess I left the top off the liquid paper."
6. "I wasn't sleeping! I was meditating on the mission statement and envisioning a new paradigm!"
7. "This is one of the seven habits of highly effective people!"
8. "I was testing the keyboard for drool resistance."
9. "I'm in the management training program."
10. "I'm actually doing a 'Stress Level Elimination Exercise Plan' (SLEEP) I learned at the last mandatory seminar you made me attend."
11. "This is in exchange for the six hours last night when I dreamed about work!"
12. "I was doing a highly specific Yoga exercise to relieve work-related stress. Are you discriminatory towards people who practice Yoga?"
13. "The coffee machine is broke...."
14. "Someone must've put decaf in the wrong pot."
15. "Boy that cold medicine I took last night just won't wear off!"
16. "It worked well for Reagan, didn't it?"
17. "I was cross-training for telecommuting. Next, I watch the Walton's."
18. "Ah, the unique and unpredictable circadian rhythms of the workaholic!"
19. "I wasn't sleeping. I was trying to pick up my contact lenses without using my hands."
20. "I thought you [boss] were gone for the day."

THE HOT AIR BALLOON

A man flying in a hot air balloon realizes he is lost. He reduces his altitude and spots a man in a field down below. He lowers the balloon further and shouts, "Excuse me, can you tell me where I am?" The man below says, "Yes, you're in a hot air balloon, about 30 feet above this field."

"You must be an engineer," says the balloonist.

"I am. How did you know?"

"Everything you told me is technically correct, but it's of no use to anyone."

The man below says, "You must be in management."

"I am. But how did you know?"

"You don't know where you are, or where you're going, but you expect me to be able to help. You're in the same position you were before we met, but now it's my fault."

QUOTES - FROM ACTUAL EMPLOYEE PERFORMANCE EVALUATIONS

1. Since my last report, this employee has reached rock bottom and has started to dig.
2. I would not allow this employee to breed.
3. This employee is really not so much of a has-been, but more of a definite won't be.
4. Works well when under constant supervision and cornered like a rat in a trap.
5. When she opens her mouth, it seems that it is only to change feet.
6. He would be out of his depth in a parking lot puddle.
7. This young lady has delusions of adequacy.
8. He sets low personal standards and then consistently fails to achieve them.
9. This employee is depriving a village somewhere of an idiot.
10. This employee should go far, and the sooner he starts the better.
11. Got a full 6 pack, but lacks the plastic thing to hold it all together.
12. A gross ignoramus - 144 times worse than an ordinary ignoramus.
13. He doesn't have ulcers, but he's a carrier.
14. I would like to go hunting with him sometime.
15. He's been working with glue too much.
16. He would argue with a signpost.
17. He brings a lot of joy whenever he leaves the room.
18. When his IQ reaches 50, he should sell.

19. If you see two people talking and one looks bored, he's the other one.
20. A photographic memory, but with the lens cover glued on.

YOU'VE BEEN IN CORPORATE AMERICA TOO LONG WHEN...

1. You ask the waiter what the restaurant's core competencies are.
2. You decide to re-organize your family into a "team-based organization."
3. You refer to dating as test marketing.
4. You can spell "paradigm."
5. You actually know what a paradigm is.
6. You understand your airline's fare structure.
7. You write executive summaries on your love letters.
8. Your Valentine's Day cards have bullet points.
9. You think that it's actually efficient to write a ten-page presentation with six other people you don't know.
10. You celebrate your wedding anniversary by conducting a performance review.
11. You believe you never have any problems in your life, just "issues" and "improvement opportunities."
12. You calculate your own personal cost of capital.
13. You explain to your bank manager that you prefer to think of yourself as "highly leveraged" as opposed to "in debt."
14. You end every argument by saying "let's talk about this off-line."
15. You can explain to somebody the difference between "re-engineering," "down-sizing," "right-sizing," and "firing people.
16. You talk to the waiter about process flow when dinner arrives late.
17. You refer to your significant other as "my Co-CEO."
18. You start to feel sorry for Dilbert's boss.
19. You believe the best tables and graphs take an hour to comprehend.

20. You account for your tuition as a capital expenditure instead of an expense.
21. You insist that you do some more market research before you and your spouse produce another child.
22. Your "deliverable" for Sunday evening is clean laundry and paid bills.
23. You use the term "value-added" without falling down laughing.

Death and Dying Humor

BERNIE SCHWARTZ

A mortician was working late one night. It was his job to examine the dead bodies before they were sent off to be buried or cremated.

As he examined the body of Bernie Schwartz, who was about to be cremated, he made an amazing discovery: Bernie Schwartz had the longest penis he had ever seen! "I'm sorry Mr. Schwartz," said the mortician, "But I can't send you off to be cremated with a tremendously huge penis like this. It has to be saved for posterity."

And with that the coroner used his tools to remove the dead man's schlong. The coroner stuffed his prize into a briefcase and took it home.

The first person he showed was his wife. "I have something to show you that you won't believe," he said, and opened his briefcase.

"Oh my god!" she screamed, "Bernie Schwartz is dead!"

WHEN I DIE...

When I die, I want to go like my grandfather...quietly in his sleep. Not screaming like the rest of the people in his car.

THE QUESTION

Driving with my young boys to a funeral, I tried to prepare them by talking about burial and what we believe happens after death. The boys behaved well during the service. But at the grave site I discovered my explanations weren't as thorough as I'd thought. In a loud voice, my four-year-old asked, "Mom?" "Yes," I whispered. "What's in the box?"

COLD

A drunk stumbles out of a bar and he needs to pee, so he makes his way into the nearby cemetery. He walks right to the edge of a freshly dug grave, loses his balance and falls in.

There's a puddle of water in the hole, and he spends the rest of the night yelling, "Help me, I'm cold! Someone help me, I'm cold!"

At closing time, another drunk walks over to the cemetery to pee, and hears the noise. He gets to the open grave, looks down and says, "Of course you're cold, you stupid son-of-a-bitch, you kicked all the dirt off yourself!"

WORKER DEAD AT DESK FOR 5 DAYS
(NEW YORK TIMES 1/22/03)

Bosses of a publishing firm are trying to work out why no one noticed that one of their employees had been sitting dead at his desk for FIVE DAYS before anyone asked if he was feeling okay. George Turklebaum, 51, who had been employed as a proof-reader at a New York firm for 30 years, had a heart attack in the open-plan office he shared with 23 other workers. He quietly passed away on Monday, but nobody noticed until Saturday morning when an office cleaner asked why he was still working during the weekend.

His boss Elliot Wachiaski said: "George was always the first guy in each morning and the last to leave at night, so no one found it unusual that he was in the same position all that time and didn't say anything. He was always absorbed in his work and kept much to himself."

A post mortem examination revealed that he had been dead for five days after suffering a coronary. Ironically, George was proofreading manuscripts of medical textbooks when he died.

You may want to give your co-workers a nudge occasionally.

Moral of the story: Don't work too hard. Nobody notices anyway

COLLEAGUES

Some of my colleagues act like they are walking around just to save funeral expenses.

LIFE AFTER DEATH

"Do you believe in life after death?" the boss asked one of his younger employees.

"Yes sir." the employee responded.

"Well, then, that makes everything just fine," the boss continued. "About an hour after you left yesterday to go to your grandfather's funeral, he stopped in to see you."

EMAIL MIX-UP

After being nearly snowbound for two weeks last winter, a Seattle man departed for his vacation in Miami Beach, where he was to meet his wife the next day at the conclusion of her business trip to Minneapolis. They were looking forward to pleasant weather and a nice time together. Unfortunately, there was some sort of mix up at the boarding gate, and the man was told he would have to wait for a later flight. He tried to appeal to a supervisor but was told the airline was not responsible for the problem and it would do no good to complain.

Upon arrival at the hotel the next day, he discovered that Miami Beach was having a heat wave, and its weather was almost as uncomfortably hot as Seattle's was cold. The desk clerk gave him a message that his wife would arrive as planned. He could hardly wait to get to the pool area to cool off, and quickly sent his wife an e-mail, but due to his haste, he made an error in the e-mail address.

His message, therefore, arrived at the home of an elderly preacher's wife whose even older husband had died only the day before. When the grieving Widow opened her e-mail, she took one look at the monitor, let out an anguished scream, fainted, and fell to the floor. Her family rushed to her room where they saw this message on the screen:

"Dearest wife, Departed yesterday as you know. Just now got checked in. Some confusion at the gate. Appeal was denied. Received confirmation of your arrival tomorrow. Your loving husband.

P.S. Things are not as we thought. You're going to be surprised at how hot it is down here."

EPITAPHS (SOME SHARED BY PATTY WOOTEN, R.N.)

In a Thrumont, Md., cemetery
Here lies an Atheist
All dressed *up*
And no place to go

In the Boot Hill Cemetery, Arizona
Here lies
Lester Moore
Four slugs
From a forty-four
No Les
No More

In a New Mexico cemetery
Here lies
Johnny Yeast
Pardon me
For not rising

An attorney's *epitaph in Rockford,* Illinois
Goembel, John E.
1867-1946
"The defense rests"

A lawyer's epitaph in England
Sir John Strange
Here lies an honest lawyer,
And that is Strange.

In a cemetery in Scotland
Here beneath this stone we lie
Back to back my wife and I
And when the angels trump shall trill
If she gets up then I'll lie still!

In a North Carolina cemetery
Come blooming youths, as you pass by
And on these lines do cast an eye
As you are now, so once was I;
As I am now, so must you be;
Prepare for death and follow me.

To which someone, who saw this, added
To follow you
I am not content
How do I know
Which way you went

On the grave of Ezekial Aikle in East Dalhousie Cemetery, Nova Scotia
Here lies
Ezekial Aikle
Age 102
The Good
Die Young.

In a London, England cemetery
Ann Mann
Here lies Ann Mann,
Who lived an old maid
But died an old Mann.

Dec. 8, 1767

In a Ribbesford, England, cemetery:
Anna Wallace
The children of Israel wanted bread
And the Lord sent them manna,
Old clerk Wallace wanted a wife,
And the Devil sent him Anna.

In memory of an accident in a Uniontown, Pennsylvania cemetery
Here lies the body
of Jonathan Blake
Stepped on the gas
Instead of the brake.

In a Silver City, Nevada, cemetery
Here lays Butch,
We planted him raw.
He was quick on the trigger,
But slow on the draw.

In a Georgia cemetery
"I told you I was sick!"

John Penny's epitaph in the Wimborne, England, cemetery
Reader if cash thou art
In want of any
Dig 4 feet deep
And thou wilt find a Penny.

On Margaret Daniels grave at Hollywood Cemetery Richmond, Virginia
She always said her feet were killing her
but nobody believed her.

On a grave from the 1880's in Nantucket, Massachusetts
Under the sod and under the trees

Lies the body of Jonathan Pease.
He is not here, there's only the pod:
Pease shelled out and went to God.

In a cemetery in Albany, New York
Harry Edsel Smith of Albany, New York
Born 1903 - Died 1942
Looked up the elevator shaft to see if
the car was on the way down. It was.

SAD DAY

What with all the sadness and trauma going on in the world at the moment, it is worth reflecting on the death of a very important person which almost went un-noticed last week

Larry La Prise, the man who wrote the song "The Hokey Pokey" died peacefully at age 93.

The most traumatic part for his family was getting him into the coffin. They put his left leg in…and then the trouble started.

THE LIVING WILL

I, _____, being of sound mind and body, do not wish to be kept alive indefinitely by artificial means.

Under no circumstances should my fate be put in the hands of pinhead politicians who couldn't pass ninth-grade biology if their lives depended on it. Nor in the hands of lawyers/doctors who are interested simply in running up the bills.

If a reasonable amount of time passes and I fail to ask for at least one of the following: beer, margarita, scotch and soda, martini, vodka and OJ, steak, shrimp or crab legs, a lottery ticket, bowl of ice cream, waffles, chocolate, or sex…it should be presumed that I won't ever get better.

When such a determination is reached, I hereby instruct my appointed person and attending physicians to pull the plug, reel in the tubes and call it a day.

At this point, it is time to call a New Orleans Jazz Funeral Band to come do their thing at my funeral, and ask all of my friends to raise their glasses to toast the good times we have had.

Signature: _____
Date: _____

P.S. I hear that in Ireland they have a Nursing Home with a Pub. The patients are happier and they have a lot more visitors. If I need a nursing home, send me there!

MEMORIAL STONE

Joe's will provided $30,000 for an elaborate funeral. As the last guests departed the affair, his wife, Helen, turned to her oldest friend. "Well, I'm sure Joe would be pleased," she said. "I'm sure you're right," replied Jody, who lowered her voice and leaned in close. "How much did this really cost"?

"All of it," said Helen. "Thirty-thousand." "No!" Jody exclaimed. "I mean, it was very nice, but $30,000?"

Helen answered. "The funeral was $ 6,500. I donated $500 to the church. The wake, food and drinks were another $500. The rest went for the memorial stone." Jody computed quickly. "Twenty-two thousand five hundred for a memorial stone? My gosh, how big is it!?"

"Two and a half carats."

REMEMBERING AN ICON

The Pillsbury Doughboy died recently of a yeast infection and trauma complications from repeated pokes in the belly. He was 71. Doughboy was buried in a lightly greased coffin. Dozens of celebrities turned out to pay their respects, including Mrs. Butterworth, Hungry Jack, the California Raisins, Betty Crocker, the Hostess Twinkies, and Captain Crunch. The grave site was piled high with flours.

Aunt Jemima delivered the eulogy and lovingly described the Doughboy as a man who never knew how much he was kneaded. Doughboy rose quickly in show business, but his later life was filled with turnovers. He was not considered a very smart cookie, wasting much of his dough on half-baked schemes. Despite being a little flaky at times, he was still a crusty old man and was considered a positive roll model for millions.

Doughboy is survived by his wife Play Dough, two children, John Dough and Jane Dough, plus they had one in the oven. He is also survived by his elderly father, Pop Tart.

The funeral was held at 350 for about 20 minutes.

FROM WOODY ALLEN

"I don't want to become immortal through my work. I want to become immortal through not dying."

"I'm not afraid of dying - I just don't want to be there when it happens!"

THE SUPER BOWL

A man had 50 yard line tickets for the Eagles-Patriots Super Bowl Game in Jacksonville, Florida. As he sat down, a man approached him and asked him if the seat next to him was available. "Yes," he said sadly, "the seat is empty." "This is incredible", exclaimed the man. "Who in their right mind would have a seat like this for the Super Bowl, the biggest sports event in the world, and not use it?"

Somberly, the man replied, "Well...the seat actually belongs to me. I was supposed to come here with my wife, but she passed away. This is the first Super Bowl we have not been together since we got married in 1967."

"Oh, I'm sorry to hear that. That's terrible. But couldn't you find someone else - a friend or relative or even a neighbor to take the seat?"

Shaking his head he replied, "No. They're all at her funeral."

THE POKER GAME

Six retired Floridians were playing poker in the condo clubhouse when Meyerwitz loses $500 on a single hand, clutches his chest and drops dead at the table. Showing respect for their fallen comrade, the other five continue playing standing up.

Finkelstein looks around and asks, "So, who's gonna' tell his wife?" They draw straws. Goldberg picks the short one. They tell him to be discreet, be gentle and not to make a bad situation any worse. "Discreet? I'm the most discreet person you'll ever meet. Discretion is my middle name; leave it to me."

Goldberg goes over to the Meyerwitz apartment and knocks on the door. The wife answers and asks what he wants. Goldberg declares: "Your husband just lost $500 and is afraid to come home." "Tell him to drop dead!" says the wife. "I'll go tell him," says Goldberg.

GETTING THEM BACK

When I was younger I hated going to weddings ...it seemed that all of My aunts and the grandmotherly types used to come up to me, poking me in the ribs and cackling, telling me, "You're next." They stopped that after I started doing the same thing to them at funerals.

Disability Humor

A SATURDAY STROLL

Two women were out for a Saturday stroll. One had a Doberman and the other, a Chihuahua.

As they walked down the street, the one with the Doberman said to her friend, "Let's go over to that bar for a drink."

The lady with the Chihuahua said, "We can't go in there. We've got dogs with us." The one with the Doberman said, "Just watch, and do as I do."

They walked over to the bar and the one with the Doberman put on a pair of dark glasses and started to walk in. The bouncer at the door said, "Sorry, lady, no pets allowed."

The woman with the Doberman said, "You don't understand. This is my guide dog." The bouncer said, "A Doberman?" The woman said, "Yes, they're using them now. They're very good." The bouncer said, "OK, come on in."

The lady with the Chihuahua thought that convincing him that a Chihuahua was a seeing-eye dog may be a bit more difficult, but thought, "What the heck," so she put on her dark glasses and walked in. Once again the bouncer said, "Sorry, lady, no pets allowed." The woman said, "You don't understand. This is my guide dog."

The bouncer said, "A Chihuahua?" The woman said, "A Chihuahua? You mean they gave me a damn Chihuahua?!"

DISABILITY ONE-LINERS

- Quadriplegics' T-shirt ... Recovering Workaholic ~ I haven't lifted my finger in years.
- When my friend Tony accidentally rolled his wheelchair through his new neighbor's wet cement he left a bad impression.
- How many dyslexics does it change to take a light bulb?
- Rehab! Rehab! I need some duck tape - my duck has a quack in it.
- After a Physical Therapy session I float like an anchor and sting like a moth.
- T-shirt: It's 2:30 in the morning, I'm legally blind and you're looking darn good to me.
- Laughter is the best medicine, but in certain situations the Heimlich maneuver may be more appropriate.
- There aren't nearly enough crutches in the world for all the lame excuses why your homework's not done!
- When the guy who bowled from a wheelchair was filmed for an ad, he became a roll model.
- Some people with disabilities can't cook for themselves so they're forced to eat from 3 basic food groups: canned, frozen and take out.
- Storyteller with Crutches - - - > Tales from the Crip.
- Money is like an arm or leg: use it or lose it. ~ Henry Ford
- He's unarmed now!
- Where is it written that the fun and games have to stop just because someone loses an eye?
- Dyslexics have more fnu!
- Make like an amputee and depart.
- What's the difference between my monthly Disability check and a sofa? A sofa supports a family.

- Walking is merely the state of perpetual falling over, we simply alternate which leg catches us.
- Thought I had Tourette's, but I just like talking dirty to you.
- The high cost of low living takes most of my disability check.
- Whenever I feel blue, I start breathing again.
- Dyslexics untie!
- The pharmacist told me to take these pills as often as I can get the cap off.
- As far as I know there is nowhere called 'Wheelchair' - so how can you be wheelchair-bound?

DYSLEXIC RIDDLE

Did you hear about the agnostic, dyslexic, insomniac?
She stayed up all night wondering if there really is a Dog.

ON THE BEACH

A man was lying on a blanket at the beach He had no arms or legs. Three women were walking past and felt sorry for the poor man.
The first woman said "Have you ever had a hug"
The man said "No", so she gave him a hug and walked on.
The second woman said "Have you ever had a kiss".
The man said "No", so she gave him a kiss and walked on.
The third woman walked over to him, knelt down and whispered in his ear, "Have you ever been f#&*%d?
The fellow looked up in amazement and said "No."
The woman smiled and said "Well, you will be when the tide comes in."

WHICH ONE?

I rear-ended a car this morning.
I tell you, I knew right then and there that it was going to be a really bad day!

The driver got out of the other car, and wouldn't you know it! He was a dwarf!!

He looked up at me and said "I am NOT Happy!"

So I said, "OK, then, which one are you?"

(NOTE: This is not to imply that people who are dwarfs are considered as having a disability, but we were a little 'light' in this category and thought it might fit.)

UGLY SUIT

When the store manager returned from lunch, he noticed his clerk's hand was bandaged, but before he could ask about the bandage, the clerk said he had some very good news for him.

"Guess what, sir?" the clerk said. "I finally sold that terrible, ugly suit we've had so long!"

"Do you mean that repulsive pink-and-blue double- breasted thing?" the manager asked.

"That's the one!"

That's great!" the manager cried, "I thought we'd never get rid of that monstrosity! That had to be the ugliest suit we've ever had! But tell me. Why is your hand bandaged?"

"Oh," the clerk replied, "after I sold the guy that suit, his guide dog bit me!"

SNIP, SNIP

There was a midget who complained to his buddy that his testicles ached all the time. As he was always talking on and on about his problem, his friend suggested that he go to the doctor and see what he could do to relieve the problem.

The midget took his advice and went to the doctor and told him what the problem was. The doctor told him to drop his pants so he could have a look. The midget dropped his pants, and the doctor put him up onto the examining table and proceeded to look for the trouble.

The doctor put one finger under his left testicle and told the midget to cough, which he did. "Ah!" mumbled the doc and putting his finger under the right one asked him to cough again, which he did. "Ahhh!" said the doctor and reached for his surgical scissors.

Snip, snip, snip on the right side and then snip, snip, snip on the left side. He told the midget to pull up his pants and see if it still ached.

The midget was delighted as he walked around the doc's office and his testicles were not aching.

"What did you do Doc?" he asked.

The doctor replied, "I cut two inches off the tops of your cowboy boots."

(NOTE: See note about dwarfs above...same goes for midgets.)

FROM GERI JEWELL

"You know the hardest thing about having cerebral palsy and being a woman? It's plucking your eyebrows. That's how I originally got pierced ears."

FROM DOUG TAYLOR

I was flying from San Francisco to Los Angeles. By the time we took off, there had been a 45-minute delay and everybody on board was ticked.

Unexpectedly, we stopped in Sacramento on the way. The flight attendant explained that there would be another 45-minute delay, and if we wanted to get off the aircraft, we would reboard in 30 minutes.

Everybody got off the plane except one gentleman who was blind. I noticed him as I walked by and could tell he had flown before because his guide dog lay quietly underneath the seats in front of him throughout the entire flight.

I could also tell he had flown this very flight before because the pilot approached him and, calling him by name, said, "Keith, we're in Sacramento for almost an hour. Would you like to get off and stretch your legs?"

Keith replied, "No thanks, but maybe my dog would like to stretch his legs."

Picture this... all the people in the gate area came to a completely quiet standstill when they looked up and saw the pilot walk off the plane with the guide dog! The pilot was even wearing sunglasses. People scattered. They not only tried to change planes, they also were trying to change airlines!

YOU MIGHT JUST HAVE ADHD WHEN...

...you find your pencil in your book bag, look up, and the rest of the class is no longer in the room.

...you lost your car keys more than once in the last ten minutes.

...you need an extra recycling box for the plastic medication bottles you discard each week.

...the stack of papers on your desk is as high as you are.

...you find the peanut butter in the freezer and you have no idea how it got there.

...you tell your child to organize her room and she tells you NEVER to use the "O" word in her presence.

...your family has been awarded the "patrons of the year" award at your neighborhood pharmacy.

...you count 108 surgical stitches on your body but you can't remember how they got there.

...you go to work every day for eight months after you retire.

...you can't remember the key word you thought up that would remind you of what you were trying to remember.

BLIND GOLFERS

A Catholic Priest, an Indian Doctor, a rich Chinese Businessman and an Italian were waiting one morning for a particularly slow group of golfers in front of them. The Italian fumed, "What's with those jerks? We must have been waiting for fifteen minutes!" The Indian Doctor chimed in, "I don't know, but I've never seen such poor golf!" The Chinese Businessman called out "Move it, time is money" The Catholic Priest said, "Here comes George the greens keeper. Let's have a word with him."

"Hello, George!" said the Catholic Priest, "What's wrong with that group ahead of us? They're rather slow, aren't they?" George the greens keeper replied, "Oh, yes. That's a group of blind fire fighters. They lost their sight saving our clubhouse from a fire last year, so we always let them play for free anytime." The group fell silent for a moment.

The Catholic Priest said, "That's so sad. I think I will say a special prayer for them tonight."

The Indian Doctor said, "Good idea. I'm going to contact my Ophthalmologist colleague and see if there's anything he can do for them."

The Chinese Businessman replied, "I think I'll donate $50,000 to the fire-fighters in honor of these brave souls."

The Italian said, "Why can't they f#&*ng play at night?"

THE GUIDE DOG

A man who was blind went for a walk with his guide dog. While on the walk, he encountered a friend he had not seen in awhile. They were catching up on what had been happening in their lives, when the dog lifted its leg and started urinating on his master's shoe. His friend noticed it but didn't say anything. The man with blindness reached in a pocket, pulled out a dog treat and started to feed it to the dog. His friend felt he had to say something and said, "Before you give your dog a treat, you might want to consider if you might be rewarding him for inappropriate behavior as he just peed on your shoe." His friend replied, "I'm not trying to reward him. I just want to find out where his head is so I can kick him in the ass."

Education Humor

STUDENT ANECDOTES

A kindergarten teacher was observing her classroom of children while they drew. She would occasionally walk around to see each child's artwork. As she got to one little girl who was working diligently, she asked what the drawing was. The girl replied, "I'm drawing God." The teacher paused and said, "But no one knows what God looks like. Without missing beat, or looking up from her drawing the girl replied, "They will in a minute."

On the first day of school, the Kindergarten teacher said, "If anyone has to go to the bathroom, hold up two fingers." A little voice from the back of the room asked, "How will that help?"

A teacher was giving a lesson on the circulation of the blood. Trying to make the matter clearer, he said, "Now, boys, if I stood on my head, the blood, as you know, would run into it, and I would turn red in the face." "Yes, sir," the boys said. "Then why is it that while I am standing upright in the ordinary position, the blood doesn't run into my feet?" A little fellow shouted, "'Cause yer feet ain't empty."

The children had all been photographed, and the teacher was trying to persuade them each to buy a copy of the group picture. "Just think how nice it will be to look at it when you are all grown up and say: 'There's Jennifer; she's a lawyer, or that's Michael. He's a doctor." A small voice at the back of the room rang out, "And there's the teacher. She's dead."

A new teacher was trying to make use of her Psychology courses. She started her class by saying, "Everyone who thinks you're stupid, stand up." After a few seconds, little Johnny stood up. The teacher said, "Do you think you're stupid, Johnny?" "No, ma'am," he said, "but I hate to see you standing there all by yourself."

The child comes home from his first day at school. Mother asks, "What did you learn today?" The kid replies, "Not enough. I have to go back tomorrow."

One day the first grade teacher was reading the story of Chicken Little to her class. She came to the part of the story where Chicken Little tried to warn the farmer. She read, ".... and so Chicken Little went up to the farmer and said, 'The sky is falling, the sky is falling!' The teacher paused then asked the class, "And what do you think that farmer said?" One little girl raised her hand and said, "I think he said: 'Holy shit! A talking chicken!'"

GOOD ANSWER

Teacher: George, name one important thing we have today that we did not have ten years ago.
George: Me!

THE TOP SIGNS A COLLEGE-STUDENT AUTHOR IS A PLAGIARIST
(© CHRIS WHITE)

-   Very few college students can write a first-person account of serving in the Roosevelt Administration.

- In the first 100 pages, you find over a dozen instances of "[INSERT CHARACTER NAME HERE]."
- "Can I get an advance? I need to renew my membership at termpaper.com."
- As you open the manila envelope containing the first draft, your office door is blown off its hinges. When the smoke clears, you find yourself surrounded by an elite team of LucasFilm lawyers, all with subpoenas drawn and pointed at your head.
- Her dedication and acknowledgments sections both mention her Canon copier.
- His book, "Religionetics," reads like a bad science fiction novel.
- "Romeo, Romeo, wherefore art thou, Romeo? I require a ride to the mall and, like, the battery on mine cell phone doth die!"
- The heartwarming passage of the four boys from boyhood innocence to the first glimmer of adult understanding is marred by Kenny's sudden death.
- Her novel begins, "Call me Shemale."
- "He quickly administered first aid. He held her eye open and rinsed gently with water for 15-20 minutes. He called a poison control center or a doctor for treatment advice."
- The dedication: "This book wouldn't have been possible without help from my good friend, Clifford Notes."

CHILDREN'S ANSWERS IN MUSIC EDUCATION (FROM THE MISSOURI SCHOOL MUSIC NEWSLETTER - SHARED BY BILL EDWARDS - EDWARDS _ BILL@COLSTATE.EDU)

- It is important to be able to reach the brakes on any piano.
- Just about any animal skin can be stretched over a frame to make a pleasant sound once the animal is removed.
- It is easy to teach anyone to play the maracas. Just grip the neck and shake him in rhythm.

- The plural form of musical instrument is known as orchestra.
- A contra-bassoon is like a bassoon, only the opposite.
- The most dangerous part about playing cymbals is near the nose.
- The main trouble with a French horn is it's too tangled up.
- For some reason, they always put a treble clef in front of every line of flute music. You just watch.
- The concertmaster of an orchestra is always the person who sits in the first chair of the first violins. This means that when a person is elected concertmaster, he has to hurry up and learn how to play a violin real good.
- Question: Is the saxophone a brass or a woodwind instrument? Answer: Yes.
- Question: What are kettle drums called? Answer: Kettle drums.
- When electric currents go through them, guitars start making sounds. So would anybody.
- A trumpet is an instrument when it is not an elephant sound.
- A harp is a nude piano.
- My very best liked piece of music is the Bronze Lullaby.
- Probably the most marvelous fugue was the one between the Hatfields and the McCoys.
- Most authorities agree that music of antiquity was written long ago.
- Caruso was at first an Italian. Then someone heard his voice and said he would go a long way. So that's why he came to America.
- I know what a sextet is but I'm not allowed to say.
- Music sung by two people at the same time is called a duel.
- Handel was half German, half Italian, and half English. He was rather large.
- Refrain means don't do it. A refrain in music is the part you better not try to sing.

THE FIELD TRIP

As a special treat, a teacher took her class to visit the museum of natural history. One child returned home excited about the trip and told his mother, "The teacher took us to a dead circus."

EXCUSE NOTES (REPORTED TO BE TRUE)

1. Dear School: Please excuse John from being absent on January 28, 29, 30, 31, 32 and, also, 33.
2. Please excuse Johnny for being. It was his father's fault.
3. Carlos was absent yesterday because he was playing football. He was hurt in the growing part.
4. Please excuse Sandra from being absent yesterday. She was in bed with gramps.
5. Ralph was absent yesterday because of sour trout.
6. Please excuse Gloria. She's been sick and under the doctor.
7. Lillie was absent from school yesterday as she had a gang over.
8. Please excuse Blanch from P.E. for a few days. Yesterday she fell out of a tree and misplaced her hip.
9. Please excuse Joyce from Jim today. She is administrating.
10. Please excuse Joey for Friday. He had loose vowels.
11. Please excuse Sarah for being absent. She was sick and I had her shot.
12. My son is under doctor's care and should not take P.M. Please execute him.

WASTING HER TIME

A little girl had just finished her first week of school. "I'm just wasting my time," she said to her mother. "I can't read, I can't write - and they won't let me talk!"

KINDERGARTEN

A group of kindergartners were trying very hard to become accustomed to the first grade. The biggest hurdle they faced was that the teacher insisted on **no** baby talk!

"You need to use 'Big People' words," she was always reminding them.

She asked Chris what he had done over the weekend. "I went to visit my Nana." "No, you went to visit your grandmother. Use 'Big People' words!"

She then asked Mitchell what he had done "I took a ride on a choo-choo."

She said "No, you took a ride on a train. You must remember to use 'Big People' words."

She then asked little Alex what he had done. "I read a book," he replied. "That's wonderful!" the teacher said. "What book did you read?"

Alex thought real hard about it, then puffed out his chest with great pride, and said, "Winnie the Shit."

EDUCATION RIDDLES

Teacher: Why are you late?
Webster: Because of the sign.
Teacher: What sign?
Webster: The one that says, "School Ahead, Go Slow."

Teacher: Cindy, why are you doing your multiplication on the floor?
Cindy: You told me to do it without using tables!

Teacher: What is the chemical formula for water?
Sarah h i j k l m n o!!
Teacher: What are you talking about?
Sarah: Yesterday you said it's h to o!

Teacher: David, go to the map and find North America.

David:	Here it is!
Teacher:	Correct. Now class, who discovered America?
Class:	David!

Bobby:	I don't think I deserve a zero on this test!
Teacher:	Neither do I, but it's the lowest grade I can give you.

Teacher:	Tommy, why do you always get so dirty?
Tommy:	Well, I'm a lot closer to the ground than you are.

Teacher:	Ellen, give me a sentence starting with "i."
Ellen:	I is...
Teacher:	No, Ellen. Always say, "I am."
Ellen:	All right.... "I am the ninth letter of the alphabet."

Teacher:	I hope I didn't see you looking at someone else's paper, Billy.
Billy:	I hope so too, Teacher.

Teacher:	Mark, your composition on "My Dog" is exactly the same as your brother's. Did you copy his?
Desmond:	No teacher, it's the same dog!

Teacher:	How fast does light travel?
Student:	I'm not sure, but I do know it always gets here too early in the morning.

Sylvia:	Dad, can you write in the dark?
Father:	I think so. What do you want me to write?
Sylvia:	Your name on this report card.

THE FINAL EXAM

At Duke University there were four sophomores taking Chemistry and all of them had an "A" so far. These four friends were so confident that the weekend before finals they decided to visit some friends and have a big party. They had a great time, but, after all the hearty partying, they slept all day Sunday and didn't make it back to Duke until early Monday morning. Rather than taking the final then, they decided that after the final they would explain to their professor why they missed it. They said that they visited friends but on the way back they had a flat tire. As a result, they missed the final.

The professor agreed they could make up the final the next day. The guys were excited and relieved. They studied that night for the exam. The Professor placed them in separate rooms and gave them a test booklet. They quickly answered the first problem, worth 5 points. Cool, they thought!

Each one in a separate room, thinking this was going to be easy, they turned the page.

On the second page was written.... For 95 points: Which tire? _____.

TEACHING ANECDOTES

When making papier-mâché my students were to rip newspaper into strips and soak them in the glue mixture. Some were having problems getting the correct width, so I demonstrated how to hold the newspaper and rip the strips one-inch wide. One of my third grade boys watched me admiringly and said, "Mrs. Lutz, you are the best stripper I have ever seen."
Bonnie Lutz - Evansville, Minnesota

As I distributed a quiz to my seventh grade English class, one student asked how they should prepare the paper's heading. I responded, "Write your name, and then wait." After a few seconds, I heard a shy girl's voice from the back of the room ask, "Well, I can understand why you want us to write our names on the paper, but why would you want to know our weight?" As soon as she realized what I'd meant, no one giggled more about this incident than the girl who asked the question did.
Robert Ritzer - Ramsex, New Jersey

I was teaching a class of first graders about Wolfgang Amadeus Mozart, whose birthday is in January. I introduced the book I had on young Mozart by saying, "This week, we will celebrate the birthday of a very famous musician." Two or three of my little ones exclaimed, "We didn't know it was your birthday this week, Mrs. Lennon!" (It put me on cloud nine for the rest of the day!)
Hope Lennon - Newark, Delaware

I was a band director from 1948-81. Once, while teaching at a junior high, I took my kindergarten son to see his first symphony concert. After tuning up, the orchestra program began. He was impressed. After intermission the tune up began again. My young man nudged me and said, "Dad, they played this song before."
Bill Wilson - Western Springs, Illinois

One of my kindergartners missed his bus; I walked with him to the principal's office to call for someone to pick him up. When he got to the office, he looked all around and very seriously asked, "Where are the clowns?" I'm sure I looked quite confused, and he quite innocently added, "My dad said that there was a bunch of clowns in this office."
Sue Warner - Elizabethtown, Kentucky

While discussing fossil hunting with my third graders, I wanted them to understand that paleontologists do not find articulated skeletons. They find just lots of bones from different dinosaurs. I explained that the stuff that holds our bones together doesn't survive the process of decay. Then I asked if they remembered what we call this matter. Evan, one of my brightest, enthusiastically waved his arm and declared with great confidence: "Snot!' At first, I thought he was being intentionally disruptive and gave him a behavior warning. He was hurt and whined, "But you told us it was that stuff in our noses!" Then I realized that in our previous discussion of cartilage, I'd told them, "That thing in your nose (meaning the septum) is the same stuff that holds your bones together."
Joe Midzalkowski - Polk County, Florida

When a principal I worked for retired, all the children in the elementary school wrote him goodbye letters. At his farewell banquet, he read from several. One boy wrote, "You were a good principal while you lasted." Another wrote, "Did you always want to be principal, or did they make you?"
Joan Mary Macey - Binghamton, New York

THE TOP 15 INDICATIONS IT'S TIME TO RETIRE FROM TEACHING
(© 2000 CHRIS WHITE WWW.TOPFIVE.COM)

15. "I'll sleep with you for an A" now sounds like too much damn work on your part.
14. You keep accidentally pinning notes for your students' parents to your own shirt.
13. Your Social Security check is now larger than your paycheck.
12. You ask a 17-year-old football player over to mow your lawn, and neither one of you fantasizes about anything else happening.
11. That wasn't the chalk that snapped while you were at the blackboard -- it was your wrist.
10. You once had the author autograph a copy of "The Canterbury Tales."
9. Thanks to the Internet, now the kids know everything about those years you spent as a struggling actress.
8. Your third grade kids think your whoopee cushion is hilarious -- only you don't have a whoopee cushion.
7. You don't just teach Latin -- it's your native language.
6. Recurring humiliation every morning when your artificial hip sets off the school's metal detectors.
5. Under the school's zero tolerance drug policy, you've been disciplined for your excessive use of Vick's Vap-o-Rub.
4. Your students' cell phones or PDAs have more memory than you do.
3. Every time a student boots a computer in the library, you point and scream, "Witch! Witch! Spawn of Satan!!!
2. Every year, it gets tougher to go 50 minutes without taking a leak.
1. Your local Kansas school board just came in and hammered your globe flat.

THE LIBRARY BOOK

The boy took home a library book whose cover read *How to Hug* only to find that it was Volume VII of the encyclopedia.

GOOD BEHAVIOR

The fourth-grade teacher had to leave the room for a few minutes. When she returned, she found the children in perfect order. Everybody was sitting absolutely quiet. She was shocked and stunned and said, "I've never seen anything like it before. This is wonderful. But, please tell me, what came over all of you? Why are you so well-behaved and quiet?"

Finally, after much urging, a little girl said, "Well, one time you said that if you ever came back and found us quiet, you would drop dead."

THE LESSON (SHARED BY WENDEL WICKLAND)

Then Jesus took his disciples up the mountain and gathering them around him, he taught them saying:

Blessed are the poor in spirit for theirs is the kingdom of heaven,
Blessed are the meek,
Blessed are they that mourn,
Blessed are the merciful,
Blessed are they that thirst for justice,
Blessed are you when persecuted,
Blessed are you when you suffer,
Be glad and rejoice for your reward is great in heaven.

Then Peter said, "Are we supposed to know this?"
And Andrew said, "Do we have to write this down?"
And James said, "Will we have a test on this?"
And Phillip said, "I don't have any paper."
And Bartholomew said, "Do we have to turn this in?"
And John said, "The other disciples didn't have to learn this."
And Matthew said, "May I go to the bathroom?"
And Judas said, "What does this have to do with the real world?"

Then one of the Pharisees who was present asked to see Jesus' lesson plan and inquired of Jesus,

"Where is your anticipatory set and your objectives in the cognitive and affective domains?"

And Jesus wept.

YOU MIGHT BE A TEACHER IF...

- You can tell it's a full moon without ever looking outside.
- When out in public, you feel the urge to talk to strange children and correct their behavior.
- You think people should be required to get a government permit before being allowed to reproduce.
- Meeting a child's parents INSTANTLY answers the question, "Why is this kid like this?"
- You move your dinner partner's glass away from the edge of the table.
- You ask if anyone needs to go to the bathroom as you enter a theater with a group of friends.
- You hand a tissue to anyone who sneezes.
- You refer to "snack time" as "happy hour".
- You ask guests if they have remembered their scarves and mittens as they leave your home.
- You say, "I like the way you did that" to the mechanic who repairs your car.
- You ask, "Are you sure you did your best?" to the mechanic who fails to repair your car.
- You sing the "Alphabet Song" to yourself as you look up a number in the phone book.
- You fold your spouse's fingers over the coins as you hand him/her the money for the tollbooth.
- You ask a quiet person at a party if he has something to share with the group.
- You declare "no cuts" when a shopper squeezes ahead of you in a checkout line.

- You want to slap the next person who says, "Must be nice to have all your holidays and summers free."

SHOW AND TELL
(BY AN ANONYMOUS 2ND GRADE TEACHER)

I've been teaching now for about fifteen years. I have two kids myself, but the best birth story I know is the one I saw in my own second-grade classroom a few years back.

When I was a kid, I loved show-and-tell. So I always have a few sessions with my students. It helps them get over shyness and usually, show-and-tell is pretty tame. Kids bring in pet turtles, model airplanes, pictures of fish they catch, stuff like that.

And I never, ever place any boundaries or limitations on them. If they want to lug it to school and talk about it, they're welcome.

Well, one day this little girl, Erica, a very bright, very outgoing kid, takes her turn and waddles up to the front of the class with a pillow stuffed under her sweater. She holds up a snapshot of an infant. "This is Luke, my baby brother and I'm going to tell you about his birthday. First, Mom and Dad made him as a symbol of their love and then Dad put a seed in my Mom's stomach and Luke grew in there. He ate for nine months through an "umbrella cord.""

She's standing there with her hands on the pillow and I'm trying not to laugh and wishing I had my camcorder with me. The kids are watching her in amazement.

"Then, about two Saturdays ago, my Mom starts saying and going, 'Oh, oh, oh!' Erica puts a hand behind her back and groans. "She walked around the house for, like an hour, 'Oh, oh, oh!' Now the kid's doing this hysterical duck walk, holding her back and groaning.

"My Dad called the middle wife. She delivers babies, but she doesn't have a sign on the car like the Domino's man." "They got my Mom to lie down in bed like this." Then Erica lies down with her back against the wall.

"And then, pop! My Mom had this bag of water she kept in there in case he got thirsty, and it just blew up and spilled all over the bed, like psshhheew!" Now Erica has her legs spread and her little hands are miming water flowing away. It was too much!

"Then the middle wife starts saying 'push, push' and 'breathe, breathe'. They started counting, but never even got past ten."

"Then, all of a sudden, out comes my brother. He was covered in yucky stuff, they all said was from Mom's play-center so there must be a lot of stuff inside there."

Then Erica stood up, took a big theatrical bow and returned to her seat. I'm sure I applauded the loudest. Ever since then, if it's show-and-tell day, I bring my camcorder, just in case another Erica comes along.

CHILDREN'S ANSWERS TO SCIENCE EXAMINATION QUESTIONS (ALLEGEDLY TRUE)

Q: Name the four seasons.
A: Salt, pepper, mustard and vinegar.

Q: Explain one of the processes by which water can be made safe to drink.
A: Flirtation makes water safe to drink because it removes large pollutants like grit, sand, dead sheep and canoeists.

Q: How can you delay milk turning sour?
A: Keep it in the cow.

Q: What causes the tides in the oceans?
A: The tides are a fight between the Earth and the Moon. All water tends to flow towards the moon, because there is no water on the moon, and nature hates a vacuum.

Q: What happens to your body as you age?
A: When you get old, so do your bowels and you get intercontinental.

Q: What happens to a boy when he reaches puberty?
A: He says good-bye to his boyhood and looks forward to his adultery.

Q: Name a major disease associated with cigarettes.
A: Premature death.

Q: What is artificial insemination?
A: When the farmer does it to the bull instead of the cow

Q: How are the main parts of the body categorized? (e.g., abdomen.)
A: The body is consisted into three parts -- the brainium, the borax and the abdominal cavity. The brainium contains the brain; the borax contains the heart and lungs, and the abdominal cavity contains the five bowels, A, E, I, O, and U.

Q: What is the fibula?
A: A small lie.

Q: What does "varicose" mean?
A: Nearby.

Q: Give the meaning of the term "Caesarian Section"
A: The Caesarian Section is a district in Rome.

Q: What does the word "benign" mean?
A: Benign is what you will be after you be eight.

Ethnic and Nationality Humor

THE BEST BAR

Y'know" said the Scotsman, "I still prefer the pubs back home in Glasgow.... there's a little bar called McTavish's. Now the landlord there goes out of his way for the locals so much that when you buy 4 drinks he will buy the 5th drink for you."

"Well", said the Englishman, "at my local, the Red Lion, the barman there will buy you your 3rd drink after you buy the first 2."

"Ahhhhh, that's nothing", said the Irishman. "Back home in Dublin there's Ryan's Bar. Now the moment you set foot in the place they'll buy you a drink, then another, all the drinks you like. Then when you've had enough drinks they'll take you upstairs and see that you get laid. All on the house." The Englishman and Scotsman immediately scorn the Irishman's claims. But he swears every word is true.

"Well," said the Englishman "did this actually happen to you?"

"Not me meself, personally, no," said the Irishman.

"But it did happen to me sister."

THE EYE TEST

A Polish immigrant goes to the DMV to apply for a driver's license and of course he has to take an eye test.

The clerk shows him the eye chart: **C Z W I X N O S T A C Z**

"Can you read this?" the clerk asks.

"Read it?" the guy says, "Hell, I know the guy!"

POLISH-ITALIAN

Did you hear about the guy who was half Polish and half Italian? He made himself an offer he couldn't understand.

RED NECK VACATION

Billy Bob and Luther were talking one afternoon when Billy Bob tells Luther, "Ya know, I reckon I'm 'bout ready for a vacation. Only this year I'm gonna do it a little different. The last few years, I took your advice about where to go.

Three years ago you said to go to Hawaii. I went to Hawaii and Earlene got pregnant.

Then two years ago, you told me to go to the Bahamas, and Earlene got pregnant again.

Last year you suggested Tahiti and darned if Earlene didn't get pregnant again."

Luther asks Billy Bob, "So, what you gonna do this year that's different?"

Billy Bob says, "This year I'm taking Earlene with me."

THE TEXAN AND THE ISRAELI

A farmer on a Kibbutz was talking to a Texan. The Texan says, "How big is your farm?"

"Well," the Israeli responds, "it's two hundred feet by three hundred feet. How big is your ranch?"

The Texan says, "I could get in my truck and drive from sunrise to sunset and never get to the end of my land."

The Israeli farmer says, "I once had a truck like that too."

THANK GOD

An Irishman who had a little too much to drink is driving home from the city one night and, of course, his car is weaving violently all over the road.

A cop pulls him over. "So," says the cop to the driver, where have ya been?

"Why, I've been to the Happy Hog," slurs the drunk.

"Well," says the cop, "it looks like you've had quite a few to drink this evening."

"I did all right," the drunk says with a smile.

"Did you know," says the cop, standing straight and folding his arms across his chest, "that a few intersections back, your wife fell out of your car?"

"Oh, thank God," sighs the drunk. "For a minute there, I thought I'd gone deaf."

FILIPINO CONTORTIONIST

What do you call a Filipino contortionist?
A Manila folder.

THE GENERIC ETHNIC JOKE

A person belonging to an ethnic group whose members are commonly considered to have certain stereotypical mannerisms met another person belonging to a different ethnic group with a different set of imputed stereotypical mannerisms. The first person acted in a manner consistent with the stereotypes associated with his ethnic group, and proceeded to make a remark which might be considered to establish conclusively his membership in that group, whereupon his companion proceeded to make a remark with a double meaning, the first meaning of which could be interpreted to indicate his agreement with his companion, but the other meaning of which serves to corroborate his membership in his particular ethnic group. The first person took offense at his remark, and reacted in a stereotypical way!

GRITS AND AN RC COLA

Man: "Let me have some grits and an RC Cola."

Guy behind the counter: "You must be from Mississippi."

Man: "What the hell kinda stereotypical remark is that? If I walked in here and asked for a sausage would you think I was Polish?"

Guy: "No."

Man: If I walked in here and asked for some chow mein would you think I was Chinese?"

Guy: "No."

Man: If I walked in here and asked for some pizza would you think I was Italian?"

Guy: "No."

Man: "Then why the hell do you think I'm from Mississippi?"

Guy: "Because this is a hardware store."

JOINT VENTURE

Did you hear about the African American and the Mexican who opened a restaurant together?

It's called "Nacho Mama."

MARCUS

Marcus came into the kitchen where his mother was making dinner. His birthday was coming up and he thought this was a good time to tell his Mother what he wanted.

"Mom, I want a bike for my birthday." Marcus was a bit of a troublemaker. He had gotten into trouble at school and at home. Marcus's mother asked him if he thought he deserved to get a bike for his birthday. "Of course", he said.

Marcus's mother, being a Christian woman, wanted him to reflect on his behavior over the last year. "Go to your room, Marcus, and think about how you have behaved this year. Then write a letter to God and tell him why you deserve a bike for your birthday." Marcus stomped up the steps to his room and sat down to write God a letter.

Letter 1: Dear God, I have been a very good boy this year and I would like a bike for my birthday. I want a red one. Your friend, Marcus.

Marcus knew that it was not true. He had not been a good boy this year, so he tore it up and started over.

Letter 2: Dear God, I have been an OK boy this year. I still would like a bike for my birthday. Marcus.

Marcus knew he could not send this letter to God either. So, Marcus wrote a third letter.

Letter 3: Dear God, I know I haven't been a good boy this year. I am very sorry. I will be a good boy if you just send me a bike for my birthday. Please! Thank you, Marcus.

Marcus knew that it was not true. By now he was very upset. He went downstairs and told his mother that he needed to go to church. She thought her plan had worked. Just be home for dinner," she told him.

Marcus walked down the street to the church on the corner. He went to the altar. Marcus looked around to see if anyone was looking as he bent down and picked up a statue of the Virgin Mary.

He slipped it up under his shirt and ran out the church going back home. He ran to his room and shut the door. Marcus began to write his letter to God.

Letter 4: Dear God, I got your mama. If you want to see her again, send the bike. Signed, You know who.

THE CATSKILLS

Two elderly Jewish women are dining at a resort in the Catskill Mountains. One of them says, "The food at this place is disgusting." "Yes," says her friend, "and such small portions."

A JOB FOR THE NORWEGIAN

A Norwegian man wanted a job, but the foreman wasn't too keen to hire him. He told the Norwegian that first he would have to pass a math test.

The Norwegian agreed. "Here's your first question, the foreman said. Without using numbers, represent the number nine.

"Without numbers?" the Norwegian says, "Dat's easy." and proceeded to draw a picture of three trees. "What's this?" the boss asked.

"Ave you got no brain? Tree and tree and tree make nine, "said the Norwegian.

"Fair enough," said the foreman, while thinking to himself that he had been outsmarted.

"Here's your second question. Use the same rules, but this time the number is 99."

The Norwegian stares into space for a while, then picks up the picture that he has just drawn and makes a smudge on each tree. "Ere you go."

The boss scratches his head and says, "How on earth do you figure that to represent 99?" "Vell, each of dose trees is dirty now. So, it's dirty tree, dirty tree, and dirty tree, and dat is 99."

The foreman is now worried that he's actually going to have to hire this Norwegian, so he says, "all right, last question. Same rules again, but represent the number 100.

"The Norwegian stares into space some more, then he picks up the picture again and makes a little mark at the base of each tree and says, "Ere you go. One hundred."

The boss looks at the attempt. "You must be nuts if you think that represents a hundred!"

The Norwegian leans forward and points to the marks at the base of each tree and says,

"A little dog came along and crap by each tree. So now you got dirty tree and a turd, dirty tree and a turd, and dirty tree and a turd, which makes one hundred.....So, when I start?!"

HOT AND THIRSTY

German: "I'm hot and thirsty, I must have beer."
Frenchman: "I'm hot and thirsty, I must have wine."
Russian: "I'm hot and thirsty, I must have vodka."
Jew: "I'm hot and thirsty, I must have diabetes."

RUSSIAN BRIDE

What does the bride of a Russian man get on her wedding night that is long and hard?

A new last name.

BOUDREAUX'S DIET

Boudreaux was terribly overweight, so his doctor put him on a diet.

The Doc says," Boudreau, I want you to eat regularly for 2 days, then skip a day, and repeat this procedure for 2 weeks. The next time I see you, you should have lost at least five pounds."

When Boudreaux returns, the doctor is shocked to see he's lost nearly 60 pounds!

Why that's amazing!' the doctor says, "Did you follow my instructions?" Boudreaux nods.

"I tell you though, by God, I thought I wuz gonna drop dead on dat turd day," he says.

"From the hunger, you mean?" asks the doctor.

"Hell no! From all dat damn skippin!"

THE BEST TOAST

John O'Reilly hoisted his beer and said, "Here's to spending the rest of me life between the legs of me wife!" That won him the top prize at the pub for the Best Toast of the Night! He went home and told his wife, Mary, "I won the prize for the Best Toast of the Night". She said, "Aye, did ye now. And what was your toast?" John said, "Here's to spending the rest of me life, sitting in church beside me wife." "Oh, that is very nice indeed, John!" Mary said. The next day, Mary ran into one of John's drinking buddies on the street corner. The man chuckled leeringly and said, "John won the prize the other night at the pub with a toast about you, Mary." She said, "Aye, he told me, and I was a bit surprised myself. You know, he's only been there twice in the last four years. Once he fell asleep, and the other time I had to pull him by the ears to make him come."

JEWISH WOMEN

The waiter walks over to the table of four elderly Jewish women and asks, "Is anything OK?"

CANADIAN SEX

Why do Canadian couples both like having sex doggie style?
So they can both keep watching the hockey game.

LEAVING EARLY

There were these three guys, a Polish guy, an Italian guy, and a Jewish guy. They all worked together at a factory. Everyday they notice that their boss leaves work a little early. So one day they meet together and say that today when the boss leaves, they'll all leave early too.

The boss left and so did they. The Jewish guy goes home and goes to rest so he can get an early start. The Italian guy goes home and cooks dinner. The Polish guy goes home and walks to his bedroom.

He opens the door slowly and sees his wife in bed with his boss so he shuts the door and leaves.

The next day the Italian and Jewish guys are talking and plan to go home early again. They ask the Polish guy if he wants to leave early again and he says, "no." They ask him why not and he said, "because yesterday I almost got caught!"

WHY IN THE WORLD...

The Chinese man wakes up his wife about 3:00 am and says, "How about some 69?" She replies, "Why in the world would you want Beef and Broccoli in the middle of the night?!"

STRANGE COINCIDENCE

A man stumbles up to the only other patron in a bar and asks if he could buy him a drink. "Why, of course," comes the reply. The first man then asks, "Where are you from?" "Why, I'm from Ireland," replies the second man. The first man responds: "You don't say, I'm from Ireland too! Let's have another round to Ireland." "Of course," says the second. Curious, the first man asks: "Where in Ireland?" "Dublin," comes the reply. "I can't believe it, me too! Let's have another round of drinks to Dublin." "Of course." The second man can't help himself so he asks, "What school did you attend?" "Saint Mary's", replies the first man. "I graduated in '62." "Me too!!", says the second man. "This is becoming unbelievable!" They say in unison. About that time, in comes one of the regulars and sits down at the bar. "What's up?" he asks the bartender. "Nothing much," replied the bartender. "The O'Malley twins are drunk again!"

JAPANESE MEN

What do Japanese men do when they have erections?
Vote.

THE GORILLA AND THE REDNECK

A small zoo in Tennessee obtained a very rare species of gorilla. Within a few weeks the gorilla, a female, became very difficult to handle. Upon examination, the veterinarian determined the problem. The gorilla was in heat. To make matters worse, there was no male gorilla available.

Thinking about their problem, the Zoo Keeper thought of Bobby Lee Walton, a redneck part-time worker responsible for cleaning the animal cages.

Bobby Lee, like most rednecks, had little sense but possessed ample ability to satisfy a female of any species.

The Zoo Keeper thought they might have a solution. Bobby Lee was approached with a proposition. Would he be willing to mate with the gorilla for $500.00?

Bobby Lee showed some interest, but said he would have to think the matter over carefully. The following day, he announced that he would accept their offer, but only under four conditions.

1. "First", Bobby Lee said, "I ain't gonna kiss her on the lips." The Keeper quickly agreed to this condition.
2. "Second", he said, you can never tell anyone about this The Keeper again readily agreed to this condition.
3. "Third", Bobby Lee said, "I want all the children raised Southern Baptist." Once again it was agreed.
4. And last, Bobby Lee said "I'll need another week to come up with the $500.00.

Everyday Humor

THE TELEMARKETER

The phone rings and there's about two seconds of silence. You know what's going on. The computer is searching for an idle sales representative who will shortly come on the line, ask you how you are and mispronounce your name.   Here's how one person handled one such call recently.

Q. "Hello, may I speak with (name omitted)."
A. "Bernie? Oh thank God you called! I'm on the way to the funeral home. Have you picked up the cats?"
Q. "I'm sorry. I'm sorry."
A. "Have you picked up the cats?"
Q. (Dumbfounded pause). "No." (Hangs up).

LETTERS DEAR ABBY ADMITTED SHE
WAS AT A LOSS TO ANSWER

Dear Abby - A couple of women moved in across the hall from me. One is a middle-aged gym teacher and the other is a social worker in her mid twenties. These two women go everywhere together and I've never seen a man go into or leave their apartment. Do you think they could be Lebanese?

Dear Abby - What can I do about all the Sex, Nudity, Fowl Language, and Violence on My VCR?

Dear Abby - I have a man I can't trust. He cheats so much, I'm not even sure the baby I'm carrying is his.

Dear Abby - I am a twenty-three year old liberated woman who has been on the pill for two years. It's getting expensive and I think my boyfriend should share half the cost, but I don't know him well enough to discuss money with him.

Dear Abby - I've suspected that my husband has been fooling around, and when confronted with the evidence, he denied everything and said it would never happen again.

Dear Abby - Our son writes that he is taking Judo. Why would a boy who was raised in a good Christian home turn against his own?

Dear Abby - I joined the Navy to see the world. I have seen it. Now how do I get out?

Dear Abby - My forty year old son has been paying a psychiatrist $50.00 an hour every week for two and a half years. He must be crazy.

Dear Abby - I was married to Bill for three months and I didn't know he drank until one night he came home sober.

Dear Abby - My mother is mean and short tempered. I think she is going through mental pause.

Dear Abby - You told some woman whose husband had lost all interest in sex to send him to a doctor. Well, my husband lost all interest in sex and he is a doctor. Now, what do I do?

THE DEER

While a Texan was busily preparing for the first day of deer hunting season, his wife started nagging that he never asked her to go along. After several hours of arguments, the wife won. That next morning they drove out to the country, and he placed his wife in a tree about 100 yards from his blind. Just as the hunter reached the blind, he heard a loud bang coming from the wife's position. As he ran up to her, he saw that she was holding her gun on a man nearby and shouting, "It's my deer! Get away from it!! The sheepish-looking stranger just nodded slowly and said, "OK, lady.. It's your deer. Just let me get my saddle off of it!"

THE NAME CHANGE (SHARED BY HERMAN E. GABEL, JR.)

A man goes before the judge requesting he be allowed to legally change his name. The Judge asks, "What is your current name." "Sam Stinks," replies the man. "Well," says the Judge, "I can understand why you would want to change your name. Do you have a name you would like to change it to?" "Yes," replied the man, "Steve."

EMBARRASSING STORIES

I walked into a hair salon with my husband and three kids in tow and asked loudly, "How much do you charge for a shampoo and a blow job?" I turned around and walked back out and never went back. My husband didn't say a word.....he knew better.

I was at the golf store comparing different kinds of golf balls. I was un-happy with the women's type I had been using. After browsing for several minutes, I was approached by one of the good-looking gentlemen who work at the store. He asked if he could help me. Without thinking, I looked at him and said, "I think I like playing with men's balls."

My sister and I were at the mall and passed by a store that sold a variety of candy and nuts. As we were looking at the display case, the boy behind the counter asked if we needed any help. I replied, "No, I'm just looking at your nuts". My sister started to laugh hysterically, the boy grinned, and I turned beet-red and walked away. To this day, my sister has never let me forget.

While in line at the bank one afternoon, my toddler decided to release some pent-up energy and ran amok. I was finally able to grab hold of her after receiving looks of disgust and annoyance from other patrons. I told her that if she did not start behaving "right now" she would be punished. To my horror, she looked me in the eye and said in a voice just as threatening, "If you don't let me go right now, I will tell

Grandma that I saw you kissing Daddy's pee-pee last night". The silence was deafening after this enlightening exchange. Even the tellers stopped what they were doing. I mustered up the last of my dignity and walked out of the bank with my daughter in tow. The last thing I heard when the door closed behind me were screams of laughter.

Have you ever asked your child a question too many times? My three year old son had a lot of problems with potty training and I was on him constantly. One day we stopped at Taco Bell for a quick lunch in between errands. It was very busy, with a full dining room. While enjoying my taco, I smelled something funny, so of course, I checked my seven month old daughter, and she was clean. Then I realized that Danny had not asked to go potty in awhile, so I asked him if he needed to go. He said "No". I kept thinking, "Oh Lord, that child has had an accident and I don't have any clothes with me." Then I said, "Danny, are you sure you didn't have an accident?" "No", he replied. I just knew that he must have had an accident, because the smell was getting worse. So, I asked one more time, "Danny, did you have an accident?" This time he jumped up, yanked down his pants, bent over and spread his cheeks and yelled "See Mom, it's just farts!!", while 30 people nearly choked to death on their tacos laughing! He calmly pulled up his pants and sat down. An older couple made me feel better by thanking me for the best laugh they'd ever had.

We had a female news anchor who, the day after it was supposed to have snowed and didn't, turned to the weatherman and asked: "So Bob, where's that eight inches you promised me last night?" Not only did he have to leave the set, but half the crew did too, they were laughing so hard.

Calling in sick to work makes me uncomfortable. No matter how legitimate my excuse, I always get the feeling that my boss thinks I'm lying. On one recent occasion, I had a valid reason but lied anyway, because the truth was just too darned humiliating. I simply mentioned that I had sustained a head injury, and I hoped I would feel up to coming in the next day. By then, I reasoned, I could think up a doozy to explain the bandage on the top of my head. The accident occurred mainly because I had given in to my wife's wishes to adopt a cute little kitty.

Initially, the new acquisition was no problem. Then one morning, I was taking my shower after breakfast when I heard my wife, Deb, call out to me from the kitchen. 'Honey! The garbage disposal is dead again. Please come reset it.' 'You know where the button is,' I protested through the shower pitter-patter and steam. 'Reset it yourself!' 'But I'm scared!' she persisted. 'What if it starts going and sucks me in?'

There was a meaningful pause and then, 'C'mon, it'll only take you a second.' So out I came, dripping wet and butt naked, hoping that my silent outraged nudity would make a statement about how I perceived her behavior as extremely cowardly. Sighing loudly, I squatted down and stuck my head under the sink to find the button. It is the last action I remember performing.

It struck without warning, and without any respect to my circumstances. No, it wasn't the hexed disposal, drawing me into its gnashing metal teeth. It was our new kitty, who discovered the fascinating dangling objects she spied hanging between my legs. She had been poised around the corner and stalked me as I reached under the sink. And, at the precise moment when I was most vulnerable, she leapt at the toys I unwittingly offered and snagged them with her needle-like claws. I lost all rational thought to control orderly bodily movements, blindly rising at a violent rate of speed, with the full weight of a kitten hanging from my masculine region.

Wild animals are sometimes faced with a 'fight or flight' syndrome. Men, in this predicament, choose only the 'flight' option. I know this from experience. I was fleeing straight up into the air when the sink and cabinet bluntly and forcefully impeded my ascent. The impact knocked me out cold.

When I awoke, my wife and the paramedics stood over me. Now there are not many things in this life worse than finding oneself lying on the kitchen floor butt naked in front of a group of 'been-there, done-that' paramedics. Even worse, having been fully briefed by my wife, the paramedics were all snorting loudly as they tried to conduct their work, all the while trying to suppress their hysterical laughter......and not succeeding.

Somehow I lived through it all. A few days later I finally made it back in to the office, where colleagues tried to coax an explanation out of me about my head injury. I kept silent, claiming it was too painful to talk about, which it was. 'What's the matter?' They all asked, 'Cat got your tongue?' If they only knew.

NEW KIND OF CAR

Two guys sat down for lunch in the office cafeteria. "Hey, whatever happened to Pete in payroll?" one asked. "He got this hare brained notion he was going to build a new kind of car," his coworker replied.

"How was he going to do it?" "He took an engine from a Pontiac, tires from a Chevy, seats from a Lincoln, hubcaps from a Caddy and well, you get the idea." "So what did he end up with?"

"Ten years to life."

AMAZINGLY SIMPLE HOME REMEDIES

- If you're choking on an ice cube, simply pour a cup of boiling water down your throat. Presto! The blockage will instantly remove itself.
- Avoid cutting yourself when slicing vegetables by getting someone else to hold them while you chop.
- Avoid arguments with the Mrs. about lifting the toilet seat, by using the sink.
- For high blood pressure sufferers: Simply cut yourself and bleed for a few minutes, thus reducing the pressure in your veins. (*Remember to use a timer...and possibly duct tape.*)
- A mouse trap, placed on top of your alarm clock, will prevent you from rolling over and going back to sleep after you hit the snooze button. (*Use duct tape to secure the mouse trap.*)
- If you have a bad cough, take a large dose of laxatives -- then you'll be afraid to cough.
- You only need two tools in life -- WD-40 and duct tape. If it doesn't move and should, use the WD-40. If it shouldn't move and does, use the duct tape.

- Remember: Everyone seems normal until you get to know them.

THE DRUNK

A drunk staggers into a Catholic church, enters a confessional, and sits down but says nothing.

The Priest coughs a few times to get his attention but the drunk continues to sit there. Finally the Priest pounds three times on the wall.

The drunk mumbles "Ain't no use knockin. There's no paper on this side, either."

NEIL ARMSTRONG - A TRUE STORY

On July 20, 1969, as commander of the Apollo 11 lunar module, Neil Armstrong was the first person to set foot on the moon. His first words after stepping on the moon, "that's one small step for man, one giant leap for mankind," were televised to earth and heard by millions. But just before he reentered the lander, he made the enigmatic remark "Good luck, Mr. Gorsky."

Many people at NASA though it was a casual remark concerning some rival soviet cosmonaut. However, upon checking, there was no Gorsky in either the Russian or American space programs. Over the years many people questioned Armstrong as to what the "Good luck, Mr. Gorsky" statement meant, but Armstrong always just smiled.

On July 5, 1995, in Tampa bay, Florida, while answering questions following a speech, a reporter brought up the 26-year-old question to Armstrong. This time he finally responded. Mr. Gorsky had died, so Neil Armstrong felt he could answer the question. In 1938 when he was a kid in a small Midwest town, he was playing baseball with a friend in the backyard. His friend hit the ball, which landed in his neighbor's yard by the bedroom windows. His neighbors were Mr. and Mrs. Gorsky. As he leaned down to pick up the ball, young Armstrong heard Mrs. Gorsky shouting at Mr. Gorsky. "Sex! You want sex?!" You'll get sex when the kid next door walks on the moon!" A true story.

PROBLEM SOLVING

Question: You are driving in a car at a constant speed. On your left side is a drop off (the ground is 18-20 inches below the level you are traveling on), and on your right side is a fire engine traveling at the same speed as you. In front of you is a galloping horse which is the same size as your car and you cannot overtake it. Behind you is another galloping horse. Both horses are also traveling at the same speed as you. What must you do to safely get out of this highly dangerous situation?

Answer: Get your drunken ass off the merry-go-round.

TOP TEN THINGS NOT TO SAY TO A POLICE OFFICER

10. Do you know why you pulled me over? I think one of us should know why.
9. Gee, Officer! That's terrific. The officer that stopped me earlier today only gave me a warning, too!
8. Which one are you - Andy or Barney?
7. I thought you had to be in good physical condition to be a police officer.
6. Sorry, Officer, I didn't realize my radar detector wasn't plugged in.
5. You must've been doin' about 125 mph to keep up with me. Good job!
4. Officer, your eyes look glazed - have you been eating donuts?
3. You're not gonna check the trunk, are you?
2. Aren't you the guy from the Village People?
1. Could you hold my beer while I get my license out?

SOME THINGS YOU JUST CAN'T EXPLAIN

A farmer is sitting in the village pub getting pissed. A man comes in and asks the farmer, "Hey, why are you sitting here on this beautiful day getting drunk?"

Farmer: "Some things you just can't explain."

Man: "So what happened that is so horrible?"

Farmer: "Well, if you must know, today I was sitting by my cow milking her. Just as I got the bucket about full, she took her left leg and kicked it over."

Man: "That's not so bad, what's the big deal?"

Farmer: "Some things you just can't explain."

Man: "So then what happened?"

Farmer: "I took her left leg and tied it to the post on the left with some rope. Then I sat down and continued to milk her. Just as I got the bucket about full she took her right leg and kicked it over."

Man: "Again? So what did you do then?"

Farmer: "I took her right leg and tied it to the post on the right."

Man: "And then what."

Farmer: "I sat back down and continued to milk her and just as I got the bucket just about full, the stupid cow knocked over the bucket with her tail."

Man: "Wow, you must have been pretty upset."

Farmer: "Some things you just can't explain."

Man: "So then what did you do?"

Farmer: "Well, I didn't have any more rope, so I took off my belt and tied her tail to the rafter. At that moment, my pants fell down and my wife walked in."

Some things you just can't explain.

THE FIRE TRUCK

A fire started on some grassland near a farm. The county fire department was called to put out the fire.

The fire was more than the county fire department could handle.

Someone suggested that a nearby volunteer bunch be called. Despite some doubt that the volunteer outfit would be of any assistance, the call was made.

The volunteers arrived in a dilapidated old fire truck.

They rumbled straight towards the fire, drove right into the middle of the flames and stopped! The firemen jumped off the truck and frantically started spraying water in all directions. Soon they had snuffed out the center of the fire, breaking the blaze into two easily controlled parts.

Watching all this, the farmer was so impressed with the volunteer fire department's work and was so grateful that his farm had been spared, that right there on the spot he presented the volunteers with a check for $1,000.

A local news reporter asked the volunteer fire captain what the department planned to do with the funds.

"That ought to be obvious," he responded, wiping ashes off his coat. "The first thing we're gonna do is get the brakes fixed on our fire truck!"

Gender Humor

UCLA RESEARCH

A study conducted by UCLA's Department of Psychiatry has revealed that the kind of face a woman finds attractive on a man can differ depending on where she is in her menstrual cycle.

For example: *If she is ovulating,* she is attracted to men with rugged and masculine features.

However, *if she is menstruating or menopausal,* she tends to prefer a man with scissors lodged in his temple and a bat jammed up his ass while he is on fire.

BECAUSE I AM A MAN

Because I'm a man, when I lock my keys in the car I will fiddle with a wire clothes hanger and ignore your suggestions that we call a road service until long after hypothermia has set in.

Because I'm a man, when the car isn't running very well, I will pop the hood and stare at the engine as if I know what I'm looking at. If another man shows up, one of us will say to the other, "I used to be able to fix these things, but now with all these computers and everything, I wouldn't know where to start." We will then drink beer.

Because I'm a man, when I catch a cold, I need someone to bring me soup and take care of me while I lie in bed and moan. You never get as sick as I do, so for you this isn't a problem.

Because I'm a man, I can be relied upon to purchase basic groceries at the store, like milk or bread. I cannot be expected to find exotic items like "cumin" or "tofu." For all I know, these are the same thing.

Because I'm a man, when one of our appliances stops working, I will insist on taking it apart, despite evidence that this will just cost me twice as much once the repair person gets here and has to put it back together

Because I'm a man, I must hold the television remote control in my hand while I watch TV. If the thing has been misplaced, I may miss a whole show looking for it (though one time I was able to survive by holding a calculator).

Because I'm a man, I don't think we're all that lost, and no, I don't think we should stop and ask someone. Why would you listen to a complete stranger? I mean, how the hell could he know where we're going?

Because I'm a man, there is no need to ask me what I'm thinking about. The answer is always either sex or football. I have to make up something else when you ask, so don't

Because I'm a man, I do not want to visit your mother, or have your mother come visit us, or talk to her when she calls, or think about her any more than I have to. Whatever you got her for Mother's Day is okay; I don't need to see it. And don't forget to pick up something for my mother too.

Because I'm a man, I think what you're wearing is fine. I thought what you were wearing five minutes ago was fine, too. Either pair of shoes is fine. With the belt or without it--looks fine. Your hair is fine. You look fine. Can we just go now?

Because I'm a man, I will share equally in the housework. You just do the laundry, the cooking, the gardening, the cleaning, the vacuuming, and the dishes, and I'll do the rest.

A BEER BEFORE IT STARTS

A man came home from work, sat down in his favorite chair, turned on the TV, and said to his wife, "Quick, bring me a beer before it starts."

She looked a little puzzled, but brought him a beer. When he finished it, he said, "Quick, bring me another beer. It's gonna' start."

This time she looked a little angry, but brought him a beer. When it was gone, he said, "Quick, another beer before it starts."

"That's it!" She blows her top, "You bastard! You waltz in here, flop your fat ass down, don't even say hello to me and then expect me to run around like your slave. Don't you realize that I cook and clean and wash and iron all day long?"

The husband sighed. "See, just like I said, it's starting."

COWBOY OR...

An old cowboy sat down at the Starbucks and ordered a cup of coffee.

As he sat sipping his coffee, a young woman sat down next to him.

She turned to the cowboy and asked, "Are you a real cowboy?"

He replied, "Well, I've spent my whole life breaking colts, working cows, going to rodeos, fixing fences, pulling calves, bailing hay, doctoring calves, cleaning my barn, fixing flats, working on tractors, and feeding my dogs, so I guess I am a cowboy."

She said, "I'm a lesbian. I spend my whole day thinking about women. As soon as I get up in the morning, I think about women. When I shower, I think about women. When I watch TV, I think about women. I even think about women when I eat. It seems that everything makes me think of women."

The two sat sipping in silence.

A little while later, a man sat down on the other side of the old cowboy and asked, "Are you a real cowboy?"

He replied, "I always thought I was, but I just found out that I'm a lesbian!"

WOMEN AND MEN: SHOWERING DIFFERENCES

How to Shower Like a Woman

1. Take off clothing and place it in sectioned laundry hamper according to lights and darks.
2. Walk to bathroom wearing long dressing gown. If you see your husband along the way, cover up any exposed areas.
3. Look at your womanly physique in the mirror - make mental note to do more sit-ups
4. Get in the shower. Use face cloth, arm cloth, leg cloth, long loofah, wide loofah, and pumice stone.
5. Wash your hair once with cucumber and sage shampoo with 43 added vitamins.
6. Wash your hair again to make sure it's clean.
7. Condition your hair with grapefruit mint conditioner enhanced with natural avocado oil. Leave on hair for 15 minutes.
8. Wash your face with crushed apricot facial scrub for 10 minutes until red.
9. Wash entire rest of body with ginger nut and Jaffa cake body wash.
10. Rinse conditioner off hair.
11. Shave armpits and legs.
12. Turn off shower.
13. Squeegee off all wet surfaces in shower. Spray mold spots with Tilex.
14. Get out of shower. Dry with towel the size of a small country. Wrap hair in super absorbent towel.
15. Check entire body for zits, tweeze hairs.
16. Return to bedroom wearing long dressing gown and towel on head.
17. If you see husband along the way, cover up any exposed areas.

How to Shower Like a Man

1. Take off clothes while sitting on the edge of the bed and leave them in a pile.
2. Walk naked to the bathroom. If you see wife along the way, shake wiener at her making the 'woo-woo' sound.
3. Look at your manly physique in the mirror. Admire the size of your wiener and scratch your ass.
4. Get in the shower.
5. Wash your face
6. Wash your armpits.
7. Blow your nose in your hands and let the water rinse them off.
8. Make fart noises (real or artificial) and laugh at how loud they sound in the shower.
9. Spend majority of time washing privates and surrounding area. Wash your butt, leaving those coarse butt hairs stuck on the soap.
11. Shampoo your hair.
12. Make a Shampoo Mohawk.
13. Pee.
14. Rinse off and get out of shower.
15. Partially dry off. Fail to notice water on floor because curtain was hanging out of tub the whole time.
16. Admire wiener size in mirror again.
17. Leave shower curtain open, wet mat on floor, light and fan on.
18. Return to bedroom with towel around your waist. If you pass wife, pull off towel, shake wiener at her and make the 'woo-woo' sound again.
19. Throw wet towel on bed.

THE MESSAGE

A very attractive lady goes up to the bar of a restaurant in a quiet pub. She gestures alluringly to the bartender who comes over immediately.

When he arrives, she seductively signals that he should bring his face closer to hers. When he does, she begins to gently caress his full beard face with both hands.

She asked "are you the manager."

"Actually, no," the bartender replied.

"Can you get him for me? I need to speak to him" she says, running her hands beyond his beard and into his hair.

"I'm afraid I can't," breathes the bartender. "Is there anything I can do?"

"Yes, there is. I need you to give him a message," she continues, running her forefinger across the bartender's lips and slyly popping a couple of her fingers into his mouth and allowing him to suck them gently.

"What should I tell him?" the bartender manages to say.

"Tell him," she whispers, "there is no toilet paper, hand soap, or paper towels in the ladies room.

LAWS FOR WOMEN TO LIVE BY

1. Don't imagine you can change a man - unless he's in diapers.
2. What do you do if your boyfriend walks out? You shut the door.
3. If they put a man on the moon - they should be able to put them all up there.
4. Never let your man's mind wander - it's too little to be out alone.
5. Go for younger men. You might as well - they never mature anyway.
6. Men are all the same - they just have different faces, so that you can tell them apart.
7. Definition of a bachelor: a man who has missed the opportunity to make some woman miserable.
8. Women don't make fools of men - most of them are the do-it-yourself types.
9. Best way to get a man to do something - suggest they are too old for it.
10. Love is blind - but marriage is a real eye-opener.

11. If you want a committed man - look in a mental hospital.
12. The children of Israel wandered around the desert for 40 years. Even in biblical times, men wouldn't ask for directions.
13. If he asks what sort of books you're interested in, tell him checkbooks.
14. Remember a sense of humor does not mean that you tell him jokes, it means that you laugh at his.
15. Sadly, all men are created equal.

THE MOOD RING

Dear Abby,
My husband is not happy with my mood swings. The other day, he bought me a mood ring so he would be able to monitor my moods.

When I'm in a good mood it turns green. When I'm in a bad mood it leaves a big red mark on his forehead. Maybe next time he'll buy me a diamond.

Sincerely,
Bitchy in Boston

MEN'S GUIDE TO HORMONES

Dangerous	Safer	Safest	Ultra Safe
What's for dinner?	Can I help you with dinner?	Where would you like to go for dinner	Here, have some wine.
Are you wearing that?	Wow, you sure look good in brown.	WOW! Look at you!	Here, have some wine.
What are you so worked up about?	Could we be overreacting?	Here's my paycheck.	Here, have some wine.

Should you be eating that?	You know, there are a lot of apples left.	Can I get you a piece of chocolate with that?	Here, have some wine.
What did you do all day?	I hope you didn't overdo it today.	I've always loved you in that robe.	Here, have some more wine.

ONCE UPON A TIME

Once upon a time in a land far away, a beautiful, independent, self-assured princess happened upon a frog as she sat contemplating ecological issues on the shores of an unpolluted pond in a verdant meadow near her castle.

The frog hopped into the princess' lap and said: "Elegant Lady, I was once a handsome prince, until an evil witch cast a spell upon me.

One kiss from you, however, and I will turn back into the dapper, young prince that I am and then, my sweet, we can marry and set up housekeeping in your castle with my mother, where you can prepare our meals, clean our clothes, bear my children, and forever feel grateful and happy doing so."

That night, as the princess dined sumptuously on lightly sautéed frog legs seasoned in a white wine and onion cream sauce, she chuckled and thought to herself: I don't f#%*g think so.

WHAT'S IN A NAME

A woman scanned the guests at a party and spotted an attractive man standing alone. She approached him.

"Hi....My name is Carmen", she told him.

"That's a beautiful name," he replied, "Is it a family name?"

"No," she replied. "I gave it to myself. It reflects the things I like most - cars and men."

"What's your name?" she asked.

He said, "B. J. Titsenbeer."

ONE WISH

A man walking along a California beach was deep in prayer. All of a sudden, he said out loud, "Lord grant me one wish."

Suddenly the sky clouded above his head and in a booming voice the Lord said, "Because you have tried to be faithful to me in all ways, I will grant you one wish."

The man said, "I have a terrible fear of flying and I also have hydrophobia so I am fearful of riding in a boat or ship. Please build a bridge to Hawaii so I can drive over anytime I want."

The Lord said, "Your request is very materialistic. Think of the enormous challenges for that kind of undertaking. The supports required to reach the bottom of the Pacific! The concrete and steel it would take! I can do it, but it is hard for me to justify your desire for worldly things. Take a little more time and think of another wish, a wish you think would honor and glorify me."

The man thought about it for a long time. Finally he said, "Lord, I wish that I could understand women. I want to know how they feel inside, what they are thinking when they give me the silent treatment, why they cry, what they mean when they say 'nothing', and how I can make a woman truly happy."

The Lord replied, "You want two lanes or four lanes on that bridge?"

ADVICE FOR WOMEN

- If you want someone willing to make a fool of himself simply over the joy of seeing you... buy a dog.
- If you want someone who will eat whatever you put in front of him and never says it's not quite as good as his mother made it... buy a dog.
- If you want someone always willing to go out, at any hour, for as long and wherever you want ... buy a dog.
- If you want someone to scare away burglars, without a lethal weapon which terrifies you and endangers the lives of your family and all the neighbors... buy a dog.

- If you want someone who will never touch the remote, doesn't care about football, and can sit next to you and watch a romantic movie... buy a dog.
- If you want someone who is content to get up on your bed just to warm your feet and whom you can push off if he snores... buy a dog.
- If you want someone who never criticizes what you do, doesn't care if you are pretty or ugly, fat or thin, young or old, who acts as if every word you say is especially worthy of listening to, and loves you unconditionally, perpetually... buy a dog.
- But on the other hand, if you want someone who will never come when you call, ignores you totally when you come home, leaves hair all over the place, walks all over you, runs around all night, only comes home to eat and sleep, and acts as if your entire existence is solely to ensure his happiness... Then, my friend...buy a cat.

WHY MEN ARE NOT SECRETARIES

Husband's note on refrigerator to his wife:
"Someone from the Guyna College called. They said Pabst beer is normal."

FBI POSITION OPEN

The FBI had an opening for an assassin. After all the background checks, interviews, and testing were done there were 3 finalists: two men and a woman.

For the final test, the FBI agents took one of the men to a large metal door and handed him a gun.

"We must know that you will follow your instructions no matter what the circumstances. Inside the room you will find your wife sitting in a chair. Kill Her!"

The man said, "You can't be serious, I could never shoot my wife." The agent said, "Then you're not the right man for this job. Take your wife and go home."

The second man was given the same instructions. He took the gun and went into the room. All was quiet for about 5 minutes. The man came out with tears in his eyes, "I tried, but I can't kill my wife."

The agent said, "You don't have what it takes. Take your wife and go home."

Finally, it was the woman's turn. She was given the same instructions, to kill her husband. She took the gun and went into the room. Shots were heard, one after another. They heard screaming, crashing, banging on the walls. After a few minutes, all was quiet. The door opened slowly and there stood the woman. She wiped the sweat from her brow.

"This gun is loaded with blanks" she said. "I had to beat him to death with the chair."

RULES FOR MEN

1: Under no circumstances may two men share an umbrella.
2: It is ok for a man to cry only under the following circumstances:
   a. When a heroic dog dies to save its master.
   b. After wrecking your boss' car.
   c. One hour, 12 minutes, 37 seconds into "The Crying Game."
3: Any Man who brings a camera to a bachelor party may be legally killed by his buddies.
4: Unless he murdered someone in your family, you must bail a friend out of jail within 12 hours.
5: If you've known a guy for more than 24 hours, his sister is off limits forever unless you actually marry her.
6: Moaning about the brand of free beer in a buddy's fridge forbidden. However complain at will if the temperature is unsuitable.

7: No man shall ever be required to buy a birthday present for another man. In fact, even remembering your buddy's birthday is strictly optional.

8: On a road trip, the strongest bladder determines pit stops, not the weakest.

9: When stumbling upon other guys watching a sporting event, you may ask the score of the game in progress, but you may never ask who's playing.

10: It is permissible to drink a fruity alcohol drink only when you're sunning on a tropical beach... and it's delivered by a model and only when it's free.

11: Unless you're in prison, never fight naked.

12: Friends don't let friends wear Speedos. Ever! Issue closed. (American variation).

13: If a man's fly is down, that's his problem, you didn't see anything.

14: Women who claim they "love to watch sports" must be treated as spies until they demonstrate knowledge of the game and the ability to drink as much as the other sports watchers.

15: A man in the company of a hot, suggestively dressed woman must remain sober enough to fight.

16: Never hesitate to reach for the last beer or the last slice of pizza, but not both, that's just greedy.

17: If you compliment a guy on his six-pack, you'd better be talking about his choice of beer.

18: Never join your girlfriend or wife in discussing a friend of yours, except if she's withholding sex pending your response.

19: Phrases that may not be uttered to another man while he is lifting weights.
   a. Yeah, Baby, Push it!
   b. C'mon, give me one more! Harder!
   c. Another set and we can hit the showers!

20: Never talk to a man in a bathroom unless you are on equal footing: i.e. both waiting in line, etc. For all other situations, an almost imperceptible nod is all the conversation you need.

21: It is acceptable for you to drive her car. It is not acceptable for her to drive yours.

22: Thou shall not buy a car in the colors of brown, pink, lime green, orange or sky blue.

23: The girl who replies to the question "What do you want for Christmas?" with "If you loved me, you'd know what I want!" gets an Xbox. End of story.

24: There is no reason for guys to watch Ice Skating or Men's Gymnastics. Ever.

MEN AND WOMEN: A FEW DIFFERENCES

Social: If Laura, Suzanne, Debra and Rose go out for lunch, they will call each other Laura, Suzanne, Debra and Rose. If Mike, Charlie, Bob and John go out, they will affectionately refer to each other as Fat Boy, Big Man, Hot Dog, and Scrappy.

When the bill arrives, Mike Charlie, Bob and John will each throw in $20, even though it's only for $32.50. None of them will have anything smaller and none will actually admit they want change back. When the girls get their bill, out come the pocket calculators.

Money: A man will pay $2 for a $1 item he wants. A woman will pay $1 for a $2 item on sale that she doesn't want.

Bathrooms: A man has six items in his bathroom: a toothbrush, comb, shaving cream, razor, a bar of soap, and a towel from the Holiday Inn. The average number of items in the typical woman's bathroom is 337. A man would not be able to identify most of these items.

Arguments: A woman has the last word in any argument. Anything a man says after that is the beginning of a new argument.

Cats: Women love cats. Men say they love cats, but when women aren't looking, men kick cats.

Marriage: A woman marries a man expecting he will change, but he doesn't. A man marries a woman expecting that she won't change and she does.

Dressing Up: A woman will dress up to go shopping, water the garden, empty the garbage, and get the mail. A man will dress up for weddings and funerals.

Natural: Men wake up as good-looking as they went to bed. Women somehow deteriorate during the night.

Offspring: A woman knows all about her children. She knows about dentist appointments and romances, best friends, favorite foods, secret fears and hopes and dreams. A man is vaguely aware of some short people living in the house.

Thought for the Day: A married man should forget his mistakes. There's no use in both partners remembering them and the wife will remind him of them at regular intervals.

REDNECK PICKUP LINES

1. Did you fart cuz you just blew me away?
2. Are yer parents retarded cuz ya sure are special.
3. My Love fer you is like diarrhea...I can't hold it in.
4. Do you have a library card cuz I'd like to sign you out.
5. Is there a mirror in yer pants cuz I can see myself in em.
6. If you 'n I were Squirrels, I'd store my nuts in yer hole.
7. You might not be the best lookin girl here, but beauty's only a light switch away.
8. Man - "Fat Penguin!" Woman - "WHAT?" Man - "I just wanted to say sumthin that would break the ice."
9. I know I'm not no Fred Flintstone, but I bet I can make yer bed-rock.
10. I can't find my puppy; can you help me find him? I think he went inta this cheap motel room.
11. Yer eyes are as blue as window cleaner.
12. If yer gunna' regret this in the mornin', we kin sleep til' 'noon.
13. Yer face reminds me of a wrench, ever time I think of it my nuts tighten up.

THE SILENT TREATMENT

Mike and Joan were having some problems at home and were giving each other the "silent treatment." But then Mike realized that he would need his wife to wake him at 5:00 am for an early morning drive with some pals to a golf match.

Not wanting to be the first to break the silence (and so lose the "war"), he wrote on a piece of paper, "Please wake me at 5:00 am."

The next morning, Mike woke up, only to discover it was 9:00 am and that his friends left for the golf course without him.

Furious, he was about to go and see why his wife hadn't awakened him when he noticed a piece of paper by the bed. The paper said, "It is 5:00 am. Wake up."

Men simply are not equipped for these kinds of contests.

THE SENSITIVE MAN

A woman meets a man in a bar. They talk; they connect; they end up leaving together. They get back to his place, and as he shows her around his apartment, she notices that one wall of his bedroom is completely filled with soft, sweet, cuddly teddy bears.

There are three shelves in the bedroom with hundreds and hundreds of cute, cuddly teddy bears, carefully placed in rows covering the entire wall! It was obvious that he had taken quite some time to lovingly arrange them and she was immediately touched by the amount of thought he had put into organizing the display. There were small bears all along the bottom shelf, medium-sized bears covering the length of the middle shelf, and huge, enormous bears running all the way along the top shelf. She found it strange for an obviously masculine guy to have such a large a collection of Teddy Bears, but doesn't mention this to him, and actually is quite impressed by his sensitive side.

They share a bottle of wine and continue talking and, after a while, she finds herself thinking, "Oh my God! Maybe, this guy could be the one! Maybe he could be the future father my children?" She turns to him and kisses him lightly on the lips. He responds warmly.

They continue to kiss, the passion builds, and he romantically lifts her in his arms and carries her into his bedroom where they rip off each other's clothes and make hot, steamy love.

She is so overwhelmed that she responds with more passion, more creativity, and more heat than she has ever known, and even did a few things she had never done with any other man.

After an intense, explosive night of raw passion with this sensitive guy, they are lying there together in the afterglow. The woman rolls over, gently strokes his chest and asks coyly, "Well, how was it?" The guy gently smiles at her, strokes her cheek, looks deeply into her eyes, and says....

"Help yourself to any prize from the middle shelf!"

Guy Walks Into A Bar Jokes

This guy walks into a bar, sits down, and orders a beer. As he sips the beer, he hears a soothing voice say "nice tie!" Looking around he notices that the bar is empty except for himself and the bartender at the end of the bar. A few sips later the voice says "beautiful shirt."

At this, the man calls the bartender over, "Hey...I must be losing my mind," he tells the bartender. "I keep hearing these voices saying nice things, and there's not a soul in this place but us."

"It's the peanuts," answers the bartender.

"What?" says the man.

"It's the peanuts," says the barkeep, "they're complimentary..."

This horse walks into a bar and the bartender says "Hey, buddy, why the long face..."

This neutron walks into a bar. "I'd like a beer" he says. The bartender promptly serves up a beer.

"How much will that be?" asks the neutron. "For you?" replies the bartender, "no charge..."

This hamburger walks into a bar, and the bartender says, "I'm sorry, but we don't serve food here..."

A termite walks into a bar and says, "Is the bar tender here?"

A piece of rope walks into a bar and the bartender says, "We don't serve your kind." The rope goes outside, ties himself in a knot and frays one end of himself. He walks back into the bar and the bartender says, "Weren't you just in here?" The rope replies, "No, I'm a frayed knot."

My dad was a magician... one day he was walking down the street and he turned into a bar.

This grasshopper walks into a bar, and the bartender says "Hey! We have a drink named after you!" The grasshopper replies "Really? You have a drink named Steve?!"

A mushroom walks into a bar and the bartender says, "I'm sorry, but we don't serve food here..." the mushroom replies "Why not?, I'm a fungi..."

This skeleton walks into a bar and says, "I'd like a beer and a mop..."

An amnesiac walks into a bar. He asks, "Do I come here often?"

A guy walks into a bar wearing an open shirt and is met by the bouncer who tells him he must wear a necktie to gain admission. The guy goes out to his car and looks for a necktie but discovers that he just doesn't have one, however, he finds a set of jumper cables in his trunk. In desperation he ties these around his neck, manages to fashion an acceptable knot and lets the ends dangle free. He goes back to the bar and the bouncer carefully looks him over for a few minutes and then says, "Well, OK, I guess you can come in--just don't start anything."

A guy walks into a bar. "OUCH!" he says.

A dyslexic guy walks into a bra.

A guy walks into a bar. The owner, seeing a new customer, sends over his best looking waitress. She gives the new customer a menu and asks "Can I help you?" He looks at her and says "Yes, I'd like a quickie". The waitress is annoyed, and says "Take a look at the menu and I'll come back for your order in a couple of minutes". She returns a couple of minutes later and again asks for his order. He responds "I'd like a quickie". Now the waitress is really miffed and says "I'll be back for you order when you've reviewed the menu" About 10 minutes later she returns and says "Are you ready to order now?" The customer answers "yes, I'd like a quickie". The waitress hauls off and slugs the customer, sending him sprawling on the floor, with the table on top of him. A fellow at the next table leans over and says to the customer: "You know, I think that's pronounced 'quiche'."

Charles Dickens walks into a bar and orders a martini. The bartender asks, "Olive or twist?" (thanks to Ric and Funny2.com)

A Times New Roman twelve point font walks into a bar. The bartender says, "Sorry, we don't serve your type here!"

A guy walks into a bar in Dublin and asks for three glasses of Guinness. He takes a sip from each glass and continues doing this until they're all empty, then asks for 3 more. The bartender says, "You know, these start to go flat the minute I pour them you'd really be better off getting one at a time." The guy says, "No, you don't understand. You see, I had two brothers. One moved to America and one moved to Australia. We vowed that we would always drink this way to remind us how it was when we were together." He becomes a regular at the bar and everyone knows his routine. Then, one day he comes in and asks for two glasses of Guinness. He drinks them the same way and then asks for two more. The bartender says, "I don't mean to intrude on your grief, but I'd just like to say how sorry we all are for your loss." The guy says, "No, you don't understand. Everyone is okay; it's just that I quit drinking."

A kangaroo walks into a bar. He orders a beer. The bartender says, "That'll be $10. We don't get many kangaroos coming in here, you know." The kangaroo says, "At $10 a beer, it's not hard to understand."

So this guy walks into a bar, gets out a little piano and a little man about a foot tall. The little man starts playing exquisite music on the piano. Another guy walks up and says, "Hey, where'd you get that little guy?" The first guy says, "I've got a genie in a lamp. So the second guy says, "Can I make a wish?" "Knock yourself out," says the first guy, and hands him the lamp. The second guy rubs the lamp, and says, "I wish for a million bucks." Suddenly, the room is filled with ducks. The second guy says, "Hey! I asked for bucks, not ducks!" "Yeah," says the first guy, "the genie's got a hearing problem. You didn't really think I asked for a twelve-inch-pianist?"

A Canadian guy walks into a bar; on the stool next to him is some footwear. He says to the bartender, "What's this - a boot?" (thanks to Tony Horvath and Funny2.com)

Celine Dion walks into a bar. The bartender says, "So, why the long face?"

A guy walks into a bar and orders a beer. "Listen," he says to the bartender. "If I show you the most amazing thing you've ever seen, is my beer on the house?" "We'll See," says the bartender. So the guy pulls out a hamster and a tiny piano out of a bag, puts them on the bar, and the hamster begins to play.
"Impressive," says the bartender, "but I'll need to see more." "Hold on," says the man. He then pulls out a bullfrog, and it sings "Old Man River." A patron jumps up from his table and shouts "That's absolutely incredible! I'll give you $100 right now for the frog." "Sold," says the guy. The patron takes the bullfrog and leaves.

"It's none of my business," says the bartender, "but you just gave away a fortune."

"Not really," says the guy. "The hamster is also a ventriloquist."

A Rabbi, a Priest and a Minister walk into a bar. The bartender says, "What is this, some kind of joke?"

Health, Dieting and Fitness Humor

THE TOP 10 ADDITIONAL WARNINGS THE FDA IS CONSIDERING PLACING ON BEER AND ALCOHOL BOTTLES

10. WARNING: Consumption of alcohol may make you think you are whispering when you are not.
9. WARNING: Consumption of alcohol is a major factor in dancing like a weirdo.
8. WARNING: consumption of alcohol may cause you to tell the same boring story over and over again until your friends want to smash your head in!
7. WARNING: consumption of alcohol may cause you to thay shings like thish.
6. WARNING: consumption of alcohol may lead you to believe that ex-lovers are hoping you will phone them at 4:00 in the morning.
5. WARNING: consumption of alcohol may leave you wondering what the hell happened to your pants.

4. WARNING: consumption of alcohol is the leading cause of inexplicable rug burns.
3. WARNING: consumption of alcohol may create the illusion that you are tougher, handsomer and smarter than some really, really big guy named Chuck.
2. WARNING: consumption of alcohol may lead you to believe you are invisible.
1. WARNING: consumption of alcohol may lead you to think people are laughing **with** you.

GOOD HEALTH

Good health is merely the slowest possible rate at which one can die.

DENTAL PATIENT COMMUNICATION SYSTEM
(© R. BRUCE BAUM)

Dear Patient:

In an attempt to better meet the needs of our patients we are initiating a patient communication system. Therefore, during any dental procedures, feel free to wave the finger of the appropriate hand to communicate any of the following:

LEFT HAND

Baby finger – Saliva is running down my neck and will soon get to my belly button.

Ring finger – Why don't you have any of those framed diplomas like the other dentists?

Middle finger – You're really hurting me and I feel like cursing.

Index finger – The last tool you were using broke in my mouth and I swallowed part of it.

Thumb – The way this chair is tilted, all the blood is moving toward my brain so that my lower torso is completely numb.

RIGHT HAND

Baby finger – I think tying this tooth to a doorknob and slamming the door would take a lot less time and energy.

Ring finger – Don't waste space – I think there's still room for some tools, gauze, or a couple of fingers on the left side of my mouth.

Middle finger – Yeeoowwww! That pain is excruciating!

Index finger – Ha, ha, ha, ha, ha. That was one funny story!

Thumb –Did you say you do or do not accept my dental plan?

AEROBICS INSTRUCTOR RIDDLES

Q. Why did the aerobics instructor cross the road?
A. Someone on the other side could still walk.

Q. How many aerobics instructors does it take to change a light bulb?
A. Four!...Three!...Two!...One!

Q. An ethical lawyer, an honest politician, and a merciful aerobics instructor all fall out of an airplane. Which one hits he ground first?
A. It doesn't matter - none of them exist.

Q. What do you call an aerobics instructor who doesn't cause pain and agony?
A. Unemployed.

Q. What's the difference between an aerobics instructor and a dentist?
A1. A dentist lets you sit down while he hurts you.
A2. A dentist hurts you. An aerobics instructor makes you hurt yourself.

THE TODDLER MIRACLE DIET

People are always on the lookout for a new diet. The trouble with most diets is that you don't get enough to eat (the starvation diet), you don't get enough variation (the liquid diet) or you go broke (the all-meat diet). Consequently, people tend to cheat of their diets, or quit after 3 days. Well, now there's the new *Toddler Miracle Diet*. Over the years you may have noticed that most two year olds are trim. Now the formula to their success is available to all in this new diet. You may want to consult your doctor before embarking on this diet; otherwise, you may be seeing him afterwards. Good Luck!!

DAY ONE: Breakfast: One scrambled egg, one piece of toast with grape jelly. Eat 2 bites of egg, using your fingers; dump the rest on the floor. Take 1 bite of toast, and then smear the jelly over your face and clothes.

Lunch: Four crayons (any color), a handful of potato chips, and a glass of milk (3 sips only, then spill the rest).

Dinner: A dry stick, two pennies and a nickel, 4 sips of flat Sprite.

Bedtime snack: Throw a piece of toast on the kitchen floor.

DAY TWO: Breakfast: Pick up stale toast from kitchen floor and eat it. Drink half bottle of vanilla extract or one vial of vegetable dye.

Lunch: Half tube of "Pulsating Pink" lipstick and a handful of Purina Dog Chow (any flavor). One ice cube, if desired.

Afternoon snack: Lick an all-day sucker until sticky, take outside, drop in dirt. Retrieve and continue slurping until it is clean again. Then bring inside and drop on rug.

Dinner: A rock or an uncooked bean, which should be thrust up your left nostril. Pour Grape Kool-Aid over mashed potatoes; eat with spoon.

DAY THREE: Breakfast: Two pancakes with plenty of syrup, eat one with fingers, rub in hair. Glass of milk; drink half, stuff other pancake in glass. After breakfast, pick up yesterday's sucker from rug, lick off fuzz, and put it on the cushion of best chair.

Lunch: Three matches, peanut butter and jelly sandwich. Spit several bites onto the floor. Pour glass of milk on table and slurp up.

Dinner: Dish of ice cream, handful of potato chips, some red punch. Try to laugh some punch through your nose, if possible.

FINAL DAY: Breakfast: A quarter tube of toothpaste (any flavor), bit of soap, an olive. Pour a glass of milk over bowl of corn flakes; add half a cup of sugar. Once cereal is soggy, drink milk and feed cereal to dog.

Lunch: Eat breadcrumbs off kitchen floor and dining room carpet. Find that sucker and finish eating it.

Dinner: A glass of spaghetti and chocolate milk. Leave meatball on plate. Stick of mascara for dessert.

DIETS AND DYING: A CONCLUSION

1. The Chinese eat very little fat and suffer fewer heart attacks than the British or Americans.
2. The French eat a lot of fat and also suffer fewer heart attacks than the British or Americans.
3. The Japanese drink very little red wine and suffer fewer heart attacks than the British or Americans.
4. The Italians drink excessive amounts of red wine and also suffer fewer heart attacks than the British or Americans.
5. The Germans drink a lot of beer and eat lots of sausages and fats and suffer fewer heart attacks than the British or Americans.

Conclusion: Eat and drink what you like. Speaking English is apparently what kills you.

EXERCISE: QUOTATIONS FROM THE EXPERTS

- It is well documented that for every minute that you exercise, you add one minute to your life. This enables you at 85 years old to spend an additional 5 months in a nursing home at $5000 per month.

- My grandmother started walking five miles a day when she was 60. She's 87 years old today, and we don't know where the hell she is. (Attributed to Ellen DeGeneres)
- The only reason I would take up exercising is so that I could hear heavy breathing again.
- I joined a health club last year, spent about 400 bucks. I haven't lost a pound. Apparently you have to go there.
- I signed up for an exercise class and was told to wear loose-fitting clothing. If I **had** any loose-fitting clothing, I wouldn't have signed up in the first place!
- I have to exercise early in the morning before my brain figures out what I'm doing.
- I like long walks, especially when they are taken by people who annoy me.
- I have flabby thighs, but fortunately my stomach covers them.
- The advantage of exercising every day is that you die healthier.
- If you are going to try cross-country skiing, start with a small country.
- I don't exercise because it makes the ice jump right out of my glass.

FROM MARTY OF AUSTIN, TEXAS
(FROM THETOPFIVE.COM © CHRIS WHITE, 2000)

Not being much of a cook, I tend to eat a lot of pre-prepared packaged foods, particularly when my wife is away and I'm feeding just myself. One of my favorites in recent years has been packages of (pre-cooked) roasted chicken pieces that you can buy in most supermarkets in the US and UK. A couple of years ago, I was shopping in the grocery section of Marks & Spencers in Glasgow, and saw what was apparently a new variant alongside the familiar roasted chicken pieces... individual pieces of chicken, but breaded rather than roasted. I picked out a package, deciding that it would make part of a tasty lunch when I returned to my flat.

By the time I returned home, it was getting well into the afternoon and I was quite hungry. I quickly set out the rest of my meal and settled down to try my newly purchased chicken drumsticks.

Upon taking the first bite, I was a bit disappointed. Marks & Spencers' packaged foods are normally quite tasty, but this seemed somewhat bland and chewy. As I took my second bite and was reflecting on the sad state of quality control these days, my eyes locked on a bright orange label on the chicken packaging still sitting on the table in front of me: "Ready to Cook" I didn't swallow the second bite.

Of course, for Christmas that year, I received a rubber chicken and a "How to Cook Chicken" cookbook from my smart-ass siblings.

CLEANLINESS

In the bathroom, an accountant, a lawyer and a farmer were standing side-by-side using the urinal. The accountant finished, zipped up and started washing and literally scrubbing his hands...clear up to his elbows...he used about 20 paper towels before he finished. He turned to the other two men and commented, "I graduated from Harvard and they taught us to be sanitary."

The lawyer finished, zipped up and quickly wet the tips of his fingers, grabbed one paper towel and commented, "I graduated from the Wharton Law School and they taught us to be environmentally conscious."

The farmer zipped up and as he was walking out the door said, "I graduated from the University of Kentucky...and they taught us not to pee on our hands."

PREGNANCY: QUESTIONS AND ANSWERS

Q: Should I have a baby after 35?
A: No, 35 children is enough.

Q: I am two months pregnant now. When will my baby move?
A: With any luck, right after he finishes college.

Q: What is the most common pregnancy craving?
A: For men to be the ones who get pregnant.

Q: What is the most reliable method to determine a baby's sex?
A: Childbirth.

Q: The more pregnant I get, the more often strangers smile at me. Why?
A: Because you are fatter than they are.

Q: My wife is five months pregnant and so moody that sometimes she's borderline irrational.
A: So what's your question?

Q: My childbirth instructor says it's not pain I'll feel during labor, but pressure. Is she right?
A: Yes, in the same way that a tornado might be called an air current.

Q: When is the best time to get an epidural?
A: Right after you find out you're pregnant.

Q: Is there any reason I have to be in the delivery room while my wife is in labor?
A: Not unless the word "alimony" means anything to you.

Q: Is there anything I should avoid while recovering from childbirth?
A: Yes, pregnancy.

Q: Do I have to have a baby shower?
A: Not if you change the baby's diaper very quickly.

Q: Our baby was born last week. When will my wife begin to feel and act normal again?
A: When the kids are in college.

MILITARY DIETS

An English soldier, an American solider and a Russian soldier found themselves sharing a tent while on a military exercise and the conversation turned towards how well fed each of them was.

"In the Russian Army we have 2000 calories of food a day," said the Russian

"Well," said the Englishman, "In the British Army we are given 4000 calories of food a day."

"That's nothing," said the American, "in the US Army we have 8000 calories of food a day".

At this the Russian got very annoyed. "Nonsense," he said, "how could one man eat so much cabbage?"

Dear Diary

For my fiftieth birthday this year, my husband (the dear) purchased a week of personal training at the local health club for me. Although I am still in great shape since playing on my high school softball team, I decided it would be a good idea to go ahead and give it a try. I called the club and made my reservations with a personal trainer I'll call Rick, who identified himself as a 26-year-old aerobics instructor and model for athletic clothing and swimwear. My husband seemed pleased with my enthusiasm to get started. The club encouraged me to keep a diary to chart my progress

Monday: Started my day at 6:00am. Tough to get out of bed, but found it was well worth it when I arrived at the health club to find Rick waiting for me. He is something of a Greek God - with blond hair, dancing eyes and a dazzling white smile. Woo Hoo!! Rick gave me a tour and showed me the machines. He took my pulse after five minutes on the treadmill. He was alarmed that my pulse was so fast, but I attribute it to standing next to him in his Lycra aerobic outfit. I enjoyed watching the skillful way in which he conducted his aerobics class after my workout today. Very inspiring. Rick was encouraging as I did my sit-ups, although my gut was already aching from holding it in the whole time he was around. This is going to be a fantastic week!

<u>Tuesday</u>: I drank a whole pot of coffee, but I finally made it out the door. Rick made me lie on my back and push a heavy iron bar into the air - then he put weights on it! My legs were a little wobbly on the treadmill, but I made the full mile. Rick's rewarding smile made it all worthwhile. I feel great!! It's a whole new life for me.

<u>Wednesday</u>: The only way I can brush my teeth is by lying on the toothbrush on the counter and moving my mouth back and forth over it. I believe I have a hernia in both pectorals. Driving was OK as long as I didn't try to steer or stop. I parked on top of a compact car in the club parking lot. Rick was impatient with me, insisting that my screams bothered other club members. His voice is a little too perky for early in the morning and when he scolds, he gets this nasally whines that is very annoying. My chest hurt when I got on the treadmill, so Rick put me on the stair monster. Why the hell would anyone invent a machine to simulate an activity rendered obsolete by elevators? Rick told me it would help me get in shape and enjoy life. He said some other shit too.

<u>Thursday</u>: Rick was waiting for me with his vampire-like teeth exposed as his thin, cruel lips were pulled back in a full snarl. I couldn't help being a half an hour late; it took me that long to tie my shoes. Rick took me to work out with dumbbells. When he was not looking, I ran and hid in the men's room. He sent Lars to find me, then as punishment, put me on the rowing machine - which I sank.

<u>Friday</u>: I hate that bastard Rick more than any human being has ever hated any other human being in the history of the world. Stupid, skinny, anemic little cheerleader. If there were a part of my body I could move without unbearable pain, I would beat him with it. Rick wanted me to work on my triceps. I don't have any triceps! And if you don't want dents in the floor, don't hand me the &*@*#$ barbells or anything that weighs more than a sandwich. (Which I am sure you learned in the sadist school you attended and graduated magna cum laude from.) The treadmill flung me off and I landed on a health and nutrition teacher. Why couldn't it have been someone softer, like the drama coach or the choir director?

165

<u>Saturday</u>: Rick left a message on my answering machine in his grating, shrilly voice wondering why I did not show up today. Just hearing him, made me want to smash the machine with my planner. However, I lacked the strength to even use the TV remote and ended up catching eleven straight hours of the *$@#&& Weather Channel.

<u>Sunday</u>: I'm having the Church van pick me up for services today so I can go and thank God that this week is over. I will also pray that next year my husband (the bastard) will choose a gift for me that is fun -- like a root canal or a hysterectomy!

HOW TO LOOSE WEIGHT WITHOUT EXERCISE

Proper weight control and physical fitness cannot be attained by dieting alone. Many people who are engaged in sedentary occupations do not realize that calories can be burned by the hundreds by engaging in strenuous activities that do not require physical exercise.

Here's the guide to calorie-burning activities and the number of calories per hour they consume.

Beating around the bush	75
Jumping to conclusions	100
Climbing the walls	150
Swallowing your pride	50
Passing the buck	25
Throwing your weight around (depending on your weight)	50-300
Dragging your heels	100
Pushing your luck	250
Making mountains out of molehills	500
Hitting the nail on the head	50
Wading through paperwork	300
Bending over backwards	75
Jumping on the bandwagon	200
Balancing the books	25
Running around in circles	350

Eating crow	225
Tooting your own horn	25
Climbing the ladder of success	750
Pulling out the stops	75
Adding fuel to the fire	160
Wrapping it up at the day's end	12

To which you may want to add your own favorite activities, including:

Opening a can of worms	50
Putting your foot in your mouth	300
Flying off the handle	75
Starting the ball rolling	90
Going over the edge	25
Picking up the pieces after	350

THE TRUTH ABOUT HEALTH AND FITNESS: QUESTIONS AND ANSWERS (SOURCE:WWW.WHOOHOO.NET/HEALTH)

Q: How can I calculate my body/fat ratio?

A: Well, if you have a body, and you have body fat, your ratio is one to one. If you have two bodies, your ratio is two to one, etc.

Q: I've heard that cardiovascular exercise can prolong life. Is this true?

A: How could that be true? Your heart is only good for so many beats, and that's it. Everything wears out eventually, so how could speeding up your heart make you live longer? That's like saying you can extend the life of your car by driving it more. Want to live longer? Take a nap.

Q: My wife says I should cut down on meat, and eat more fruits and vegetables.

A: Your wife just doesn't grasp logistical efficiencies the way you do. Look, what does a cow eat? Corn. And what's corn - a vegetable. So a steak is nothing more than an efficient mechanism of delivering vegetables to your system. Need grain? Eat chicken. Beef is also a good source of field grass. And a pork chop can give you 100% of your recommended daily allowance of slop.

Q: Is beer bad for you?

A: I normally don't like to answer questions which deal with my religious values, but I find this question so ridiculous I simply have to say something. Look, it goes to the earlier point about vegetables. As we all know, scientists divide everything in the world into three categories: animal, mineral, and vegetable. Well, we all know that beer is not an animal, and it's not on the periodic table of elements, so that only leaves one thing, right? My advice: Have a burger and a beer and tell everyone you're on a vegetarian diet.

Q: At the gym, a guy asked me to "spot" for him while he did the bench press. What did he mean?

A: "Spotting" for someone means you stand over him while he blows air up your shorts. It's an accepted practice at health clubs, though if you find that it becomes the **only** reason why you're going in, you probably ought to reevaluate your exercise program.

Q: What are some of the advantages of participating in a regular exercise program?

A: Can't think of a single one, sorry.

Q: I'm getting a little soft around the middle. Will sit-ups help this?

A: Definitely not! Look, when you exercise a muscle, it gets bigger, right? You should only be doing sit-ups if you want a bigger stomach.

Q: I thought it would be good for me to carry my clubs when I play golf, but last weekend some idiot almost ran over me with the golf cart!

A: Uh, sorry, we were in a hurry to get to the clubhouse for cocktails. I was reaching into my cooler and didn't see you.

Q: There's a lot of equipment available at the gym today, like the treadmill, the stair-stepper, etc. Which one do you recommend?

A: The strato-lounger.

Holiday Humor

THE SPECIAL OCCASION

This is more embarrassing for my mother than for me because I wasn't quite four years old when it happened. My mother taught me to read when I was 3 years old (her first mistake). One day I was in the bathroom and noticed one of the cabinet doors was ajar. I read the box in the cabinet. I then asked my mother why she was keeping napkins in the bathroom. Didn't they belong in the kitchen? Not wanting to burden me with unnecessary facts she told me that those were for special occasions. Now fast forward a few months. It's Thanksgiving Day, and my folks are leaving to pick up the pastor and his wife for Dinner. Mom had assignments for all of us while they were gone. Mine was to set the table. You guessed it! When they returned, the pastor came in first and immediately burst into laughter. Next came his wife who gasped, then began giggling. Next came my father, who roared with laughter. Then came mom, who almost died of embarrassment when she saw each place setting on the table with a "special occasion" napkin at each plate, with the fork carefully arranged on top. I had even tucked the little tails in so they didn't hang off the edge. My mother asked me why I used these and, of course, my response sent the other adults into further fits of laughter. "But Mom, you said they were for special occasions!!"

DOWN THE CHIMNEY

The five year old twins climbed up on their roof. Bobby said, "C'mon, let's jump down the chimney! Just like Santa does!"

Billy, "No!" Bobby, "Why not?" Billy, "I'm afraid to go down a chimney like Santa." Bobby, "Maybe you have Claustrophobia."

HOLIDAY EATING TIPS

1. Avoid carrot sticks. Anyone who puts carrots on a holiday buffet table knows nothing of the Christmas spirit. In fact, if you see carrots, leave immediately. Go next door, where they're serving rum balls.
2. Drink as much eggnog as you can…and quickly. Like fine single-malt scotch, it's rare. In fact, it's even rarer than single-malt scotch. You can't find it any other time of year but now. So drink up! Who cares that it has 10,000 calories in every sip? It's not as if you're going to turn into an eggnog-alcoholic or something. It's a treat. Enjoy it. Have one for me. Have two. It's later than you think. It's Christmas!
3. If something comes with gravy, use it. That's the whole point of gravy. Gravy does not stand alone. Pour it on. Make a volcano out of your mashed potatoes. Fill it with gravy. Eat the volcano. Repeat.
4. As for mashed potatoes, always ask if they're made with skim milk or whole milk. If it's skim, pass. Why bother? It's like buying a sports car with an automatic transmission.
5. Do not have a snack before going to a party in an effort to control your eating. The whole point of going to a Christmas party is to eat other people's food for free. Lots of it. Hello?
6. Under no circumstances should you exercise between now and New Year's. You can do that in January when you have nothing else to do. This is the time for long naps, which you'll

need after circling the buffet table while carrying a 10-pound plate of food and that vat of eggnog.

7. If you come across something really good at a buffet table, like frosted Christmas cookies in the shape and size of Santa, position yourself near them and don't budge. Have as many as you can before becoming the center of attention. They're like a beautiful pair of shoes. If you leave them behind, you're never going to see them again.

8. Same for those little cream puffs and tiny éclairs. Same for pies… Apple. Pumpkin. Mincemeat. Have a slice of each. Or, if you don't like mincemeat, have two apples and one pumpkin. Always have three. When else do you get to have more than one dessert? Labor Day!

9. Did someone mention fruitcake? Granted, it's loaded with the mandatory celebratory calories, but avoid it at all cost. I mean, have some standards.

10. One final tip: If you don't feel terrible when you leave the party or get up from the table, you haven't been paying attention. Reread tips; start over, but hurry, January is just behind Christmas.

TEN SIGNS YOU'RE TOO OLD FOR TRICK OR TREATING

10. You get winded from knocking on the door.
9. You have to have another kid chew the candy for you.
8. You ask for high fiber candy only.
7. When someone drops a candy bar in your bag, you lose your balance and fall over.
6. People say, "Great Keith Richards mask!" and you're not wearing a mask.
5. When the door opens you yell, "Trick or..." and can't remember the rest.
4. By the end of the night, you have a bag full of restraining orders.
3. You have to carefully choose a costume that won't dislodge your hairpiece.

2. You're the only Power Ranger in the neighborhood with a walker.
1. You avoid going to houses where your ex-wives live.

THE HOLLANDAISE

A man goes to his dentist because he feels something is wrong with his mouth. The dentist examines him and says, "That new upper plate I put in for you six months ago is completely corroded. What have you been eating?"

The man replies, "All I can think of is that about four months ago my wife made some asparagus with hollandaise sauce. I loved the hollandaise so much I now put it on everything – meat, toast, fish, vegetables, you name it."

"Well," says the dentist, "that's probably the problem. Hollandaise sauce is made with lots of lemon juice, which is highly corrosive. It's eaten away your upper plate. I'll make you a new plate, and this time I'll use chrome."

"Why chrome?" asks the patient.

The dentist replies, "It's simple. Everyone knows there's no plate like chrome for the hollandaise!"

NEW YEAR'S EVE

"An optimist stays up until midnight to see the new year in. A pessimist stays up to make sure the old year leaves." *Bill Vaughan*

MARTHA STEWART'S HOLIDAY CALENDAR (THE HUMOR DIGEST CONTRIBUTED BY KEN BROUSSEAU, SR.)

December 1: Blanch carcass from Thanksgiving turkey. Spray paint gold, turn upside down and use as a sleigh to hold Christmas Cards.

December 2: Have Mormon Tabernacle Choir record outgoing Christmas message for answering machine.

December 3: Using candlewick and hand-gilded miniature pinecones, fashion cat-o-nine-tails. Flog gardener.

December 4: Repaint Sistine Chapel ceiling in ecru, with mocha trim.

December 5: Get new eyeglasses. Grind lenses myself.

December 6: Fax family Christmas newsletter to Pulitzer committee for consideration.

December 7: Debug most recent version of *Windows*.

December 10: Align carpets to adjust for curvature of Earth.

December 11: Lay Faberge egg.

December 12: Take dog apart. Disinfect. Reassemble.

December 13: Collect dentures from the poor and homeless. They make excellent pastry cutters, particularly for decorative pie crusts.

December 14: Install plumbing in gingerbread house.

December 15: Replace air in mini-van tires with Glade "holiday scents" in case tires are shot out at mall.

December 17: Child-proof the Christmas tree with garland of razor wire.

December 19: Adjust legs of chairs so each Christmas dinner guest will be same height when sitting at his or her assigned seat.

December 20: Dip sheep and cows in egg whites and roll in confectioner's sugar to add a festive sparkle to the pasture.

December 21: Drain city reservoir; refill with mulled cider, orange slices and cinnamon sticks.

December 22: Float votive candles in toilet tank.

December 23: Seed clouds for white Christmas.

December 24: Do my annual good deed. Go to several stores. Be seen engaged in last minute Christmas shopping, thus making many people feel less inadequate than they really are.

December 25: Bear son. Swaddle. Lay in color coordinated manger scented with homemade potpourri.

December 26: Organize spice racks by genus and phylum.

December 27: Build snowman in exact likeness of God.

December 31: New Year's Eve! Give staff their resolutions. Call a friend in each time zone of the world as the clock strikes midnight in that country.

STATEMENTS TO AVOID ON THANKSGIVING DAY

- Whew, that's one terrific spread!"
- "I'm in the mood for a little dark meat."
- "Tying the legs together keeps the inside moist."
- "Talk about a huge breast!"
- "It's Cool Whip time!"
- "If I don't undo my pants, I'll burst!"
- "Are you ready for seconds yet?"
- "Are you going to come again?"
- "It's a little dry, do you still want to eat it?"
- "Just wait your turn, you'll get some!"
- "Don't play with your meat."
- "Just spread the legs open and stuff it in."
- "Do you think you'll be able to handle all these people at once?"
- "I didn't expect everyone to come at once!"
- "You still have a little bit on your chin."
- "Use a nice smooth stroke when you whip it."
- "How long will it take after you stick it in?"
- "You'll know it's ready when it pops up."
- "Wow, I didn't think I could handle all of that!"
- "How many are coming?"
- "That's the biggest one I've ever seen!"
- "Just lay back & take it easy...I'll do the rest."
- "How long do I beat it before it's ready?"

Humorous Quotations

- You can't be a real country unless you have a beer and an airline - it helps if you have some kind of a football team, or some nuclear weapons, but at the very least you need a beer. *Frank Zappa*
- Dad always thought laughter was the best medicine, which I guess is why several of us died of tuberculosis. *Jack Handey*
- Humor is by far the most significant activity of the human brain. *Edward De Bono*
- Tragedy is when I cut my finger. Comedy is when you walk into an open sewer and die. *Mel Brooks*
- I realize that humor isn't for everyone. It's only for people who want to have fun, enjoy life, and feel alive. *Anne Wilson Schaef*
- The time you enjoy wasting is not wasted time. *Bertrand Russell*
- Veni, Vidi, Visa: We came, we saw, we went shopping. *Jan Barrett*

- People will accept your ideas much more rapidly if you tell them Benjamin Franklin said it first. *David Comins*
- Always bite the heads off Animal Crackers first, so you don't have to hear them screaming. *Bob Greene*
- Life should NOT be a journey to the grave with the intention of arriving safely in an attractive and well preserved body. Rather, your goal should be to skid in sideways, chocolate in one hand, martini in the other, totally worn out and screaming, "WOO HOO! Whatta ride!
- A good friend will come and bail you out of jail...but, a true friend will be sitting next to you saying, "Wow...that was fun!"
- Life may not be the party we hoped for, but while we are here we might as well dance.
- It's not me who can't keep a secret it's the people I tell that can't. *Abraham Lincoln*
- When the power of love overcomes the love of power, the world will know peace. *Jimi Hendrix*
- Life is like wrestling a gorilla. You don't stop when you get tired; you stop when the gorilla gets tired.
- If life was fair, Elvis would be alive and all the impersonators would be dead. *Johnny Carson*
- Put the saddle on the stove Mama, 'cause I'm riding the range tonight! *Elias 'Wick' Baum*
- I hate quotations. *Ralph Waldo Emerson*
- Sex on television can't hurt you, unless you fall off. *Homer Simpson*
- It has been proven that Americans watch television more than any other appliance. *Steve Martin and Gary Muildier*
- Everything I read talked about the evils of drinking, so I gave up reading. *Henny Youngman*
- Teamwork is essential -- it allows you to blame someone else. *Dagwood Bumstead*
- I can resist anything except temptation. *Oscar Wilde*
- From the moment I picked up your book until I laid it down, I was convulsed with laughter. Some day I intend to read it. *Groucho Marx*

- If it weren't for electricity we'd all be watching television by candlelight. *George Gobel*
- In theory, there is no difference between theory and practice. But, in practice, there is. *Jan L.A. van de Snepscheut*
- If you don't have a sense of humor, it's just not funny! *Author unknown.*
- The problem with the designated driver program, it's not a desirable job. But if you ever get sucked into doing it, have fun with it. At the end of the night, drop them off at the wrong house. *Jeff Foxworthy*
- I went to a bookstore and I asked the woman behind the counter where the self-help section was. She said, "If I told you that would defeat the whole purpose." *Brian Kiley*
- If play is the work of childhood, then work should be the play of adulthood. *R. Bruce Baum*
- A study in the Washington Post says that women have better verbal skills than men. I just want to say to the authors of that study: "Duh!" *Conan O'Brien*
- Suppose you were an idiot... And suppose you were a member of Congress...But I repeat myself. *Mark Twain*
- Don't cry because it ended. Smile because it happened. *Author unknown.*
- If a woman has to choose between catching a fly ball and saving an infant's life, she will choose to save the infant's life without even considering if there is a man on base. *Dave Barry*
- I think that's how Chicago got started. A bunch of people in New York said, 'Gee, I'm enjoying the crime and the poverty, but it just isn't cold enough. Let's go west.' *Richard Jeni*
- Confidence is going after Moby Dick in a rowboat and taking the tartar sauce with you. *Zig Ziglar*
- If life gives you lemons, stick them down your shirt and make your boobs look bigger. *Raneboux*
- Things are going to get a lot worse before they get worse. *Lily Tomlin*
- A male gynecologist is like an auto mechanic who never owned a car. *Carrie Snow*

- If you can't be a good example, then you'll just have to serve as a horrible warning. *Catherine Aird*
- I saw my mother yesterday. Thank God she didn't see me. *Author unknown*
- After contemplating the irony of the situation, I decided to go back into the store and actually pay for my "What Would Jesus Do?" bracelet. *Ruth M.*
- We have more fun than people. *Bob Greene*
- As a kid, whenever I got sick my mom would say, "Don't worry, son. There's nothing so bad that it can't be fixed with a bottle of cheap Scotch and a couple of hookers." Or was that the old crusty guy who hung around the schoolyard? No matter -- either way, it's terrific advice. *Bob Van Voris*
- The most revolutionary act anyone can commit to is to be happy. *Patch Adams*
- On the one hand, we'll never experience childbirth. On the other hand, we can open all our own jars. *Jeff Green*
- Two roads diverged in a wood and I chose the one with the large-breasted hitchhiker on it. And that has made all the difference. *Michael Sheinbaum*
- Have you ever noticed, anybody going slower than you is an idiot, and anyone going faster than you is a maniac? *George Carlin*
- We are here on earth to do good to others. What the others are here for; I don't know. *W. H. Auden*
- I think men who have a pierced ear are better prepared for marriage. They've experienced pain and bought jewelry. *Rita Rudner*
- I'm at an age where I think more about food than sex. Last week I put a mirror over my dining room table. *Rodney Dangerfield*
- Only Irish coffee provides in a single glass all four essential food groups: alcohol, caffeine, sugar and fat. *Alex Levine*
- Kids, just because I don't care, it doesn't mean I'm not listening. *Homer Simpson*
- When in doubt, make a fool of yourself. There is a microscopically thin line between being brilliantly creative

and acting like the most gigantic idiot on earth. So, what the hell, leap. *Cynthia Heimel*

- Never take a solemn oath. People think you mean it. *Norman Douglas*
- My parents have been visiting me for a few days. I just dropped them off at the airport. They leave tomorrow. *Margaret Smith*
- Work should be more fun than fun. *Noel Coward*
- When I was born I was so surprised I didn't talk for a year and a half. *Gracie Allen*
- Be true to your teeth, and they won't be false to you. *Soupy Sales*
- Worry is the misuse of our imaginations. *Ed Foreman*
- A smile is an inexpensive way to improve your looks. *Charles Gordy*
- Nobody wants constructive criticism. It's all we can do to put up with constructive praise. *Mignon McLaughlin*
- Happiness is having a large, loving, caring, close-knit family in another city. *George Burns*
- Stress is not how you get to the top, but how you bounce at the bottom. *General Patton*
- Among those whom I like or admire, I can find no common denominator, but among those whom I love, I can: all of them make me laugh. *W. H. Auden*
- All animals, except man, know that the principal business of life is to enjoy it. *Samuel Butler*
- This wall paper is killing me. One of us will have to go. *Oscar Wilde* (on his death bed)
- This portion of "Women on the Run" is brought to you by Phillips Milk of Magnesia. *Harry Von Zell*
- Cats are intended to teach us that not everything in nature has a function. *Garrison Keillor*
- I was going to buy a copy of *The Power of Positive Thinking*, and then I thought: What the hell good would that do? *Ronnie Shakes*
- If truth is beauty, how come no one has their hair done in the library? *Lily Tomlin*

- There is no food where the flavor cannot be enhanced by the addition of peanut butter. *Herman E. Gabel, Jr.*
- More than any other time in history, mankind faces a crossroads. One path leads to despair and utter hopelessness. The other, to total extinction. Let us pray we have the wisdom to choose correctly. *Woody Allen*
- I don't have much of a sex life. I have a mirror over my bed. It says, "Objects are much larger than they appear to be." *Dennis Bruce*
- After twelve years of therapy my psychiatrist said something that brought tears to my eyes. He said, "No hablo ingles."
- I had dinner with my parents last night, and I made a classic Freudian slip. I meant to say, "Please pass the salt," but it came out, "You idiots, you ruined my childhood." *Johnathan Katz*
- My parents used to send me to spend summers with my grandparents. I hate cemeteries. *Chris Fonseca*
- People can be divided into three groups: those who make things happen, those who watch things happen and those who wonder what happened. *John Newbern*
- Any time four New Yorkers get into a cab without arguing, a bank robbery has just taken place. *Johnny Carson*
- A man is as old as the woman he feels. *Groucho Marx*
- That lowdown scoundrel deserves to be kicked to death by a jackass - and I'm just the one to do it. *Congressional candidate in Texas*
- It is indeed fitting that we gather here today to pay tribute to Abraham Lincoln, who was born in a log cabin that he built with his own hands. *Politician in a speech honoring President Lincoln*
- Why can't the Jews and Arabs sit down together and settle this like good Christians? *Overhead during a congressional debate.*
- Never let a panty line show around your ankles. *Joan Rivers*
- Don't wait up for the shrimp boats, Mama; I'm coming home with the crabs. *Elias 'Wick' Baum*

- My wife thinks I'm too nosy. At least that's what she scribbles in her diary.   *Drake Sather*
- It takes a big man to cry, but it takes a bigger man to laugh at that man.   *Jack Handey*
- My mother said, "You won't amount to anything because you procrastinate! I said, "Just you wait." *Judy Tenuta*
- My life has been one great big joke,
  A dance that's walked
  A song that's spoke,
  I laugh so hard I almost choke
  When I think about myself.

    Maya Angelou

Humorous Signs

- On a Septic Tank Truck in Oregon: "Yesterday's Meals on Wheels."
- Sign over a Gynecologist's Office: "Dr. Jones, at your cervix."
- On a Plumber's truck: "We repair what your husband fixed."
- On a Plumber's truck: "Don't sleep with a drip. Call your plumber."
- Pizza Shop Slogan: "7 days without pizza makes one weak."
- At a Tire Shop in Milwaukee: "Invite us to your next blowout."
- On a Plastic Surgeon's Office door: "Hello. Can we pick your nose?"
- At a Towing company: "We don't charge an arm and a leg. We want tows."
- On an Electrician's truck: "Let us remove your shorts"
- In a Non-smoking Area: "If we see smoke, we will assume you are on fire and take appropriate action."

- On a Maternity Room door: "Push. Push. Push"
- At an Optometrist's office: "If you don't see what you're looking for, you've come to the right place."
- On a Taxidermist's window: "We really know our stuff."
- In a Podiatrist's office: "Time wounds all heels."
- On a Fence: "Salesmen welcome! Dog food is expensive."
- At a Car Dealership: "The best way to get back on your feet -- miss a car payment."
- Outside a Muffler Shop: "No appointment necessary. We hear you coming."
- In a Veterinarian's waiting room: "Be back in 5 minutes. Sit! Stay!"
- At the electric company: "We would be delighted if you send in your payment. However, if you don't, you will be."
- In a restaurant window: "Don't stand there and be hungry, Come on in and get fed up."
- In the front yard of a funeral home: "Drive carefully. We'll wait."
- At a propane filling station, "Thank heaven for little grills."
- At a Chicago radiator shop: "Best place in town to take a leak."
- In front of an auto junkyard on Malta: "We Have Japanese Body Parts!"
- In an office: "Toilet out of order...Please use floor below."
- In a Laundromat: "Automatic washing machines: please remove all your clothes when the light goes out."
- In a London department store: "Bargain basement upstairs."
- In an office: "Would the person who took the step ladder yesterday please bring it back or further steps will be taken."
- In an office: "After tea break staff should empty the teapot and stand upside down on the draining board."
- Outside a secondhand shop: "We exchange anything - bicycles, washing machines, etc. Why not bring your wife along and get a wonderful bargain?"

- Spotted in a safari park: "Elephants please stay in your car."
- Notice in a farmer's field: "The farmer allows walkers to cross the field for free, but the bull charges."
- On a repair shop door: "We can repair anything. (please knock hard on the door - the bell doesn't work)."
- Sign at a hotel: "Help! We need inn-experienced people."
- Sign in a science teacher's room: "If it moves, it's biology. If it stinks, it's chemistry. If it doesn't work, it's physics."
- Sign in an office: "We shoot every 3rd salesman, and the 2nd one just left."
- Sign behind counter at video rental store: "We are sorry to report that we are all out of 'That Movie with That Guy Who Was in That Other Movie'. There was some confusion when ordering from our distributor. Thank You"
- Sign in beauty shop window: "Dye now!"
- Sign at a computer store: "Out for a quick byte."
- On a delivery truck from an egg farm: "Better laid than ever."
- On a clinical microbiology lab door: "Staph only."
- On a sign in front of manicure salon: "Nail your sweetheart for Valentines!"
- In a Bucharest hotel lobby: "The lift is being fixed for the next day. During that time we regret that you will be unbearable."
- In a Paris hotel elevator: "Please leave your values at the front desk."
- In a hotel in Athens: "Visitors are expected to complain at the office between the hours of 9 and 11 A.M. daily."
- In a Japanese hotel: "You are invited to take advantage of the chambermaid."
- In the lobby of a Moscow hotel across from Russian Orthodox monastery: "You are welcome to visit the cemetery where famous Russian and Soviet composers, artists, and writers are buried daily except Thursday."
- On the menu of a Swiss restaurant: "Our wines leave you nothing to hope for."

- In a Bangkok dry cleaners: "Drop your trousers here for best results."
- In an advertisement by a Hong Kong dentist: "Teeth extracted by the latest Methodists."
- In a Rome laundry: "Ladies, leave your clothes here and spend the afternoon having a good time.
- In a Copenhagen airline ticket office: We take your bags and send them in all directions."
- On the door of a Moscow hotel room: "If this is your first visit to the USSR, you are welcome to it."
- Two signs from a Majorcan shop entrance: "English well speaking." and "Here speeching American."

Marriage, Love and Relationship Humor (with a little sex)

WHERE WOULD YOU BE?

If - you had all the money your heart desires?

If - you had no worries?

If - you came home to a clean house and the finest meal is awaiting you?

If - your bathwater had been run just the way you like it?

If - you had the perfect kids?

If - your partner was awaiting you with open arms and kisses?

Where would you be? You'd be in the wrong house!

HAPPY TONIGHT

My husband came home with a tube of KY jelly and said, "This will make you happy tonight." He was right. When he went out of the bedroom, I squirted it all over the doorknob and closed the door.

WOMEN'S HUMOR

One day my housework-challenged husband decided to wash his sweatshirt. Seconds after he stepped into the laundry room, he shouted to me, "What setting do I use on the washing machine?"

"It depends," I replied. "What does it say on your shirt?" He yelled back, "University of Texas."

"It's just too hot to wear clothes today," Jack says as he stepped out of the shower, "honey, what do you think the neighbors would think if I mowed the lawn like this?" "Probably that I married you for your money," she replied.

He said - Since I first laid eyes on you, I have wanted to make love to you really badly. She said - Well, you succeeded.

He said - Shall we try swapping positions tonight?

She said - That's a good idea... you stand by the ironing board while I sit on the sofa and fart.

YOUR MOTHER

Husband: "Now look, Lucy, I don't want to seem harsh, but your mother has been living with us for twenty years now. Don't you think it's about time she got a place of her own?"

Wife: "My mother! I thought she was your mother!"

MARY LOU

A man was sitting quietly reading his paper one morning, peacefully enjoying himself, when his wife sneaks up behind him and whacks him on the back of his head with a frying pan.

Man: "What was that for?"

Wife: "What was that piece of paper in your pant's pocket with the name Mary Lou written on it?"

Man: "Oh honey. Don't you remember two weeks ago when I went to the horse races? Mary Lou was the name of one of the horses I bet on."

The wife seemed satisfied and headed on to do some work around the house, feeling a bit sheepish. Three days later he is once again sitting in his chair reading and she repeats the frying pan whacking. Man: "What's that for this time?"

Wife: "Your horse called."

THE SPELLING TEST

A woman arrived at the Gates of Heaven. While she was waiting for Saint Peter to greet her, she peeked through the gates. She saw a beautiful banquet table. Sitting all around were her parents and all the other people she had loved and who had died before her. They saw her and began calling greetings to her "Hello - How are you! We've been waiting for you! Good to see you."

When Saint Peter came by, the woman said to him, "This is such a wonderful place! How do I get in?" "You have to spell a word," Saint Peter told her. "Which word?" the woman asked. "Love."

The woman correctly spelled "Love" and Saint Peter welcomed her into Heaven.

About a year later, Saint Peter came to the woman and asked her to watch the Gates of Heaven for him that day. While the woman was guarding the Gates of Heaven, her husband arrived. "I'm surprised to see you," the woman said. "How have you been?" "Oh, I've been doing pretty well since you died," her husband told her. "I married the beautiful young nurse who took care of you while you were ill. And then I won the multi-state lottery. I sold the little house you and I lived in and bought a huge mansion. And my wife and I traveled all around the world. We were on vacation in Cancun and I went water skiing today. I fell and hit my head, and here I am. What a bummer! How do I get in?"

"You have to spell a word," the woman told him. "Which word?" her husband asked.

"Czechoslovakia."

THE FIVE SECRETS OF A PERFECT RELATIONSHIP

1. It's important to have a woman who helps at home, who cooks from time to time, who cleans up and who has a job.

2. It's important to have a woman who can make you laugh.
3. It's important to have a woman who you can trust and who doesn't lie to you.
4. It's important to have a woman who is good in bed and who likes to be with you.
5. It's very important that these four women do not know each other.

MARRIAGE - SOME THOUGHTS

- Trouble in marriage often starts when a man gets so busy earning his salt that he forgets his sugar.
- Too many couples marry for better or for worse, but not for good.
- When a man marries a woman, they become one, but the trouble starts when they try to decide which one.
- On anniversaries the wise husband always forgets the past... but never the present.
- A foolish husband remarks to his wife: "Honey, you stick to the washing, ironing, cooking, and scrubbing. No wife of mine is going to work.
- The bonds of matrimony are a good investment only when the interest is kept up.
- Many girls like to marry a military man--he can cook, sew, make bed, and is in good health...and he's already used to taking orders.

THE CHEATING WIFE

Larry returns to Buffalo from a business trip after midnight and a day early. He grabs a cab at the airport. He suspects his wife is having an affair, and he intends to catch her in the act, so en route home, he asks the cabby to be a witness. For $100, the cabby agrees.

After quietly arriving at the house, Larry and the cabby tiptoe inside, up the stairs and then into the bedroom. Larry switches on the lights, yanks the blanket back and there's his wife in bed with another man.

Enraged, he pulls out a gun and puts it to the guy's head.

The wife shrieks, "STOP, OH GOD, LARRY, STOP!! Don't do it!

"I lied! I didn't inherit money. He paid for the Porsche I gave you for your birthday and the new cabin cruiser and your Bills' seasons tickets and our house at the lake!! He pays the country club bills, too, even the dues!! OH, LARRY, STOP!! FOR GOD SAKES, STOP!!!"

Stunned, Larry slowly lowers the gun. He looks at the cabby woefully and says, "Wha-what would you do?'

The cabby says, "I'd cover his ass with that blanket before he catches a cold."

PENNANCE

A married Irishman went into the confessional and said to his priest, "I almost had an affair with another woman." The priest said, "What do you mean, almost?" The Irishman said, "Well, we got undressed and rubbed together, but then I stopped." The priest said, "Rubbing together is the same as putting it in. You're not to see that woman again. For your penance, say five Hail Mary's and put $50 in the poor box."

The Irishman left the confessional, said his prayers, and then walked over to the poor box. He paused for a moment and then started to leave. The priest, who was watching, quickly ran over to him saying, "I saw that. You didn't put any money in the poor box!" The Irishman replied, "Yeah, but I rubbed the $50 on the box, and according to you, that's the same as putting it in!"

HAPPIEST WOMAN IN THE WORLD

A couple is lying in bed. The husband says, "I am going to make you the happiest woman in the world."

The wife says..... "I'll miss you."

THE DIAMOND CURSE

A buxom blonde wore, at a charity ball, an enormous diamond. "It happens to be the third most famous diamond in the whole world," she boasted. "The first is the Hope Diamond, then comes the Kohinoor and then comes this one, which is called The Lipshitz Diamond."

"What a diamond!"

"How lucky you are!"

"Wait, wait, nothing in life is all luck," said the diamonded lady. "Unfortunately, with this famous Lipshitz Diamond one must accept the famous Lipshitz curse!"

The ladies buzzed and asked, "And what's the Lipshitz curse?"

"Mr. Lipshitz," sighed the lady.

GOOD SEX

The sex was so good even the neighbors had a cigarette.

RED SKELTON'S TIPS FOR A HAPPY MARRIAGE

NOTE: For those readers too young to know who Red Skelton is, he was a very funny comedian on early live television.

1. Two times a week, we go to a nice restaurant, have a little beverage, and then come good food and companionship. She goes on Tuesdays, I go on Fridays.
2. We also sleep in separate beds. Hers is in Ontario and mine is in Tucson.
3. I take my wife everywhere, but she keeps finding her way back.
4. I asked my wife where she wanted to go for our anniversary. "Somewhere I haven't been in a long time!" she said. So I suggested the kitchen.
5. We always hold hands. If I let go, she shops.
6. She has an electric blender, electric toaster and electric bread maker. Then she said "There are too many gadgets and no place to sit down!" So I bought her an electric chair.
7. My wife told me the car wasn't running well because there was water in the carburetor. I asked where the car was, she told me "In the lake."

8. She got a mudpack and looked great for two days. Then the mud fell off.
9. She ran after the garbage truck, yelling "Am I too late for the garbage?" The driver said "No, jump in!"
10. Remember. Marriage is the number one cause of divorce.
11. Statistically, 100% of all divorces start with marriage.
12. I married Miss Right. I just didn't know her first name was **Always.**
13. I haven't spoken to my wife in 18 months. I don't like to interrupt her.
14. The last fight was my fault. My wife asked "What's on the TV?" I said "Dust!"

LOUD SEX

A wife went in to see a therapist and said, "I've got a big problem, doctor. Every time we're in bed and my husband climaxes, he lets out this ear splitting yell."

"My dear, that's completely natural. I don't see what the problem is", the therapist explained.

"The problem is," she complained, "It wakes me up!"

BREAKING UP IN COLLEGE (WHEN SHARING THE SAME MAJOR) - FROM BILL STEBBINS' HUMOR LIST

Psychology - Girl accuses guy of just using her as a substitute for his Mother.

Sociology - Each claims to have been oppressed in the relationship.

Archeology - One tries to bury the past, and accuses the other of trying to dig it up.

Theatre - "OH! Life is... ENDED... as we KNOW it!"

Biology - "You just wanted to get in my genes!"

Physics - Both resign themselves to the fact that what goes up must come down.

Journalism - "Today was the end of an era. Jack, 19, and Jill, 18, called an end to their relationship of 2 weeks..."

Women's Studies - "HE did it!"

Business - Both decide that they're spending way too much money together, and that it's simply cheaper to be single.

History - Each party argues the breakup was caused by something the other party did in the past.

Geography - Both people decide to simply move far away to avoid each other.

Anatomy - "I never liked your body anyway."

Economics - One party demands more than the other can supply.

THE WOMAN'S PERFECT BREAKFAST

- She's sitting at the table with her gourmet coffee.
- Her son is on the cover of the Wheaties box.
- Her daughter is on the cover of Business Week.
- Her boyfriend is on the cover of Playgirl.
- And her husband is on the back of the milk carton

THE PROPOSAL

A college senior took his new girlfriend to a football game. The young couple found seats in the crowded stadium and were watching the action. A substitute was put into the game, and as he was running onto the field to take his position, the boy said to his girlfriend, "Take a good look at that fellow. I expect him to be our best man next year." His girlfriend snuggled closer to him and said, "That's the strangest way I ever heard of for a fellow to propose to a girl. Regardless of how you said it, I accept!"

LEMON JUICE

There once was a religious young woman who went to Confession. Upon entering the confessional, she said, "Forgive me, Father, for I have sinned." The priest said, "Confess your sins and be forgiven." The young woman said, "Last night my boyfriend made mad passionate love to me seven times." The priest thought long and hard and then said, "Squeeze seven lemons into a glass and then drink the juice." The young woman asked, "Will this cleanse me of my sins?" The priest said, "No, but it will wipe that smile off of your face."

MARRIAGE COUNSELING (SHARED BY LARRY UNGER)

A husband and wife came for counseling after 20 years of marriage. When asked what the problem was, the wife went into a passionate, painful tirade listing every problem they had ever had in the twenty years they had been married.

She went on and on and on: neglect, lack of intimacy, emptiness, loneliness, feeling unloved and unlovable, an entire laundry list of unmet needs she had endured over the course of their marriage.

Finally, after allowing this to go on for a sufficient length of time, the therapist got up, walked around the desk and, after asking the wife to stand, embraced and kissed her passionately as her husband watched with a raised eyebrow. The woman shut up and quietly sat down as though in a daze.

The therapist turned to the husband and said, 'This is what your wife needs at least three times a week.

Can you do this?'

The husband thought for a moment and replied, 'Well, I can drop her off here on Mondays and Wednesdays, but on Fridays, I fish.

SEXUALITY MYTHS

A man boarded an airplane and took his seat. As he settled in, he glanced up and saw a very beautiful woman boarding the plane. He soon realized she was heading straight towards his seat. Lo and behold, She took the seat right beside his. Eager to strike up a conversation, he blurted out, "Business trip or vacation?" She turned, smiled and said, "Business. I'm going to the Annual Nymphomaniac Convention in Chicago."

He swallowed hard. Here was the most gorgeous woman he had ever seen sitting next to him and she was going to a meeting for nymphomaniacs. Struggling to maintain his composure, he calmly asked, "What's your business role at this convention?" "Lecturer," she responded. "I use my experience to debunk some of the popular myths about sexuality."

"Really!" he said, "what myths are those?" "Well," she explained, "one popular myth is that American men are the most well-endowed when, in fact, it's the Native American Indian who is most likely to possess that trait. Another popular myth is that French men are the best lovers, when actually it is the men of Jewish descent. We have, however, found that the best potential lover in all categories is the Southern redneck."

Suddenly, the woman became a little uncomfortable and blushed. "I'm sorry," she said, "I shouldn't really be discussing this with you. I don't even know your name."

"Tonto," the man said, "Tonto Goldstein. But my friends call me 'Bubba'."

ITALIAN LOVE STORY! (SHARED BY LARRY UNGER)

At Saint Mary's Catholic Church they have a weekly husband's marriage seminar. At the session last week, the Priest asked Luigi, who was approaching his 50th wedding anniversary, to take a few minutes and share some insight into how he had managed to stay married to the same woman all these years.

Luigi replied to the assembled husbands, 'Well, I've a-tried to treat-a her nice, spend the money on her, but best of all is that I took-a her to Italy for the 20th anniversary!'

The Priest responded, 'Luigi, you are an amazing inspiration to all the husbands here! Please tell us what you are planning for your wife for your 50th anniversary.'

Luigi proudly replied, 'I'm a-gonna go and get her.'

HE THINKS HE KNOWS YOU

A man and woman were traveling along in their car when a police officer pulls them over. The officer walks up to the window and says "Did you know you were speeding back there." The lady (who is almost deaf) said to her husband, "What did he say, what did he say?" The man turns to his wife and said "He said I was speeding." The officer then said "Where are you from?" The man replied "Chicago" The wife then says "What did he say, what did he say?" The man turns to his wife and said, "He wanted to know where we came from." The officer then said "Shit, you know, I had my worst sex ever in Chicago." The lady then says "What did he say, what did he say?" The man turns back and says "He says he thinks he knows you."

DEAR PROCTOR AND GAMBLE

Dear Proctor and Gamble Company,

I am writing to say what an excellent product Tide is! I've used Tide all through my married life, as my Mom always told me it was the best. Now that I am in my fifties, I find it even better!

In fact, about a month ago, I spilled some red wine on my new white blouse. My inconsiderate and uncaring husband started to berate me about how clumsy I was, and generally started becoming a pain in the neck.

One thing led to another, and somehow I ended up with a lot of his blood on my white blouse! I grabbed my bottle of liquid Tide with bleach alternative, and to my surprise and satisfaction, all of the stains came out!

In fact, the stains came out so well, the detectives who came by yesterday told me that the DNA tests on my blouse were negative, and then my attorney called and said that I would no longer be considered a suspect in the disappearance of my husband. What a relief! Going through menopause is bad enough without being a murder suspect!

I thank you, once again, for having such a great product. Well, gotta go. I have to write a letter to the Hefty bag people!

MARRIAGE IS...

Marriage is the process of finding out what kind of person your spouse would really have preferred.

THE NEWLYWEDS

The newlyweds finally made it to the hotel room on their wedding day. As the groom was taking off his pants, his new bride noticed that his knees were badly scarred. She inquired about it and her husband told her, "When I was a child I had the kneeseales." She said, "You mean the measles." "No," he replied, "I had the kneeseasles." She said, "OK." He continued to undress and after he removed his shoes and socks, she noticed his toes were all gnarled and deformed. She asked about that, and he replied, "When I was younger I had the toelio." She said, "You mean polio." He answered, "No, I had toelio." She said, "Fine." Just then he removed his underwear. She looked over and said, "Don't tell me...smallcocks"

PEST CONTROL

A woman was having a passionate affair with an inspector from a pest-control company. One afternoon they were carrying on in the bedroom together when her husband arrived home unexpectedly. "Quick," said the woman to the lover, "Into the closet!" and she pushed him in the closet, stark naked. The husband, however, became suspicious and after a search of the bedroom discovered the man in the closet.

"Who are you?" he asked him.

"I'm an inspector from Bugs-B-Gone, "said the exterminator.

"What are you doing in there?" the husband asked.

"I'm investigating a complaint about an infestation of moths," the man replied.

"Stark naked?" asked the husband.

The man looked down at himself and said, "Those little bastards!

Medical Humor

THE HICCUPS

A man goes into a drug store and asks the pharmacist if she can give him something for the hiccups.

The pharmacist promptly reaches out and slaps the man's face.

"What did you do that for?" the man asks.

"Well, you don't have the hiccups anymore do you?" she replies.

The man says, "No, but my wife out in the car still does!"

SONGS FROM THE HOSPITAL HIT PARADE

"I'll be Sewing You"
"Red Cells in the Sunset"
"It's Spleen a Long, Long Time"
"It Had to Be Flu"
"On the Bonny Banks of Glaucoma"
"Gonna' Take a Sentimental Gurney"
"The Staphs and Streps Forever"
"Old Man's Liver"
"I've Grown Accustomed to Her Brace"

"The Girl from Emphysema"
"MRI Blue?"
"My Melancolicky Baby"
"From Here to Maternity"

SARAH FINKEL - A TRUE STORY

A woman called a local hospital. "Hello. Could you connect me to the person who gives information about patients? I'd like to find out if a patient is getting better, doing as expected or getting worse."

The voice on the other end said, "What is the patient's name and room number?"

"Sarah Finkel, room 302."

I'll connect you with the nursing station."

"3rd floor Nursing Station. How can I help you?"

"I'd like to know the condition of Sarah Finkel in room 302."

"Just a moment. Let me look at her records. Mrs. Finkel is doing very well. In fact, she's had two full meals, her blood pressure is fine, to be taken off the heart monitor in a couple of hours and, if she continues this improvement, Dr. Cohen is going to send her home Tuesday at noon."

The woman said, "What a relief! Oh, that's fantastic... that's wonderful news!"

The nurse said, "From your enthusiasm, I take it you are a close family member or a very close friend!"

"Neither! I'm Sarah Finkel in 302! Nobody here tells me a thing."

SIGNS YOUR PODIATRIST IS FAKING IT
(CHRIS WHITE © 2007)

His recommendation for your athlete's foot: Amputation, before it spreads.

She prescribes Nickelodeon "Moon Boots", claiming they're good for restoring spinal Feng Shui.

He tells you that your heel spurs will come in handy next time you ride a horse.

She insists that your iPod sounds just fine.

He giggles like a loon every time someone says "phalanges."

Your insurance company just told you that "he's *so* not gellin'" isn't a covered condition.

CHARTING CHUCKLES - HOSPITAL CHART MISTAKES

1. The patient refused autopsy.
2. The patient has no previous history of suicides.
3. Patient has left white blood cells at another hospital.
4. She has no rigors or shaking chills, but her husband states she was very hot in bed last night.
5. Patient has chest pain if she lies on her left side for over a year.
6. On the second day the knee was better, and on the third day it disappeared.
7. The patient is tearful and crying constantly. She also appears to be depressed.
8. The patient has been depressed since she began seeing me in 2003.
9. Discharge status: Alive but without permission.
10. Healthy appearing decrepit 69-year old male, mentally alert but forgetful.
11. Patient had waffles for breakfast and anorexia for lunch.
12. She is numb from her toes down.
13. While in ER, she was examined, x-rated and sent home.
14. The skin was moist and dry.
15. Occasional, constant infrequent headaches.
16. Patient was alert and unresponsive
17. Rectal examination revealed a normal size thyroid.
18 She stated that she had been constipated for most of her life, until she got a divorce.
19. I saw your patient today, who is still under our car for physical therapy.
20. Both breasts are equal and reactive to light and accommodation.
21. Examination of genitalia reveals that he is circus-sized.
22. The lab test indicated abnormal lover function.
23 Skin: somewhat pale but present.
24. The pelvic exam will be done later on the floor.

25. Patient has two teenage children, but no other abnormalities.
26. Physician has been following the patient's breast for six years.
27. Since she can't get pregnant with her husband, I thought you would like to work her up.

THE DOCTOR

The young woman looked up from her hospital bed at the handsome doctor and said breathlessly, "They tell me, doctor, that you're a real lady killer."

The doctor replied, "Maybe so, but the jury threw the case out of court due to lack of evidence."

REAL MEDICAL STORIES
(SHARED BY PATTY WOOTEN, R.N.)

A man comes into the ER and yells "My wife's going to have her baby in the cab!" The ER physician grabs his stuff, rushes out to the cab, lifts the lady's dress, and begins to take off her underwear. Suddenly he notices that there are several cabs, and he's in the wrong one.

A nurse at the beginning of the shift places her stethoscope on an elderly and slightly deaf female patient's posterior chest wall. "Big breaths," instructed the nurse. "Yes, they used to be," sighed the patient.

One day I had to be the bearer of bad news when I told a wife that her husband had died of a massive myocardial infarct. Not more than five minutes later, I heard her reporting to the rest of the family that he had died of a "massive internal fart."

I was performing a complete physical, including the visual acuity test. I placed the patient twenty feet from the chart and began, "Cover your right eye with your hand." He read the 20/20 line perfectly. "Now your left." Again, a flawless read. "Now both," I requested. There was silence. He couldn't even read the large E on the top line. I turned and discovered that he had done exactly what I had asked; he was standing there with both his eyes covered. I was laughing too hard to finish the exam.

A nurses' aide was helping a patient into the bathroom when the patient exclaimed, "You're not coming in here with me. This is only a one-seater!"

During a patient's two week follow-up appointment with his cardiologist, he informed his doctor that he was having trouble with one of his medications. "Which one?", asked the doctor. "The patch. The nurse told me to put on a new one every six hours and now I'm running out of places to put it!" The doctor quickly undressed him, and discovered what he hoped he wouldn't see... Yes, the man had over fifty patches on his body! Now the instructions include removal of the old patch before applying a new one.

While acquainting myself with a new elderly patient, I asked, "How long have you been bedridden?" After a look of complete confusion she answered, "Why not for about twenty years - when my husband was alive."

THE DOCTOR'S OFFICE

A guy walks into a doctor's office with a lettuce leaf sticking out of his ear. The doctor says, "Hmmmm, that's strange." The guy replies, "That's just the tip of the iceberg."

THE PAP SMEAR

This is a laugh for all those women out there who so look forward to that wonderful time once a year when they get to be "intimate" with their OB/GYN doctor! In Sydney, Australia, one of the radio stations pays ($1000-$5000) for people to tell their most embarrassing stories. This is one of the winners:

I was due later in the week for an appointment with the gynecologist. Early one morning I received a call from the doctor's office to tell me that I had been rescheduled for early that morning at 9:30 a.m.

I had only just packed everyone off to work and school, and it was already around 8:45 a.m. The trip to his office took about 35 minutes, so I didn't have any time to spare. As most women do, I like to take a little extra effort over hygiene when making such visits, but this time I wasn't going to be able to make the full effort. So I rushed upstairs, threw off my dressing gown, wet the washcloth that was sitting next to the sink, and gave myself a quick wash in "that area" to make sure I was at least presentable.

I threw the washcloth in the clothes basket, donned some clothes, hopped in the car and raced to my appointment. I was in the waiting room only a few minutes when I was called in.

Knowing the procedure, as I'm sure you do, I hopped up on the table, looked over at the other side of the room and pretended that I was in Paris or some other place a million miles away.

I was a little surprised when the doctor said, "My, we have made an extra effort this morning, haven't we?" but I didn't respond. When the appointment was over, I heaved a sigh of relief and went home. The rest of the day was normal...some shopping, cleaning, cooking, etc.

After school when my six-year-old daughter was playing, she called out from the bathroom, "Mum, where's my washcloth?" I told her to get another one from the cupboard. She replied, "No, I need the one that was here by the sink. It had all my glitter and sparkles in it."

VETERINARIAN TESTS

A man runs into the vet's office carrying his dog, screaming for help. The vet rushes him back to an examination room and has him put his dog down on the examination table. The vet examines the still, limp body and after a few moments, tells the man that his dog, regrettably, is dead. The man, clearly agitated and not willing to accept this, demands a second opinion. The vet goes into the back room and comes out with a cat and puts the cat down next to the dog's body. The cat sniffs the body, walks from head to tail, poking and sniffing the dog's body and finally looks at the vet, meows and shakes his head. The vet looks at the man and says, "I'm sorry, but the cat thinks that your dog is dead, too."

The man is still unwilling to accept that his dog is dead. So the vet brings in a black Labrador retriever. The Lab sniffs the body, walks from head to tail, and finally looks at the vet and barks twice. The vet looks at the man and says, "I'm sorry, but the Lab thinks your dog is dead too."

The man, finally resigned to the diagnosis, thanks the vet and asks how much he owes. The vet answers, "$650."

"Six hundred and fifty dollars to tell me my dog is dead!?" exclaims the man.

"Well," the vet replies, "I would only have charged you $50 for my initial diagnosis. The additional $600 was for the cat scan and lab test."

CANCER QUOTES

"Having breast cancer is massive amounts of no fun. First they mutilate you; then they poison you; then they burn you. I have been on blind dates better than that." *Molly Ivans*

A few weeks after my [breast cancer] surgery, I went out to play catch with my golden retriever. When I bent over to pick up the ball, my prosthesis fell out. The dog snatched it, and I found myself chasing him down the road yelling "Hey, come back here with my breast!" *Linda Ellerbee*

THINGS YOU NEVER WANT TO HEAR DURING SURGERY
(© CHRIS WHITE)

1. Wait a minute, if this is her spleen, then what's that?
2. Rags! Come back with that! Bad Dog!
3. Better save that. We'll need it for the autopsy.
4. Hand me that... uh... that uh... thingie
5. Rats! Page 47 of the manual is missing!

6. Could you stop that thing from beating? It's throwing my concentration off.
7. I hate it when they're missing stuff in here.
8. "Accept this sacrifice, O Great Lord of Darkness."
9. That's cool! Now can you make his leg twitch?!
10. What do you mean he wasn't in for a sex change?
11. Nurse, did this patient sign the organ donation card?
12. Don't worry. I think it is sharp enough.
13. What do you mean, "You want a divorce"!
14. Isn't this the one with the really lousy insurance?
15. Ya' know...there's big money in kidneys...and this guy's got two of 'em.

BABY'S FIRST DOCTOR'S VISIT
(SHARED BY ELISE LAMBERT)

A woman and a baby were in the doctor's examining room, waiting for the doctor to come in for the baby's first exam.

The doctor arrived, and examined the baby, checked his weight, and being a little concerned, asked if the baby was breast-fed or bottle-fed.

"Breast-fed," she replied.

"Well, strip down to your waist," the doctor ordered. She did. He pinched her nipples, pressed, kneaded, and rubbed both breasts for a while in a very professional and detailed examination. Motioning to her to get dressed, the doctor said, "No wonder this baby is underweight. You don't have any milk."

"I know," she said, "I'm his Grandma, but I'm glad I came."

PREPARING FOR YOUR MAMMOGRAM

Many women are afraid of their first mammogram, but there is no need to worry. By taking a few minutes each day, for a week, preceding the exam and doing the following practice exercises, you will be totally prepared for the test, and best of all, you can do these simple practice exercises right in your home.

Exercise 1: Open your refrigerator door and insert one breast between the door and the main box. Have one of your strongest friends slam the door shut as hard as possible and lean on the door for good measure. Hold that position for five seconds. Repeat again in case the first time wasn't effective enough.

Exercise 2: Visit your garage at 3 AM when the temperature of the cement floor is just perfect. Take off all your clothes and lie comfortably on the floor with one breast wedged under the rear tire of the car.

Ask a friend to slowly back the car up until your breast is sufficiently flattened and chilled. Turn over and repeat for the other breast.

Exercise 3: Freeze two metal bookends overnight. Strip to the waist. Invite a stranger into the room. Press the bookends against one of your breasts. Smash the bookends together as hard as you can. Set an appointment with the stranger to meet next year and do it again. You are now properly prepared.

THE OPERATION

An older Jewish gentleman was on the operating table awaiting surgery and he insisted that his son, a renowned surgeon, perform the operation. As he was about to get the anesthesia he asked to speak to his son. "Yes, Dad, what is it?" "Don't be nervous, son; do your best. Just remember if it doesn't go well and something happens to me, your mother is going to come and live with you and your family."

HMO: QUESTIONS AND ANSWERS

Q. What does HMO stand for?

A. This is actually a variation of the phrase, "HEY MOE." Its roots go back to a concept pioneered by Moe of the Three Stooges, who discovered that a patient could be made to forget about the pain in his foot if he was poked hard enough in the eyes.

Q. I just joined an HMO. How difficult will it be to choose the doctor I want?

A. Just slightly more difficult than choosing your parents. Your insurer will provide you with a book listing all the doctors in the plan. These doctors basically fall into two categories - those who are no longer accepting new patients, and those who will see you but are no longer participating in the plan. But don't worry; the remaining doctor who is still in the plan and accepting new patients has an office just a half-day's drive away, and a diploma from a Third World country.

Q. Do all diagnostic procedures require pre-certification?
A. No. Only those you need.

Q. Can I get coverage for my pre-existing conditions?
A. Certainly, as long as they don't require any treatment

Q. What happens if I want to try alternative forms of medicine?
A. You'll need to find alternative forms of payment.

Q. What if I'm away from home and I get sick?
A. You really shouldn't do that.

Q. I think I need to see a specialist, but my doctor insists he can handle my problem. Can a general practitioner really perform a heart transplant right in his office?
A. Hard to say, but considering that all you're risking is the $20 co-payment, there's no harm in giving him a shot at it.

Q. Will health care be different in the next century?
A. No. But if you call right now, you might get an appointment by then.

MEDICAL CONDITION

A man is sitting next to a woman on a jet which is getting ready to take off. Suddenly, the man sneezes. He unzips his pants and wipes the end of his penis off with his handkerchief. He zips up, and continues reading his magazine. The woman cannot believe what she just saw. Then he sneezes again, unzips, pulls out his penis and wipes it off with a handkerchief. The woman says, "Excuse me sir, but that is disgusting and rude, and if you do it again, I am going to call the flight attendant and have you removed from this plane. He says, "I am so sorry that I have offended you. I have this very rare and embarrassing medical condition that causes me to have an orgasm every time I sneeze." The woman, disarmed by the man's honesty, and somewhat embarrassed by her own callousness, says, with sympathy, "Oh you poor man, what are you taking for it?" "Pepper," he answers.

SAVING A LIFE

Two men living way back in the Appalachian hills walk into a bar. While having a shot of whiskey, they talk about their moonshine operation. Suddenly, a woman eating a sandwich at a nearby table begins to cough. After a minute or so, it becomes apparent that she is in real distress.

One of the men looks at her and says, 'Kin ya swallar?'

The woman shakes her head no.

Then he asks, 'Kin ya breathe?'

The woman begins to turn blue and shakes her head no.

The man walks over to the woman, lifts up her dress, yanks down her drawers and quickly gives her right butt cheek a lick with his tongue.

The woman is so disgusted that she has a violent spasm and the obstruction flies out of her mouth.

As she begins to breathe again, the man walks back to the bar.

His partner says, 'Ya know, I'd heerd of that there Hind Lick Maneuver, but I ain't niver seed nobody do it!'

THE POOPIE SHEET - SHARED BY TENA GARAS, R. N.

GHOST POOPIE – The kind where you feel the poopie come out, but there is no poopie in the toilet.

CLEAN POOPIE – The kind where you poopie it out, see it in the toilet, but there is nothing on the toilet paper.

WET POOPIE – The kind of poopie where you wipe your butt 60 times and it still feels unwiped, so you have to put some toilet paper between your butt and your underwear so you won't ruin them with a stain.

SECOND WAVE POOPIE – This happens when you're done poopie-ing and you've pulled your pants up to your knees, and you realize that you have to poopie some more.

POP-A-VEIN-IN-YOUR-FOREHEAD POOPIE – The poopie where you strain so much to get it out, you practically have a stroke.

LINCOLN-LOG POOPIE – The kind of poopie that is so huge you're afraid to flush first without breaking it into pieces with the toilet brush.

GASSEY POOPIE – The poopie is so noisy everyone within earshot is giggling.

DRINKER POOPIE – The kind of poopie you have the morning after a long night of drinking. It's most noticeable trait is the skid mark on the bottom of the toilet.

CORN POOPIE – self-explanatory

GEE-I-WISH-I-COULD-POOPIE POOPIE – The kind where you want to poopie, but all you do is sit on the toilet and fart a few times.

SPINAL TAP POOPIE – That's where the poopie hurts so badly coming out you'd swear it was leaving you sideways.

WET-CHEEKS POOPIE – (The power dump). The poopie that comes out of your butt so fast your butt gets splashed with water.

LIQUID POOPIE – The kind of poopie where yellowish-brown liquid shoots out of your butt and splashes all over the toilet bowl.

SHY POOPIE - The poopie starts coming out, but suddenly it goes back in.

MEXICAN FOOD POOPIE – The poopie smells so bad your nose burns.

UPPER-CLASS POOPIE – The kind of poopie that doesn't even smell.

THE SURPRISE POOPIE – You're not even at the toilet because you are sure you're about to fart, but ooops – a poopie!

THE DANGLING POOPIE – This poopie refuses to drop into the toilet even though you know you are done poopie-ing it. You just hope a shake or two will cut it loose.

DOCTOR, DOCTOR!

Doctor, doctor, my hair's coming out. Can you give me something to keep it in?
Certainly…How about a paper bag?

Doctor, doctor, people keep ignoring me.
Next, please!

Doctor, doctor, I feel like a pair of curtains.
Pull yourself together!

Doctor, doctor, I keep thinking I'm a spoon.
Sit there and don't stir.

Doctor, doctor, I keep thinking I'm a pack of cards.
I'll deal with you later.

Doctor, doctor, I keep thinking there's two of me.
One at a time, please.

Doctor, doctor, I keep thinking I'm a dog.
Lie down on the couch and I'll examine you.
I can't. I'm not allowed on the furniture.

Doctor, doctor, my little boy's swallowed a bullet.
What shall I do?
Well, for a start, don't point him at me.

Doctor, doctor, I've lost my memory.

When did it happen?
When did what happen?

SIGNS OF A CHEAP HMO

- Annual breast exam conducted at Hooters.
- Directions to your doctor's office include, "Take a left when you enter the trailer park."
- Tongue depressors taste faintly of Fudgesicle.
- The only proctologist in the plan is "Gus" from Roto-Rooter.
- The only item listed under Preventive Care coverage is "an apple a day."
- The only expense covered 100% is embalming.
- With your last HMO, your Prozac didn't come in different colors with little M's on them.

TOP TEN COMMENTS FROM PATIENTS DURING COLONOSCOPIES
(© CHRIS WHITE)

10. "Take it easy, Doc, you're boldly going where no man has gone before."
9. "Find Amelia Earhart yet?"
8. "Can you hear me NOW?"
7. "Oh boy that was sphincterrific!"
6. "Are we there yet? Are we there yet? Are we there yet?"
5. "You know, in Arkansas, we're now legally married."
4. "Any sign of the trapped miners, Chief?"
3. "Hey! Now I know how a Muppet feels!"
2. If your hand doesn't fit, you must quit!"
1. "Could you write me a note for my wife, saying that my head is not, in fact, up there?"

One-Liners

- It used to be only death and taxes were inevitable. Now, of course, there's shipping and handling, too.
- Who was the first person to look at a cow and say, "I think I'll squeeze these dangly things here, and drink whatever comes out?"
- Who was the first person to say, "See that chicken over there... I'm gonna eat the next thing that comes out of its bottom."
- Can a hearse carrying a corpse drive in the carpool lane?
- If the professor on Gilligan's Island can make a radio out of coconut, why can't he fix a hole in a boat?
- Why does your doctor leave the room when you get undressed if they are going to look at your body anyway?
- Why does Goofy stand erect while Pluto remains on all fours? They're both dogs!
- If Wile E. Coyote had enough money to buy all that Acme stuff, why didn't he just buy dinner?
- Why do the Alphabet song and Twinkle, Twinkle Little Star have the same tune?

- Junk is something you have for years and throw out three weeks before you need it.
- Do illiterate people get the full effect of Alphabet Soup?
- Some people are like slinkies…not really good for anything, but they bring a smile to your face when pushed down the stairs.
- Did you ever notice that when you blow in a dog's face, he doesn't like it, but when you take him on a car ride, he sticks his head out the window?
- Does pushing the elevator button more than once make it arrive faster?
- A husband is someone who after taking the trash out, gives the impression he just cleaned the whole house.
- The nice part about living in a small town is that when you don't know what you're doing, someone else does.
- My next house will have no kitchen -just vending machines and a large trash can.
- Ms. Confused said, "I was worried that my mechanic might try to rip me off, I was relieved when he told me all I needed was turn-signal fluid."
- I'm so depressed… My Doctor refused to write me a prescription for Viagra. He said it would be like putting a new flagpole on a condemned building.
- For every action, there is an equal and opposite government program.
- Several high profile televangelists have written an impressive new book….It is called: "Ministers Do More Than Lay People."
- Transvestite: A guy who likes to eat, drink and be Mary!
- The difference between the Pope and your boss: The Pope only expects you to kiss his ring.
- My mind works like lightning. One brilliant flash and it is gone.
- The difference between boogers and broccoli: Kids don't eat broccoli.
- The only time the world beats a path to your door is if you're in the bathroom.

- I hate sex in the movies. Tried it once, the seat folded up, the drink spilled and that ice, well it really chilled our mood.
- Definition of a teenager? God's punishment for enjoying sex.
- The elephant to the naked man: "It's cute, but can it pick up peanuts?"

ONE-LINER SPEAKER INTRODUCTIONS

- Our speaker for the evening gives the most refreshing talks. Everywhere he goes the audiences always feel good when they wake up.
- Recently our speaker had to discontinue several of his long talks on account of his throat. Several people threatened to cut it.
- Tonight I would like to present to you _____ about whom the President of the United States once said, "Who?"
- Our speaker will not bore you with a long speech... he can do it with a short one.
- Our speaker needs no introduction... (person speaking sits down).
- You have been a wonderful audience... you stayed.
- I am sorry to announce that we have two disappointments this evening. Brad Pitt was unable to make it and _____ _____ was.
- It has been said that _____ is the greatest speaker in our field, and tonight we honor, _____ _____, the man who made that statement.

Parenting Humor

THE TOP TWELVE THINGS YOU WILL NEVER HEAR A MOTHER SAY

12. Be good and on your birthday I'll get You a BB gun!
11. How on earth can you see the TV, sitting so far back?
10. Don't bother wearing a jacket - the wind chill is bound to improve.
9. Let me smell that shirt - yeah, it's good for another week.
8. I think a cluttered bedroom is a sign of creativity.
7. Yeah, I used to skip school too.
6. Just leave all the lights on...it makes the house more cheery.
5. Could you turn the music up louder, so I can enjoy it too?
4. Run and bring me the scissors! Hurry!
3. I don't have a tissue with me - just use your sleeve.
2. The curfew is a general time to shoot for. It's not like I'm watching the clock or anything.
1. Well if Timmy's mom says its okay, that's good enough for me.

TOP TEN THINGS YOU'LL NEVER HEAR DAD SAY
(FROM JOKE-OF-THE-DAY.COM)

10. Well, how 'bout that?! I'm lost! Looks like we'll have to stop and ask for directions.
9. You know Pumpkin, now that you're thirteen, you'll be ready for unchaperoned car dates. Won't that be fun?
8. I noticed that all your friends have a certain "up yours" attitude...I like that.
7. Here's a credit card and the keys to my new car - GO CRAZY.
6. What do you mean you want to' play football? Figure skating's not good enough for you, son?
5. Your Mother and I are going away for the weekend ...you might want to consider throwing a party.
4. Well, I don't know what's wrong with your car. Probably one of those doo-hickey thingies - you know - that makes it run or something. Just have it towed to a mechanic and pay whatever he asks.
3. No son of mine is going to live under this roof without an earring or tattoos - now quit your belly-aching, and let's go to the mall.
2. Whaddya wanna go and get a job for? I make plenty of money for you to spend.
1. Father's Day? Aahh - don't worry about that - it's no big deal.

WHAT MY MOTHER TAUGHT ME...AND I AM TEACHING MY OWN CHILDREN (FROM RUBIN@PANAMA.C-COM.NET)

My mother taught me...

TO APPRECIATE A JOB WELL DONE - "If you're going to kill each other, do it outside - I just finished cleaning!"

RELIGION - "You better pray that will come out of the carpet."

About TIME TRAVEL: "If you don't straighten up, I'm going to knock you into the middle of next week!"

LOGIC: "Because I said so, that's why."

FORESIGHT - "Make sure you wear clean underwear, in case you're in an accident."

IRONY - "Keep laughing and I'll give you something to cry about."

About the sciences of OSMOSIS - "Shut your mouth and eat your supper!"

About BECOMING A CONTORTIONIST - "Will you look at the dirt on the back of your neck?"

STAMINA - "You'll sit there until all that spinach is finished."

About WEATHER - "It looks as if a tornado swept through your room."

How to solve PHYSICS PROBLEMS - "If I yelled because I saw a meteor coming toward you; would you listen then?"

About HYPOCRISY - "If I've told you once, I've told you a million times - Don't Exaggerate!"

THE CIRCLE OF LIFE - "I brought you into this world, and I can take you out."

About BEHAVIOR MODIFICATION - "Stop acting like your father!"

About ENVY - "There are millions of less fortunate children in this world who don't have wonderful parents like you have!"

BAD COCOA

A little boy never uttered a word for the first six years of his life. One day his parents served him some cocoa. To their amazement the boy said, "This cocoa is no good."

The shocked parents asked him, "Why did you wait so long to talk!?"

The boy said, "Up till now, everything's been okay."

THINGS I'VE LEARNED FROM MY BOYS
(SUBMITTED AS TRUE)

- A king size waterbed holds enough water to fill a 2000 sq. ft. house 4 inches deep.
- If you spray hair spray on dust bunnies and run over them with roller blades, they can ignite.
- A 3-year old Boy's voice is louder than 200 adults in a crowded restaurant.
- If you hook a dog leash over a ceiling fan, the motor is not strong enough to rotate a 42 pound boy wearing Batman underwear and a Superman cape. It is strong enough, however, if tied to a paint can, to spread paint on all four walls of a 20x20 ft. room.
- You should not throw baseballs up when the ceiling fan is on.
- When using a ceiling fan as a bat, you have to throw the ball up a few times before you get a hit. A ceiling fan can hit a baseball a long way.
- The glass in windows (even double-pane) doesn't stop a baseball hit by a ceiling fan.
- When you hear the toilet flush and the words "uh oh", it's already too late
- Brake fluid mixed with Clorox makes smoke, and lots of it.
- A six-year old Boy can start a fire with a flint rock even though a 36-year old man says they can only do it in the movies.
- Certain Lego's will pass through the digestive tract of a 4-year old boy.
- Play dough and microwave should not be used in the same sentence.
- Super glue is forever.
- No matter how much Jell-O you put in a swimming pool you still can't walk on water.
- Pool filters do not like Jell-O.
- VCR's do not eject "PB &J" sandwiches even though TV commercials show they do.

- Garbage bags do not make good parachutes.
- Marbles in gas tanks make lots of noise when driving.
- Always look in the oven before you turn it on; plastic toys do not like ovens.
- The fire department in Austin, Texas has a 5-minute response time.
- The spin cycle on the washing machine does not make earthworms dizzy.
- It will, however, make cats dizzy.
- Cats throw up twice their body weight when dizzy.

THE JOYS OF HAVING KIDS
(SHARED BY BILL STEBBENS - BS16@CORNELL.EDU)

- Trying to dress an active little one is like trying to thread a sewing machine while it's running.
- There are only two things a child will share willingly - communicable diseases and their mother's age.
- Cleaning your house while your kids are at home is like trying to shovel the driveway during a snowstorm.
- Kids really brighten a household; they never turn off any lights.
- An alarm clock is a device for waking people up who don't have small kids.
- Shouting to make your kids obey is like using the horn to steer your car, and you get about the same results!
- Any child can tell you that the sole purpose of a middle name is so he can tell when he's really in trouble.

THE SCHOOL PLAY

Boy: "Dad, I just got a part in the school play. I play the part of a man who's been married for twenty-five years."

Father: "That's a good start, son. Just keep right at it and one of these days you'll get a speaking part."

ON THE BALCONY

John and Sandra decided that the only way to have brief sex on a Sunday afternoon with their 8 year old son in the apartment was to send him out on the balcony with a popsicle and tell him to report on all the neighborhood activities. He began his commentary as his parents put their plan into operation:

"There's a car being towed from the parking lot" he shouted.

A few moments passed.

"An ambulance just drove by!"

A few moments passed.

"Looks like the Anderson's have company!" he called out.

"Matt's riding a new bike"

"The Coopers are having sex!"

Startled, Mother and Dad shot up in bed!!!

Dad cautiously asked "How do you know they are having sex!?"

"Jimmy Cooper is standing out on his balcony with a popsicle too."

Religious Humor

A MEMORY PROBLEM

A man standing in line at a check out counter of a grocery store was very surprised when a very attractive woman behind him said, "Hello!" Her face was beaming. He gave her that "who are you look," and couldn't remember ever having seen her before. Then, noticing his look, she figured she had made a mistake and apologized. "Look," she said "I'm really sorry but when I first saw you, I thought you were the father of one of my children," and walked out of the store.

The guy was dumbfounded and thought to himself, "What the hell is the world coming to? Here is an attractive woman who can't keep track of who fathered her children!"

Then he got a little panicky. "I don't remember her," he thought but, maybe during one of the wild parties he had been to when he was in college, perhaps he did father her child!

He ran from the store and caught her in the parking lot and asked, "Are you the girl I met at a party in college and then we got really drunk and had wild crazy sex on the pool table in front of everyone?"

"No", she said with a horrified look on her face.

"I'm your son's Sunday School teacher!"

THE CATHOLIC DOG (SHARED BY MIKE BAUM)

Muldoon lived alone in the Irish countryside with only a pet dog for company. One day the dog died, and Muldoon went to the parish priest and asked, "Father, my dog is dead. Could ya' be sayin' a mass for the poor creature?"

Father Patrick replied, "I'm afraid not; we cannot have services for an animal in the church. But there are some Baptists down the lane, and there's no tellin' what they believe. Maybe they'll do something for the creature."

Muldoon said, "I'll go right away Father. Do ya' think $5,000 is enough to donate to them for the service?"

Father Patrick exclaimed, "Sweet Mary, Mother of Jesus! Why didn't ya tell me the dog was Catholic?"

THREE MINISTERS

A Presbyterian, a Methodist, and a Baptist pastor along with their wives were on a cruise. A tidal wave came up and swamped the ship; they all drowned, and next thing you know, they're standing before St. Peter. First came the Presbyterian and his wife. St. Peter shook his head sadly. "I can't let you in. You loved money too much. You loved it so much; you even married a woman named Penny." Then came the Methodist. "Sorry, can't let you in, either. You loved food too much. You loved to eat so much; you even married a woman named Candy." The Baptist turned to his wife and whispered nervously, "It doesn't look good, Fanny."

THREE RELIGIOUS TRUTHS

1. The Jews don't recognize Jesus as the Messiah.
2. Protestants don't recognize the Pope as the leader of the Church.
3. Baptists don't recognize each other in the liquor store.

JEWISH LOGIC

Moshe is waiting on the platform at the station. He notices a man who is obviously also Jewish standing nearby and asks him for the time. But the man ignores him. Moshe then asks him again, and the man responds in the same way.

Frustrated, Moshe asks "Excuse me sir, but I've asked you for the time twice, why are you ignoring me"

Suddenly, the man looks up and says, "We're both waiting for the train, if I answer you, then when we get on the train you will come and sit next to me, we will probably start talking, and I may invite you to my house for Shabbat dinner, there you will meet my daughter, you will probably like her, you may eventually want to marry her, and to be honest with you, why would I want a son-in-law **who can't afford a watch?"**

THE SERMON

I think this Mom will never forget this particular Sunday sermon... "Dear Lord," the minister began, with arms extended toward heaven and a rapturous look on his upturned face. "Without you, we are but dust." He would have continued but at that moment my very obedient daughter (who was listening!) leaned over to me and asked quite audibly in her shrill little girl voice, "Mom, what is butt dust?"

THE NEW RELIGION

Join our *Church of Apathy* when you get good and ready, or around-to-it. This is the official church for those that don't wish to identify with a specific religion. For those that feel that atheism and agnosticism are just too much damn work. Others, who believe that their religion solves all their problems, need not apply.

We are a relatively New Religion with new attitudes. We are Apathists. We seek no converts. We distribute no pamphlets. We ring no door bells.

The Church of Apathy was thought about by its Founders for several years, before they decided to organize on December 26th, 1978, they decided not to become tax exempt, nor claim any guidance from any divine source.

In 1989 they decided to look around for a suitable church site, but that effort proved to be too much trouble, and besides they really didn't care where they met anyway. The founders thought they should have a clergy person, but so far all that applied were rejected. They asked stupid questions about our not having a prayer book with writing in it. Some complained that we didn't have a Symbol or a Logo identifying our religion. Some wanted us to light candles, bless wine, chant, sway, kneel, pray or in general "carry on" like mainstream religions....all of these candidates for the clergy person were rejected.

We recently celebrated the 30th year of our founding. We Apathists encourage those that share our deeply rooted apathy to think about joining our church as non-active members. We seek neither donations nor offerings....you keep your money, and we'll keep ours. As we have no mother church, postal address, telephone number, or website, we are sometimes difficult to locate. However if you have faith, and are not in any big rush to join our Church, you are the type of person that could benefit by being an Apathist.

We are happy to say that in over 30 years, not one of our members has been called "a dirty Apathist" to their face, they have demanded, and received "apple fritters" as their religious rights, in prisons and university cafeterias, and our Religion is not part of any college course on "Comparative Religions ", and as far as we know, none of our faithful have been healed, saved, or converted. Some have rented from Avis but we consider that as free will. Someday we would like to sponsor our own TV ministry, but we haven't figured out as yet what to preach about. We strongly believe that one should not take YES for an answer.....but if they do, they do.

We do have a motto: Don't Bother Us...and We Won't Bother You.

CONFUSED

"I'm confused," the little boy admitted to his teacher.

"I went to church last Sunday and they kept telling me to stand up for Jesus!

But then I went to the ballgame, and everyone kept yelling, 'For Christ's sake, sit down!'"

LETTERS TO GOD (SUBMITTED TO THE HUMOR DIGEST BY TOM AND CAROL - TCR@CHARTER.NET)

A teacher asked her class to write notes to God.... Here are some of the notes they handed in:

Dear God: I didn't think orange went with purple until I saw the sunset you made on Tuesday. That was cool.

Dear God: Instead of letting people die and having to make new ones, why don't you just keep the ones you have?

Dear God: Maybe Cain and Abel would not have killed each other so much if they had their own rooms. That's what my Mom did for me and my brother.

Dear God: If you watch me in church on Sunday, I'll show you my new shoes.

Dear God: In school they told us what you do. Who does it when you're on vacation?

Dear God: Are you really invisible or is it just a trick?

Dear God: Is it true my father won't get in Heaven if he uses his bowling words in the house?

Dear God: Did you mean for the Giraffe to look like that or was it an accident?

Dear God: Who draws the lines around the countries?

Dear God: I went to this wedding and they kissed right in the church. Is that okay?

Dear God: Thank you for the baby brother, but what I prayed for was a puppy.

Dear God: Please send me a pony. I never asked for anything before. You can look it up.

Dear God: I want to be just like my Daddy when I get big, but not with so much hair all over.

Dear God: You don't have to worry about me I always look both ways.

Dear God: Of all the people who work for you I like Noah and David the best.

Dear God: My brother told me about being born but it doesn't sound right. They're just kidding, aren't they?

Dear God: I would like to live 900 years just like the guy in the Bible.

Dear God: We read Thomas Edison made light. But in Sunday school they said you did it. So, I bet he stole your idea.

THE MORAL LESSON

A mother was preparing pancakes for her sons, Kevin, 5 and Ryan, 3. The boys began to argue over who would get the first pancake. Their mother saw the opportunity for a moral lesson. "If Jesus were sitting here, He would say, 'Let my brother have the first pancake, I can wait.'" Kevin turned to his younger brother and said, "Ryan, you be Jesus!"

YOU'D NEVER BELIEVE IT

Nine year old Bobby was asked by his mother what he had learned in Religious School.

"Well, Mom, our teacher told us how God sent Moses behind enemy lines on a rescue mission to lead the Israelites out of Egypt. When he got to the Red Sea, he had his engineers build a pontoon bridge and all the people walked across safely. Then he used his mobile phone unit to radio headquarters for reinforcements. They sent bombers to blow up the bridge and all the Israelites were saved."

"Now, Joey, is that really what your teacher taught you?" his mother asked. "Well, no, Mom. But if I told it the way the teacher did, you'd never believe it!"

THE HAIR DRYER

A distinguished young woman on a flight from Switzerland asked the Priest beside her, "Father, may I ask a favour?"

"Of course, what may I do for you?" "Well, I bought an expensive woman's electronic hair dryer for my mother's birthday that is unopened and well over the Customs limits, and I'm afraid they'll confiscate it. Is there any way you could carry it through Customs for me? Under your robes, perhaps?" "I would love to help you, dear, but I must warn you: I will not lie." "With your honest face, Father, no one will question you." When they got to Customs, she let the priest go ahead of her. The official asked, "Father, do you have anything to declare?" "From the top of my head down to my waist, I have nothing to declare."

The official thought this answer strange, so asked, "And what do you have to declare from your waist to the floor?" "I have a marvellous instrument designed to be used on a woman, but which is, to date, unused. Roaring with laughter, the official said, "Go ahead, Father."

THE SECRET TO SEXUAL SATISFACTION

An older Jewish man married a younger woman. After several months, the young woman complained that she had never climaxed during sex and by birthright; all Jewish women are entitled to at least one climax during sex, so they went to see the Rabbi.

The Rabbi told them to get a young, strong, virile young man to wave a towel over them while they are having sex. This, the Rabbi says, will cause the woman to climax, so the couple tried it. After several attempts, still no climax.

They went back to the Rabbi. The Rabbi says for the bride to change partners and have the virile young man have sex with her and have the husband wave the towel. They try it that night and the young woman goes into wild, screaming, ear-splitting climaxes, one after the other.

When it is over, the husband smugly looks down at the young man and says, "You see, schmuck, **that's** how you wave a towel!"

WISE MOTHER SUPERIOR

The wise old Mother Superior from county Tipperary was dying. The nuns gathered around her bed trying to make her comfortable. They gave her some warm milk to drink, but she refused it. Then one nun took the glass back to the kitchen.

Remembering a bottle of Irish whiskey received as a gift the previous Christmas, she opened and poured a generous amount into the warm milk.

Back at Mother Superior's bed, she held the glass to her lips. Mother Superior drank a little, then a little more. Before they knew it, she had drunk the whole glass down to the last drop.

"Mother," the nuns pleaded, "Please give us some wisdom before you die. She raised herself up in bed with a pious look on her face and said, "Don't sell that cow!"

BIBLE STORY

James was listening to a Bible story. His dad read: "The man named Lot was warned to take his wife and flee out of the city but his wife looked back and was turned to salt.

Concerned, James asked: "What happened to the flea?"

IN THE CLOSET

A married woman is having an affair. Whenever her lover comes over, she puts her nine year old son in the closet. One day the woman hears a car in the driveway and puts her lover in the closet, as well.

Inside the closet, the little boy says, "It's dark in here, isn't it?" "Yes it is," the man replies. "You wanna buy a baseball?" the little boy asks.

"No thanks," the man replies.

"I think you do want to buy a baseball," the little extortionist continues. "OK. How much?" the man replies after considering the position he is in. "Twenty-five dollars," the little boy replies. "Twenty-five dollars?!" the man repeats incredulously, but complies to protect his hidden position.

The following week, the lover is visiting the woman again when she hears a car in the driveway and, again, places her lover in the closet with her little boy.

"It's dark in here, isn't it?" the boy starts off. "Yes it is," replies the man. "Wanna buy a baseball glove?" the little boy asks. "OK. How much?" the hiding lover responds, acknowledging his disadvantage. "Fifty dollars," the boy replies and the transaction is completed.

The next weekend, the little boy's father says "Hey, son. Go get your ball and glove and we'll play some catch." "I can't. I sold them," replies the little boy. "How much did you get for them?" asks the father, expecting to hear the profit in terms of lizards and candy.

"Seventy-five dollars," the little boy says. "Seventy-five dollars?! That's thievery! I'm taking you to the church right now. You must confess your sin and ask for forgiveness", the father explains as he hauls the child away.

At the church, the little boy goes into the confessional, draws the curtain, sits down, and says "It's dark in here, isn't it?"

"Don't you start that shit in here now," the priest says.

THE TRAIN ROBBERY

The Israeli news reported a robbery of a train in Israel. The thieves stole 5,000 dollars and 23,000 dollars in pledges.

BIG MISTAKE

A new young monk arrives at the monastery. He is assigned to help the other monks in copying the old canons and laws of the church by hand. He notices, however, that all of the monks are copying from copies, not from the original manuscript. So, the new monk goes to the head abbot to question this, pointing out that if someone made even a small error in the first copy, it would never be picked up. In fact, that error would be continued in all of the subsequent copies. The head monk says, "We have been copying from the copies for centuries, but you make a good point, my son," So, he goes down into the dark caves underneath the monastery where the original manuscript is held in a locked vault that hasn't been opened for hundreds of years.

Hours go by and nobody sees the old abbot. So, the young monk gets worried and goes downstairs to look for him. He sees him banging his head against the wall. His forehead is all bruised and he is crying uncontrollably. The young man asks the old abbot, "What's wrong, father?" With a choking voice, the old abbot replies, "The word is **celebrate**."

PRISON QUARTET

While I was in a church in Mississippi, the pastor announced that their prison quartet would be singing the following evening. I wasn't aware there was a prison in the vicinity and I looked forward to hearing them.

The next evening, I was puzzled when four members of the church approached the stage. Then the pastor introduced them.

"This is our prison quartet," he said, "behind a few bars and always looking for the key."

TALKING TO A WALL

In Jerusalem, a female journalist heard about a very old Jewish man who had been going to the Western Wall to pray, twice a day, everyday, for a long, long time. So she went to check it out.

She went to the Western Wall and there he was!

She watched him pray and after about 45 minutes, when he turned to leave, she approached him for an interview.

"I'm Rebecca Smith from CNN. Sir, how long have you been coming to the Western Wall and praying?"

"For about 60 years."

"60 years! That's amazing! What do you pray for?"

"I pray for peace between the Christians, Jews, and the Muslims.

I pray for all the hatred to stop and I pray for all our children to grow up in safety and friendship."

"How do you feel after doing this for 60 years?"

"Like I'm talking to a wall!

GOOD REASON

A Sunday school teacher asked her children, as they were on the way to church service, "And why is it necessary to be quiet in church?" One bright little girl replied, "Because people are sleeping."

CHURCH BULLETIN BLOOPERS

1. Bertha Belch, a missionary from Africa will be speaking tonight at Calvary Memorial Church in Racine. Come tonight and hear Bertha Belch all the way from Africa.
2. Announcement in the church bulletin for a National PRAYER and FASTING Conference: "The cost for attending the Fasting and Prayer conference includes meals."
3. Our youth basketball team is back in action Wednesday at 8 PM in the recreation hall. Come out and watch us kill Christ the King.
4. Miss Charlene Mason sang "I will not pass this way again" giving obvious pleasure to the congregation.
5. "Ladies, don't forget the rummage sale. It's a chance to get rid of those things not worth keeping around the house. Don't forget your husbands."
6. Next Sunday is the family hayride and bonfire at the Fowlers'. Bring your own hot dogs and guns. Friends are welcome! Everyone come for a fun time.
7. The peacemaking meeting scheduled for today has been canceled due to a conflict.
8. The sermon this morning: "Jesus Walks on the Water" The sermon tonight: "Searching for Jesus"
9. Next Thursday there will be tryouts for the choir. They need all the help they can get.
10. Barbara remains in the hospital and needs blood donors for more transfusions. She is also having trouble sleeping and requests tapes of Pastor Jack's sermons.
11. During the absence of our Pastor, we enjoyed the rare privilege of hearing a good sermon when J.F. Stubbs spoke to the congregation.
12. The Rector will preach his farewell message after which the choir will sing "Break Forth into Joy."
13. Remember in prayer the many who are sick of our community.

14. Smile at someone who is hard to love. Say "hell" to someone who doesn't care much about you.
15. Don't let worry kill you off--let the Church help.
16. Irving Benson and Jessie Carter were married on October 24 in the church. So ends a friendship that began in their school days.
17. A bean supper will be held on Tuesday evening in the church hall. Music will follow.
18. At the evening service tonight, the sermon topic will be "What is Hell?" Come early and listen to our choir practice.
19. Eight new choir robes are needed due to the addition of several new members and to the deterioration of some older ones.
20. The senior choir invites any member of the congregation who enjoys sinning to join the choir.
21. Scouts are saving aluminum cans, bottles, and other items to be recycled. Proceeds will be used to cripple children.
22. The Lutheran men's group will meet at 6 PM. Steak, mashed potatoes, green beans, bread and dessert will be served for a nominal feel.
23. For those of you who have children and don't know it, we have a nursery downstairs.
24. Please place your donation in the envelope along with the deceased person(s) you want remembered.
25. Attend and you will hear an excellent speaker and heave a healthy lunch.
26. The church will host an evening of fine dining superb entertainment and gracious hostility.
27. Potluck supper Sunday at 5:00 PM.- prayer and medication to follow.
28. The ladies of the Church have cast off clothing of every kind. They may be seen in the basement on Friday afternoon.
29. This evening at 7 P.M. there will be a hymn sing in the park across from the Church. Bring a blanket and come prepared to sin.

30. Ladies Bible Study will be held Thursday morning at 10. All ladies are invited to lunch in the Fellowship Hall after the B.S. is done.

31. The pastor would appreciate it if the ladies of the congregation would lend him their electric girdles for the pancake breakfast next Sunday morning.

32. Low Self Esteem Support Group will meet Thursday at 7 PM.. Please use the back door.

33. The eighth-graders will be presenting Shakespeare's Hamlet in the Church basement Friday at 7 PM. The Congregation is invited to attend this tragedy.

34. Weight Watchers will meet at 7 PM at the First Presbyterian Church. Please use the large double doors at the side entrance.

35. Mrs. Johnson will be entering the hospital this week for testes.

36. The Associate Minister unveiled the church's new tithing campaign slogan last Sunday: "I Upped My Pledge - Up Yours."

37. Our next song is "Angels We Have Heard Get High."

GOD IS WATCHING

The children were lined up in the cafeteria of a Catholic elementary school for lunch. At the head of the table was a large pile of apples. The nun made a note, and posted on the apple tray: "Take only ONE. God is watching."

Moving further along the lunch line, at the other end of the table was a large pile of chocolate chip cookies. A child had written a note, "Take all you want. God is watching the apples."

THE RABBI AND THE PRIEST

A Priest and a Rabbi were sitting next to each other on an airplane. After a while, the Priest turned to the Rabbi and asked, "Is it still a requirement of your faith that you not eat pork?"

The Rabbi responded, "Yes, that is still one of our beliefs."

The Priest then asked, "Have you ever eaten pork?"

To which the Rabbi replied, "Yes, on one occasion I did succumb to temptation and tasted a ham sandwich." The Priest nodded in understanding and went on with his reading.

A while later, the Rabbi spoke up and asked the Priest, "Father, is it still a requirement of your church that you remain celibate?"

The Priest replied, "Yes, that is still very much a part of our faith."

The Rabbi then asked him, "Father, have you ever fallen to the temptations of the flesh?

The Priest replied, "Yes, Rabbi, on one occasion I was weak and broke with my faith."

The Rabbi nodded understandingly and remained silent, thinking, for about five minutes.

Finally, the Rabbi said, "Beats a ham sandwich, doesn't it?

TELLING EVERYBODY

An old man walks into a confessional. The following conversation ensues:

Man: I am 92 years old, have a wonderful wife of 70 years, many children, grandchildren, and great grandchildren. Yesterday, I picked up two college girls, hitchhiking. We went to a motel, where I had sex with each of them three times.

Priest: Are you sorry for your sins?

Man: What sins?

Priest: What kind of a Catholic are you?

Man: I'm Jewish

Priest: Why are you telling me all this?

Man: I'm telling everybody!

VERY IMPORTANT PERSON

The Pope has just finished a tour of the Napa Valley and is taking a limousine to San Francisco. Having never driven a limo, he asks the chauffeur if he can drive for a while. Since the chauffeur really doesn't have much of a choice, he climbs in the back of the limo and the Pope takes the wheel.

The Pope proceeds down Silverado, and starts accelerating to see what the limo can do. He gets to about 90 MPH, and suddenly he sees the red and blue lights of the highway patrol in his mirror. He pulls over and the trooper comes to his window.

The trooper, seeing who it is, says, "Just a moment please, I need to call in."

The trooper calls in and asks for the chief. He tells the chief that he's got a **really** important person pulled over, and asks how he should handle it.

"It's not Ted Kennedy again is it?" asks the chief.

"No Sir!" replies the trooper, "This guy's more important."

"Is it the Governor?" asks the chief.

"No! Even more important!" replies the trooper.

"Is it the president???" asks the chief.

"No! Even more important!" replies the trooper.

"Well, who the heck is it?" screams the chief.

"I don't know Sir." replies the trooper, "but he's got the Pope as his chauffeur!"

"FANTESTIC"

Two Jewish matrons, friends from the old country, were conversing on the porch swing of a large white pillared mansion in Miami Beach. The first woman says, "Ven mine first child vas born, mine husband built for me this beautiful mension." The second woman says, "Fentestic."

The first woman continues, "Ven mine second child vas born, mine husband bought for me dot fine Cadillek in de driveway." Again, the second woman says, "Fentestic."

The first woman boasts, "Den, ven mine third child vas born, mine husband bought for me this exqvisite diamond bracelet." Yet again, the second woman comments, "Fentestic."

The first woman then asks her companion, "Vat did your husband buy for you ven you had your first child?" The second woman replies, "Mine husband sent me to charm school."

"Charm school!" the first woman cries, "Oy Vey is mir! Vot for?" The first woman responds, "So instead of saying "Bullshit" I learned to say, "Fentestic!"

UNCHARTED ISLAND

Morris and Esther, an elderly Jewish couple, are sitting together on an airplane flying to the Far East.

Over the public address system, the Captain announces: "Ladies and Gentlemen, I am afraid I have some very bad news. Our engines have ceased functioning, and this plane will be going down momentarily. Luckily, I see an island below us that should be able to accommodate our landing. This island appears to be uncharted; I am unable to find it on our maps. So the odds are that we will never be rescued and will have to live on the island for a very long time if not forever.

A few minutes later the plane lands safely on the island, where upon Morris turns to his wife and asks, "Esther, did we pay our pledge to the Yeshiva yet?" "No Morris!" she responded. Morris smiles, and then asks, "Esther, did we pay our United Jewish Appeal, pledge?" "Oy no, I forgot to send the check!" Now Morris laughs. "One last thing, Esther...did you remember to send our Temple Building Fund check this month?" "Oy, Morris I forgot that one too!" Now Morris is practically choking with laughter. Esther asks Morris, "So vot are you smiling and laughing about?" Morris responds, "Don't worry, they'll find us."

TEN COMMANDMENTS

A Sunday school teacher was discussing the Ten Commandments with her five and six year-olds. After explaining the commandment "Honor thy Father and thy mother," she asked, "Is there a commandment that teaches us how to treat our brothers and sisters?" Without missing a beat, one little boy answered,

"Thou shall not kill."

THE ETERNAL JEWISH TRUTHS

- The optimist sees the bagel, the pessimist sees the hole.
- If you can't say something nice, say it in Yiddish.
- If it tastes good, it's probably not kosher.
- Why spoil a good meal with a big tip?
- WASPs leave and never say good-bye. Jews say good-bye and never leave.
- Twenty percent off is a bargain; fifty percent off is a mitzvah.
- Israel is the land of milk and honey; Florida is the land of milk of magnesia.
- Pork is forbidden, but a pig in a blanket makes a nice hors d'oeuvre.
- If your name was Lipschitz, you'd change it, too.
- Always leave a little room for the Viennese table.
- Always whisper the names of diseases.
- If you don't eat, it will kill me.
- Anything worth saying is worth repeating a thousand times.
- Where there's smoke, there may be smoked salmon.
- Never take a front-row seat at a bris.
- Next year in Jerusalem. The year after that, how about a nice cruise?
- Never leave a restaurant empty-handed.
- A schmata is a dress that your husband's ex is wearing.
- Before you read the menu, read the prices.
- There comes a time in every man's life when he must stand up and tell his mother he's an adult. This usually happens at around age 45.
- Tsuris is a Yiddish word that means your child is marrying someone who isn't Jewish.
- Without Jewish mothers, who would need therapy?

THIRTEEN CHILDREN

A man was in the hospital recovering from an operation when a nun walked into his room. She was there to cheer up the sick and lame. They start talking and she asks about his life. He talks about his wife and his thirteen children.

"My, my," says the nun. "Thirteen children, a good and proper Catholic family. God is very proud of you."

"Actually, Sister," he says, "I am not Catholic, I'm Jewish."

"Jewish!" she exclaims. "You sex maniac, you!!"

THE SAILOR AND THE PRIEST

A sailor and a priest were playing golf. The sailor was not very good at it, and uttered a loud "DAMN I missed!" each time he missed. The priest tolerated him for a few minutes and couldn't take it any more.

"Do not swear thus, my friend, or God will punish you". It didn't make a difference, the sailor continued unabated. One after another, the sailor played badly, followed up with, "DAMN I missed!"

Again, the priest said "Do not utter such profanities, or God will show you a sign." It didn't help, and the next stroke missed was followed by the loud, "DAMN I missed!"

Suddenly, a bolt of lightning dropped out of the clouds and struck the priest dead.

A voice boomed out of the clouds, "DAMN, I missed!"

JEWISH WOMAN PRESIDENT

The first Jewish woman President is elected.

She calls her Mother: "Mama, I've won the elections, you've got to come to the swearing-in ceremony."

"I don't know, what would I wear?"

"Don't worry, I'll send you a dressmaker."

"But I only eat kosher food."

"Mama, I am going to be the president, the reception will be catered by a kosher deli."

"But how will I get there?"

"I'll send a limo, just come mama."

"Ok, Ok, if it makes you happy."

The great day comes and Mama is seated between the Supreme Court Justices and the future cabinet members. She nudges the gentleman on her right. "You see that girl, the one with her hand on the Bible? Her brother's a doctor!"

WHY CHANGE CHURCHES?

I don't know why some people change churches - what difference does it make which one you stay home from? *Rev. Denny Brake*

JESUS WAS...

There were 3 good arguments that Jesus was Black:
1. He called everyone brother.
2. He liked Gospel.
3. He couldn't get a fair trial.

But then there were 3 equally good arguments that Jesus was Jewish:
1. He went into His Father's business.
2. He lived at home until he was 33.
3. He was sure his Mother was a virgin and his Mother was sure He was God.

But then there were 3 equally good arguments that Jesus was Italian:
1. He talked with His hands.
2. He had wine with His meals.
3. He used olive oil.

But then there were 3 equally good arguments that Jesus was a Californian:
1. He never cut His hair.
2. He walked around barefoot all the time.
3. He started a new religion.

But then there were 3 equally good arguments that Jesus was an American Indian:
1. He was at peace with nature.
2. He ate a lot of fish.
3. He talked about the Great Spirit.

But then there were 3 equally good arguments the Jesus was Irish:
1. He never got married.
2. He was always telling stories.
3. He loved green pastures.

But the most compelling evidence of all - 3 proofs that Jesus was a woman:
1. He fed a crowd at a moment's notice when there was no food.
2. He kept trying to get a message across to a bunch of men who just didn't get it.
3. And even when He was dead, He had to get up because there was work to do.

THE ULTIMATE BAR MITZVAH

In order to impress everyone with his millions, the father of the boy who is to be Bar Mitzvah arranged to rent the shuttle from NASA and take his family and the Rabbi into space. That created a lot of attention, and all the press was there to find out how it went.

The first person off the shuttle was the grandma, and the reporters asked, "How was the service?"

Grandma answered, "OK".

"How was the boy's speech?" "OK."

"How was the food?" "OK."

"Everything was just OK? You don't seem to have liked it? What was wrong?"

"There was no atmosphere!"

SISTER MARY MARGARET

A young nun named Sister Margaret Mary, who works for a local home health agency, was making her rounds when she ran out of gas. As luck would have it, a gas station was just a block away. She walked to the station to borrow a can to start with and drive to the station for a fill up.

The attendant regretfully told her the only gas can he owned had been loaned out, but if she would wait – it was sure to be back shortly.

Since the nun was on the way to see a patient, she decided not to wait and so she walked back to the car. After looking through the car for something to fill with gas, she spotted a bed pan she was taking to the patient.

Always resourceful, she carried it to the station, filled it with gasoline, and carried it back to her car. As she was pouring the gas into the tank, two men were watching from across the street.

One turned to the other and said, "If it starts, I'll become a Catholic!"

MINISTER'S QUESTION

Minister: "Paul, now be sincere, do you say your prayers before you eat your dinner?"

Paul: "No sir, I don't need to. My mom is a good cook."

TOP TEN AMISH SPRING BREAK ACTIVITIES

10. Drink molasses 'til you heave.
9. Wet bonnet contest.
8. Stuff as many guys as you can into a buggy.
7. Buttermilk kegger.
6. Blow past the Dairy Queen on a really bitchin' Clydesdale.
5. Get a tattoo: "Born to raise barns."
4. Cruise streets of Belleville shouting insults at people with zippers.

3. Sleep 'til 6 a.m.

2. Drive over to Allensville and kick some Mennonite ass.

1. Churn butter naked.

JEWISH TELEGRAM OR EMAIL

"Begin worrying. Details to follow."

CHURCH ENTRANCE REQUIREMENT

Three couples, an elderly couple, a middle-aged couple and a young newlywed couple wanted to join a church. The pastor said, "We have special requirements for new parishioners. You must abstain from having sex for two weeks."

The couples agreed and came back at the end of two weeks. The pastor went to the elderly couple and asked, "Were you able to abstain from sex for the two weeks?" The old man replied, "No problem at all, Pastor." "Congratulations! Welcome to the church!" said the pastor.

The pastor went to the middle-aged couple and asked, "Well, were you able to abstain from sex for the two weeks?" The man replied, "The first week was not too bad. The second week I had to sleep on the couch for a couple of nights but, yes, we made it." "Congratulations! Welcome to the church!" said the pastor.

The pastor then went to the newlywed couple and asked, "Well, were you able to abstain from sex for two weeks?"

"No Pastor, we were not able to go without sex for the two weeks," the young man replied sadly. "What happened?" inquired the pastor. "My wife was reaching for a can of paint on the top shelf and dropped it. When she bent over to pick it up, I was overcome with lust and took advantage of her right there."

"You understand, of course, this means you will not be welcome in our church," stated the pastor. "We know," said the young man, "We're not welcome at Home Depot anymore either."

THREE WISE WOMEN

Do you know what would have happened if it had been Three Wise Women instead of Three Wise Men?

They would have asked directions, arrived on time, helped deliver the baby, cleaned the stable, made a casserole, and, brought practical gifts. Yeah, and they would have made reservations at the inn, way in advance.

THE BLIND MAN

Two nuns are ordered to paint a room in the convent, and the last instruction of the Mother Superior is that they must not get even a drop of paint on their habits. After conferring about this for a while, the two nuns decide to lock the door of the room, strip off their habits, and paint in the nude. In the middle of the project, there comes a knock at the door. "Who is it?" calls one of the nuns. "Blind man," replies a voice from the other side of the door. The two nuns look at each other, shrug, and decide that no harm can come from letting a blind man into the room. They open the door. "Nice boobs," says the man. "Where do you want these blinds?"

CHRISTIAN HOME

After the christening of his baby brother in church, Jason sobbed all the way home in the back seat of the car. His father asked him three times what was wrong. Finally, the boy replied, "That preacher said he wanted us brought up in a Christian home, and I wanted to stay with you guys."

JEWISH BIBLE BLOOPERS (WRITTEN BY STUDENTS)

- The Jews were a proud people, and throughout history they had trouble with the unsympathetic Genitals.
- God asked Abraham to sacrifice Isaac on Mount Montezuma. Jacob, son of Isaac, stole his brother's birthmark.
- One of Jacob's sons, Joseph, gave refuse to the Israelites.
- Lot's wife was a pillar of salt by day and a ball of fire by night.
- Moses led the Hebrew slaves to the Red Sea, where they made unlevel bread, which is bread made without any ingredients. Afterwards, Moses went up on Mount Cyanide to get the Ten Amendments. He died before he ever reached Canada. The 5th amendment is to humor thy father and thy mother. The 7th amendment is "Thou shalt not admit adultery." Joshua led the Hebrews in the battle of Geritol.
- The greatest miracle in the Bible is when Joshua told his son to stand still, and he obeyed him.
- A Jewish person should have only one spouse – this is called monotony.
- David was a Hebrew King skilled at playing the liar. He fought with the Finkelsteins, a race of people who lived in Biblical times. Solomon, one of David's sons, had three hundred wives and seven hundred porcupines.

Sports Humor

THE BUM

A really "scruffy" looking bum stopped a man on the street and asked for $2.00.

"Will you buy booze with it?" the man asks, to which the bum replies, "No."

"Will you gamble it away?" Once again the bum replies, "No."

"Will you make bets at the golf course?"

The bum replies, "No, I don't play golf."

Then the man asks, "Will you come home with me so my wife can see what happens to a man who doesn't drink, gamble, or play golf?"

GOLF

- In primitive society, when native tribes beat the ground with clubs and yelled, it was called witchcraft; today, in civilized society, it is called golf.
- Golf is an expensive way of playing marbles.
- Golf is a game in which the slowest people in the world are those in front of you, and the fastest are those behind.

- Golf: A five mile walk punctuated with disappointments.
- The secret of good golf is to hit the ball hard, straight and not too often.
- There's no game like golf: you go out with three friends, play eighteen holes, and return with three enemies.
- Golf was once a rich man's sport, but now it has millions of poor players.
- An amateur golfer is one who addresses the ball twice: once before swinging, and once again after swinging.
- Many a golfer prefers a golf cart to a caddy because the cart cannot count, criticize or laugh.
- Don't buy a putter until you've had a chance to throw it.
- Never try to keep more than 30 separate thoughts in your mind during your golf swing.
- When your shot has to carry over a water hazard, you can either hit one more club or two more balls.
- The less skilled the player, the more likely he is to share his ideas about the golf swing.
- No matter how bad you are playing, it is always possible to play worse.
- The inevitable result of any golf lesson is the instant elimination of the one critical unconscious motion that allowed you to compensate for all of your many other errors.
- A golf match is a test of your skill against your opponents' luck.
- Counting on your opponent to inform you when he breaks a rule is like expecting him to make fun of his own haircut.
- The shortest distance between any two points on a golf course is a straight line that passes directly through the center of a very large tree.
- It's easier to get up at 6:00 AM to play golf than at 10:00 to mow the yard.
- You can hit a two acre fairway 10% of the time and a two inch branch 90% of the time.
- If you really want to get better at golf, go back and take it up at a much earlier age.

- Since bad shots come in groups of three, a fourth bad shot is actually the beginning of the next group of three.
- When you look up, causing an awful shot, you will always look down again at exactly the moment when you ought to start watching the ball if you ever want to see it again.
- There are two things you can learn by stopping your back-swing at the top and checking the position of your hands: how many hands you have, and which one is wearing the glove.
- A ball you can see in the rough from 50 yards away is not yours.
- A good drive on the 18th hole has stopped many a golfer from giving up the game.
- Golf is the perfect thing to do on Sunday because you always end up having to pray a lot.
- A good golf partner is one who's always slightly worse than you are....that's why I get so many calls to play with friends.
- If there's a storm rolling in, you'll be having the game of your life.
- It's amazing how a golfer who never helps out around the house will replace his divots, repair his ball mark s, and rake his sand traps.
- If your opponent has trouble remembering whether he shot a six or a seven, he probably shot an eight (or worse).
- It takes longer to learn to be a good golfer than it does to become a brain surgeon. On the other hand, you don't get to ride around on a cart, drink beer, eat hot dogs and fart if you are performing Brain Surgery!

GOLF QUOTATIONS

- "Its good sportsmanship not to pick up lost balls while they are still rolling." *Mark Twain*
- "One of the advantages bowling has over golf is that you seldom lose a bowling ball." *Don Carter*

- "I've had a good day when I don't fall out of the cart." *Buddy Hackett*
- "I know I am getting better at golf because I am hitting fewer spectators." *Gerald Ford*
- "Golf's three ugliest words: still your shot." *Dave Marr*
- "It took me seventeen years to get three thousand hits in baseball. I did it in one afternoon on the golf course." *Hank Aaron*
- "The reason the pro tells you to keep your head down is so you can't see him laughing." *Phyllis Diller*
- "I'm very lucky. If it wasn't for golf I don't know what I'd be doing. If my IQ had been two points lower, I'd have been a plant somewhere." *Lee Trevino*
- "I have a tip that can take 5 strokes off anyone's golf game. It is called an eraser." *Arnold Palmer*
- "Golf is a game whose aim is to hit a very small ball into an even smaller hole, with weapons singularly ill-designed for the purpose." *Winston Churchill*
- "Golf can best be defined as an endless series of tragedies obscured by the occasional miracle." - Anonymous
- "Tee your ball high...air offers less resistance than dirt." *Jack Nicklaus*
- "Why is it that when you tell yourself, 'don't hit it in the water' your body only seems to hear the word 'water'?" *Anonymous*
- "The trees taunt you; the sand mocks you; the water calls your name...and they say golf is a quiet game." *Anonymous*
- "Golf's a hard game to figure. One day you'll go out and slice it and shank it, hit into all the traps and miss every green. The next day you go out and, for no reason at all, you really stink." *Bob Hope*
- "Only a stupid golfer throws his club behind him. The smart golfer throws his club ahead so he can pick it up on the way to the next hole. *Anonymous*
- "Corollary: clubs don't float." *Anonymous*
- "He who has the fastest golf cart never has a bad lie." *Mickey Mantle*

"If there's lightning while you're golfing, take your 2 iron out of your bag and hold it high in the air. For even God can't hit a 2 iron." *Anonymous*

GOTCHAS

One day the club duffer challenged the local golf pro to a match, with a $100 bet on the side. "But," said the duffer, "since you're obviously much better than I am , to even it a bit you have to spot me two 'gotchas'." The golf pro didn't know what a 'gotcha' was, but he went along with it. And off they went. Coming back to the 19th hole, the rest of the club members were greatly amazed to see the golf pro paying the duffer $100. "What happened?" asked one of the members. "Well," said the pro, "I was teeing up for the first hole, and as I brought the club down, the jerk stuck his hand up between my legs and grabbed my balls while yelling 'Gotcha!' Have you ever tried to play 18 holes of golf waiting for the second 'gotcha'?"

DOCTORS ORDERS

Golfer: My doctor says I can't play golf.
Caddy: Ah, he's played with you too, huh?

LONG SHOT

A guy stood over his tee shot for what seemed an eternity. Looking up, looking down, measuring the distance, figuring the wind direction and speed. He was driving his partner nuts. Finally his exasperated partner says, "What's taking so long? Hit the blasted ball!" The guy answers, "My wife is up there watching me from the clubhouse. I want to make this a perfect shot." "Forget it, man-you don't stand a snowball's chance in hell of hitting her from here!"

TOP TEN REASONS GOLF IS BETTER THAN SEX...
(DAVID LETTERMAN)

#10 - A below par performance is considered good.
#9 - You can stop in the middle and have a cheeseburger and a couple of Beers.

#8 - It's much easier to find the sweet spot.

#7 - Foursomes are encouraged.

#6 - You can still make money doing it as a senior.

#5 - Three times a day is possible.

#4 - Your partner doesn't hire a lawyer if you do it with someone else.

#3 - If you live in Florida, you can do it every day.

#2 - You don't have to cuddle with your partner when you're finished.

#1 - If your equipment gets old and rusty, you can replace it.

TOP TEN THINGS THAT SOUND DIRTY IN GOLF BUT AREN'T

10. Nuts...my shaft is bent.
9. After 18 holes I can barely walk.
8. You really whacked the hell out of that sucker.
7. Look at the size of his putter.
6. Keep your head down and spread your legs a bit more.
5. Mind if I join your threesome?
4. Stand with your back turned and drop it.
3. My hands are so sweaty I can't get a good grip.
2. Nice stroke, but your follow through has a lot to be desired.
1. Hold up...I need to wash my balls first.

SPORTS COMMENTARY
(FROM LES POURCIAU - POURCIAU@MEMPHIS.EDU - THE HUMOR DIGEST)

The following are actual quotes by commentators at various sporting events.

Folks, this is perfect weather for today's game. Not a breath of air. (Curt Gowdy)

Arnie Palmer, usually a great putter, seems to be having trouble with his long putt. However, he has no trouble dropping his shorts. (Sports Broadcaster)

Well, either side could win it, or it could be a draw. (Ron Atkinson)

This is Gregoriava from Bulgaria. I saw her snatch this morning and it was amazing. (Pat Glenn - Weightlifting Commentator)

This is really a lovely horse. I once rode her mother. (Ted Walsh- Horse Racing Commentator)

The lead car is absolutely unique, except for the one behind it, which is identical. (Murray Walker)

An inch or two either side of the post and that would have been a goal. (Dave Bassett)

Ardiles strokes the ball like it is part of his own anatomy. (Jimmy Magee, RTE)

I owe a lot to my parents, especially my mother and father. (Greg Norman)

Strangely, in slow motion replay, the ball seemed to hang in the air for even longer. (David Acfield)

Sure there have been injuries and deaths in boxing - but none of them serious. (Alan Minter)

If history repeats itself, I should think we can expect the same thing again. (Terry Venables)

He dribbles a lot and the opposition doesn't like it - you can see it all over their faces. (Ron Atkinson)

Winfield goes back to the wall. He hits his head on the wall and it rolls off! It's rolling all the way back to second base! This is a terrible thing for the Padres. (Jerry Coleman)

...and Ray Illingworth is relieving himself in front of the pavilion. (John Arlott)

Ah, isn't that nice, the wife of the Cambridge president is kissing the cox of the Oxford crew. (Harry Carpenter, Crew / rowing announcer)

The Baltimore Colts are a bright team. It seems that they have their future ahead of them. (Curt Gowdy)

....and later we will have action from the men's coxless pairs. (Sue Barker, Crew/rowing)

I couldn't settle in Italy - it was like living in a foreign country. (Ian Rush)

Julian Dicks is everywhere. It's like they've got eleven Dicks on the field. (Metro Radio)

I would not say he (David Ginola) is the best left winger in the Premiership, but there are none better. (Ron Atkinson)

There goes Juantorena down the back straight, opening his legs and showing his class. (David Coleman)

One of the reasons Arnie [Palmer] is playing so well is that, before each tee-shot, his wife takes out his balls and kisses them. Oh my God, what have I just said? (US TV Commentator)

THE FISHERMAN

A visitor from Buffalo was strolling along the California surf one morning.

During his walk he came upon a fellow, fishing pole clutched in his hands, sound asleep against the side of a huge coastal rock. Just then the pole began to jerk violently.

"Hey, there!" cried the visitor as he roused the fisherman. "Look out there! You have a bite."

"So I do," yawned the drowsy one glancing out at the water. "If you don't mind, will you pull in the line for me?" The visitor, somewhat surprised, did as he was requested.

"Now, mister," continued the fisherman, "put some fresh bait on the hook and cast the line out for me."

Again the visitor complied.

After doing so he turned to the lazy angler. "You know," he declared, "anyone as lazy as you ought to get married and have a son to do these things for him."

"That's a good idea," beamed the fisherman. "Know where I could find a pregnant woman?"

WHAT WOULD YOU BE?

A first-grade teacher explains to her class that she is an Indianapolis Colts fan. She asks her students to raise their hands if they are Colts fans too. Not really knowing what a Colts fan was, but wanting to be liked by their teacher, their hands fly into the air.

There is, however, one exception. Kelly has not gone along with the crowd. The teacher asks her why she has decided to be different. "Because I'm not a Colts fan" she reports.

"Then," asks the teacher," What are you?"

"I'm a Chicago Bears fan," boasts the little girl.

The teacher asks Susie why she is a Bears fan.

"Well, my Dad and Mom are Bears fans, so I'm a Bears fan too," she responds.

"That's no reason," the teacher says. "What if your mom was a moron and your dad was an idiot. What would you be then?"

Kelly smiles and says, "Then I'd be a Colts fan."

Transportation Humor

AIRLINE HUMOR

On a Continental Flight with a very "senior" flight attendant crew, the pilot said, "Ladies and gentlemen, we've reached cruising altitude and will be turning down the cabin lights. This is for your comfort and to enhance the appearance of your flight attendants."

Heard on a Southwest Airline flight: "Ladies and gentlemen, if you wish to smoke, the smoking section on this airplane is on the wing and if you can light 'em, you can smoke 'em."

On landing, the stewardess said, "Please be sure to take all of your belongings. If you're going to leave anything, please make sure it's something we'd like to have."

There may be 50 ways to leave your lover, but there are only 4 ways out of this airplane"

"Thank you for flying Delta Business Express. We hope you enjoyed giving us the business as much as we enjoyed taking you for a ride."

As the plane landed and was coming to a stop at Ronald Reagan, a lone voice came over the loudspeaker: "Whoa, big fella. WHOA!"

After a particularly rough landing during thunderstorms in Memphis, a flight attendant on a Northwest flight announced, "Please take care when opening the overhead compartments because, after a landing like that, sure as hell everything has shifted."

From a Southwest Airlines employee: "Welcome aboard Southwest Flight 245 to Tampa. To operate your seat belt, insert the metal tab into the buckle, and pull tight. It works just like every other seat belt; and, if you don't know how to operate one, you probably shouldn't be out in public unsupervised."

"In the event of a sudden loss of cabin pressure, masks will descend from the ceiling. Stop screaming, grab the mask, and pull it over your face. If you have a small child traveling with you, secure your mask before assisting with theirs. If you are traveling with more than one small child, pick your favorite."

"Weather at our destination is 50 degrees with some broken clouds, but we'll try to have them fixed before we arrive. Thank you, and remember, nobody loves you, or your money, more than Southwest Airlines."

"Your seat cushions can be used for flotation; and, in the event of an emergency water landing, please take them with you with our compliments and paddle to shore."

"As you exit the plane, make sure to gather all of your belongings. Anything left behind will be distributed evenly among the flight attendants. Please do not leave children or spouses."

From the pilot during his welcome message: "Delta Airlines is pleased to have some of the best flight attendants in the industry. Unfortunately, none of them are on this flight!"

Heard on Southwest Airlines just after a very hard landing in Salt Lake City: The flight attendant came on the intercom and said, "That was quite a bump, and I know what y'all are thinking. I'm here to tell you it wasn't the airline's fault, it wasn't the pilot's fault, it wasn't the flight attendant's fault, it was the asphalt."

Overheard on an American Airlines flight into Amarillo, Texas, on a particularly windy and bumpy day: During the final approach, the Captain was really having to fight it. After an extremely hard landing, the Flight Attendant said, "Ladies and Gentlemen, welcome to Amarillo. Please remain in your seats with your seat belts fastened while the Captain taxis what's left of our airplane to the gate!"

Another flight attendant's comment on a less than perfect landing: "We ask you to please remain seated as Captain Kangaroo bounces us to the terminal."

An airline pilot wrote that on this particular flight he had hammered his ship into the runway really hard. The airline had a policy which required the first officer to stand at the door while the passengers exited, smile, and give them a "Thanks for flying our airline." He said that, in light of his bad landing, he had a hard time looking the passengers in the eye, thinking that someone would have a smart comment. Finally everyone had gotten off except for a little old lady walking with a cane.
She said, "Sir, do you mind if I ask you a question?"
"Why, no, Ma'am," said the pilot. "What is it?"
The little old lady said, "Did we land, or were we shot down?"

After a real crusher of a landing in Phoenix, the attendant came on the horn,"Ladies and Gentlemen, please remain in your seats until Captain Crash and the Crew have brought the aircraft to a screeching halt against the gate. And, once the tire smoke has cleared and the warning bells are silenced, we'll open the door and you can pick your way through the wreckage to the terminal."

Part of a flight attendant's arrival announcement: "We'd like to thank you folks for flying with us today. And, the next time you get the insane urge to go blasting through the skies in a pressurized metal tube, we hope you'll think of US Airways."

A plane was taking off from Kennedy Airport. After it reached a comfortable cruising altitude, the Captain made an announcement over the intercom, "Ladies and gentlemen, this is your captain speaking. Welcome to Flight Number 293, nonstop from New York to Los Angeles. The weather ahead is good and, therefore, we should have a smooth and uneventful flight. Now sit back and relax... OH, MY GOD!" Silence followed, and after a few minutes, the captain came back on the intercom and said, "Ladies and Gentlemen, I am so sorry if I scared you earlier. While I was talking to you, the flight attendant accidentally spilled a cup of hot coffee in my lap. You should see the front of my pants!" A passenger in Coach yelled, "That's nothing. You should see the back of mine!"

A mother and her son were flying Southwest Airlines from Kansas City to Chicago. The son (who had been looking out the window) turned to his mother and asked, "If big dogs have baby dogs and big cats have baby cats, why don't big planes have baby planes?" The mother (who couldn't think of an answer) told her son to ask the flight attendant. So the boy asked the flight attendant, "If big dogs have baby dogs and big cats have baby cats, why don't big planes have baby planes?" The flight attendant responded, "Did your mother tell you to ask me?" The boy said, "Yes, she did." "Well, then, tell your mother that there are no baby planes because Southwest always pulls out on time. Have your mother explain that to you."

TURN YOURSELF AROUND

A priest and a pastor from the local churches are standing by the side of the road, pounding a sign into the ground that reads: "The End Is Near! Turn Yourself Around Now -- Before It's Too Late!"

As a car sped past them, the driver yelled, "Leave us alone, you religious nuts!"

From the curve they heard screeching tires and a big splash.

The pastor turns to the priest and asks, "Do you think the sign should just say 'Bridge Out'?"

WINTER STATISTIC

Ninety-eight percent of Americans say, "Oh shit!" before going into a ditch off a slippery road. The other two percent are from Buffalo. They say, "Hold my beer and watch this..."

SOMEWHERE EXPENSIVE

My wife wanted to go somewhere expensive for our anniversary, so I took her down the street to the Sunoco station.

AIR TRAFFIC CONTROL

During a taxi, the crew of a US Air departure flight to Ft. Lauderdale made a wrong turn and came nose- to-nose with a United 727. The irate ground controller (a female) lashed out at the US Air crew screaming, "US Air 2771, where are you going? I told you to turn right on 'Charlie' taxi way; you turned right on 'Delta.' Stop right there. I know it's difficult to tell the difference between a C and a D, but get it right."

Continuing her lashing to the embarrassed crew, she was now shouting hysterically, "You've screwed everything up; it'll take forever to sort this out. You stay right there and don't move until I tell you to. You can expect progressive taxi instructions in about a half hour, and I want you to go exactly where I tell you, when I tell you, and how I tell you. You got that, US Air 2771?"

Naturally, the "ground control" frequency went terribly silent until an unknown male pilot broke the silence and asked, "Wasn't I married to you once?"

THE TRAIN COMPARTMENT

A man and a woman, who have never met before, find themselves assigned to the same sleeping room on a transcontinental train.

Though initially embarrassed and uneasy over sharing a room, the two are tired and fall asleep quickly...he in the upper bunk and she in the lower.

At 1:00 AM, he leans over and gently wakes the woman saying, "Ma'am, I'm sorry to bother you, but would you be willing to reach into the closet to get me a second blanket? I'm awfully cold."

"I have a better idea," she replies. "Just for tonight, let's pretend that we're married."

"Wow! That's a great idea!!" he exclaims.

"Good," she replies. "Get your own damn blanket!"

After a moment of silence, he farted.

AUTO ACCIDENT INSURANCE CLAIMS

The following statements from claim applications were shared in a Toronto newspaper:

- I collided with a stationary bus coming from the opposite direction.
- A pedestrian hit me and went under my car.
- The guy was all over the road. I had to swerve a number of times before I hit him.
- If the other driver had stopped a few yards behind himself, the accident would never have happened.
- In my attempt to kill a fly, I drove into a telephone pole.
- I had been driving my car for forty years when I fell asleep at the wheel and had an accident.
- I was on the way to the doctor's with rear-end trouble when my universal joint gave way, causing me to have an accident.
- My car was legally parked as it backed into the other vehicle.
- I was sure the old fellow would never make it to the other side of the roadway when I struck him.
- The pedestrian had no idea which way to go, so I ran over him.
- The indirect cause of this accident was a little guy in a small car with a big mouth.

- The telephone pole was approaching fast; I was attempting to swerve out of its path when it struck my front end.
- I pulled away from the side of the road, glanced at my mother-in-law, and headed over the embankment.

COMPLAINTS AND RESOLUTIONS

After every flight, Qantas, which has an excellent safety record, each pilot fills out a form called a "gripe sheet" which tells mechanics about problems with the aircraft. The mechanics correct the problems; document their repairs on the form, and then pilots review the gripe sheets before the next flight.

Never let it be said that ground crews lack a sense of humor. Here are some actual maintenance complaints submitted by Qantas pilots (marked with a P) and the solutions recorded (marked with an S) by maintenance engineers.

P: Left inside main tire almost needs replacement.
S: Almost replaced left inside main tire.

P: Test flight OK, except auto-land very rough.
S: Auto-land not installed on this aircraft.

P: Something loose in cockpit.
S: Something tightened in cockpit.

P: Dead bugs on windshield.
S: Live bugs on back-order.

P: Autopilot in altitude-hold mode produces a 200 feet per minute descent.
S: Cannot reproduce problem on ground.

P: Evidence of leak on right main landing gear.
S: Evidence removed.

P: DME volume unbelievably loud.
S: DME volume set to more believable level.

P: Friction locks cause throttle levers to stick.
S: That's what they're for.

P: IFF inoperative.
S: IFF always inoperative in OFF mode.

P: Suspected crack in windshield.
S: Suspect you're right.

P: Number 3 engine missing.
S: Engine found on right wing after brief search.

P: Aircraft handles funny.
S: Aircraft warned to straighten up, fly right, and be serious.

P: Target radar hums.
S: Reprogrammed target radar with lyrics.

P: Mouse in cockpit.
S: Cat installed.

P: Noise coming from under instrument panel. Sounds like a midget pounding on something with a hammer.
S: Took hammer away from midget.

GOOD NEWS

A wife phones up her husband at work for a chat.

Husband: "I'm sorry dear but I'm up to my neck in work today."

Wife: "But I've got some good news and some bad news for you dear."

Husband: "OK darling, but as I've got no time now, just give me the good news."

Wife: "Well, the air bag works."

TIPS FOR STUDENT PILOTS

- Takeoffs are optional. Landings are mandatory.
- If you push the stick forward, the houses get bigger. If you pull the stick back, they get smaller.
- Flying isn't dangerous. Crashing is dangerous.
- A "good" landing is one from which you can walk away. A "great" landing is one from which you can walk away and after which they can use the plane again.
- Learn from the mistakes of others. You won't live long enough to make all of them yourself.
- There are three simple rules for making a smooth landing. Unfortunately, no one knows what they are.
- You start with a bag full of luck and an empty bag of experience. The trick is to fill the bag of experience before you empty the bag of luck.
- Good judgment comes from experience. Unfortunately, experience usually comes from bad judgment.
- There are old pilots and there are bold pilots. There are, however, no old, bold pilots.
- Always try to keep the number of landings you make equal to the number of your takeoffs.

THE LUGGAGE MACHINE

On a recent trip from Boston to Los Angeles, the flight was delayed one hour taking off. There was lots of grumbling on the plane. And as the plane taxied to the run way the pilot came on the intercom and explained the delay as follows. "Good afternoon, this is your pilot, thank you for your patience.

We are sorry for the delay today but the machine that rips the handles off your luggage broke down and in an effort to provide the quality service you have grown to expect we have had to manually rip the baggage handles off, which took us longer."

Verbal Humor

EMPLOYMENT

- My first job was as a tailor but, I wasn't suited for it, mainly because it was a sew-sew job.
- Next I tried working in a muffler factory but, that was too exhausting.
- Then I tried to be a chef - figured it would ad a little spice to my life but, I just didn't have the thyme.
- I attempted to be a deli worker but, any way I sliced it, I couldn't cut the mustard.
- My best job was being a musician but eventually, I found that I wasn't noteworthy.
- I studied a long time to be a doctor but, I didn't have any patience.
- My next job was in a shoe factory; I tried but, I just didn't fit in.
- I became a professional fisherman but, I discovered that I couldn't live on my net income.
- I managed to get a job working for a pool maintenance company but, the work was just too draining.

- So, then I got a job in a workout center but, they said that I wasn't fit for the job.
- After many years of trying to find steady work I finally got a job as a historian until I realized there was no future in it.
- My last job was working at Starbucks but, I had to quit because it was always the same old grind.

SURGERY

Just as a surgeon was finishing up an operation and was about to close, the patient awakes, sits up, and demands to know what is going on. "I'm about to close," the surgeon says.

The patient grabs the surgeon's hand and says, "I'm not going to let you do that! I'll close my own incision!"

The doctor hands him the thread and says, "Suture self".

BAD NOVEL OPENINGS
(SHARED BY THE PUNK WITH THE STUTTER - THE-PUNK-WITH-THE-STUTTER@HOME.COM)

These are the 10 winners of the Bulwer-Lytton contest (run by the English Department of San Jose State University), wherein one writes only the first line of a bad novel:

10. "As a scientist, Throckmorton knew that if he were ever to break wind in the echo chamber he would never hear the end of it."
9. "Just beyond the Narrows the river widens."
8. "With a curvaceous figure that Venus would have envied, a tanned, unblemished oval face framed with lustrous thick brown hair, deep azure-blue eyes fringed with long black lashes, perfect teeth that vied for competition, and a small straight nose, Marilee had a beauty that defied description."
7. "Andre, a simple peasant, had only one thing on his mind as he crept along the East wall: 'Andre creep ... Andre creep ... Andre creep.'"

6. "Stanislaus Smedley, a man always on the cutting edge of narcissism, was about to give his body and soul to a back-alley sex-change surgeon to become the woman he loved."

5. "Although Sarah had an abnormal fear of mice, it did not keep her from eking out a living at a local pet store."

4. "Stanley looked quite bored and somewhat detached, but then penguins often do."

3. "Like an overripe beefsteak tomato rimmed with cottage cheese, the corpulent remains of Santa Claus lay dead on the hotel floor."

2. "Mike Hardware was the kind of private eye who didn't know the meaning of the word 'fear,' a man who could laugh in the face of danger and spit in the eye of death - in short, a moron with suicidal tendencies."

1. "The sun oozed over the horizon, shoved aside darkness, crept along the greensward, and, with sickly fingers, pushed through the castle window, revealing the pillaged princess, hand at throat, crown asunder, gaping in frenzied horror at the sated, sodden amphibian lying beside her.

FRED IS GONE

A bill collector knocked on the door of a country debtor. "Is Fred home?" he asked the woman who answered the door. "Sorry," the woman replied. "Fred's gone for cotton." The next day the collector tried again. "Is Fred here today?" "No, sir," she said, "I'm afraid Fred has gone for cotton." When he returned the third day he humphed, "I suppose Fred is gone for cotton again?" "No," the woman answered solemnly, "Fred died yesterday." Suspicious that he was being avoided, the collector decided to wait a week and investigate the cemetery himself. But sure enough, there was poor Fred's tombstone, with this inscription: "Gone, But Not for Cotton."

GREETING CARDS THAT NEVER MADE IT TO PRINTING (FROM RANDALL WOODMAN - RWOODMAN@ATTBI.COM)

My tire was thumping. I thought it was flat.
When I looked at the tire ...I noticed your cat. Sorry!

You had your bladder removed and you're on the mends.
Here's a bouquet of flowers . . . and a box of Depends.

Looking back over the years that we've been together,
I can't help but wonder . . . What the hell was I thinking?

Congratulations on your wedding day!
Too bad no one likes your husband.

I've always wanted to have someone to hold, someone to love.
After having met you . . . I've changed my mind.

As the days go by, I think of how lucky I am. . . that you're not here
to ruin it for me.

Congratulations on your promotion. Before you go…would you like
to take this knife out of my back?
You'll probably need it again.

Someday I hope to get married . . . but not to you.

So your daughter's a hooker, and it spoiled your day.
Look at the bright side, it's really good pay.

Happy birthday! You look great for your age…Almost Lifelike!

When we were together, you always said you'd die for me.
Now that we've broken up, I think it's time you kept your promise.

I knew the day would come when you would leave me for my best
friend.
So here's his leash, water bowl and chew toys.

Congratulations on your new bundle of joy.
Did you ever find out who the father was?

Heard your wife left you, how upset you must be.
But don't fret about it . . . She moved in with me.

Happy Birthday, Uncle Dad! (Not available in all states)

JUST A STAGE

I had a dream the other night. I was in the old West riding in a stagecoach. Suddenly, a man riding a horse pulls up to the left side of the stagecoach, and a rider less horse pulls up on the right. The man leans down, pulls open the door, and jumps off his horse into the stagecoach. Then he opens the door on the other side and jumps onto the other horse. Just before he rode off, I yelled out, "What was all that about?" He replied, "Nothing. It's just a stage I'm going through."

HEADLINES

- Crack Found on Governor's Daughter
- Something Went Wrong in Jet Crash, Expert Says
- Police Begin Campaign to Run Down Jaywalkers
- Is There a Ring of Debris around Uranus?
- Panda Mating Fails; Veterinarian Takes Over
- Miners Refuse to Work after Death
- Juvenile Court to Try Shooting Defendant
- War Dims Hope for Peace
- If Strike Isn't Settled Quickly, It May Last Awhile
- Cold Wave Linked to Temperatures
- Enfield (London) Couple Slain; Police Suspect Homicide
- Red Tape Holds Up New Bridges
- Man Struck By Lightning: Faces Battery Charge
- New Study of Obesity Looks for Larger Test Group
- Astronaut Takes Blame for Gas in Spacecraft
- Kids Make Nutritious Snacks
- Local High School Dropouts Cut in Half
- Hospitals are Sued by 7 Foot Doctors
- Typhoon Rips Through Cemetery; Hundreds Dead

THE METEOROLOGIST

Although he was a qualified meteorologist, a local broadcaster ran up a terrible record of forecasting for the TV news program. He became something of a local joke when a newspaper began keeping a record of his predictions and showed that he'd been wrong almost three hundred times in a single year. That kind of notoriety was enough to get him fired. He moved to another part of the country and applied for a similar job. One blank on the job application called for the reason for leaving his previous position. In the blank he wrote quite honestly, "The climate didn't agree with me."

CZECHOSLOVAKIAN MIDGET

A Czechoslovakian midget was running through the side streets trying to escape from the secret police. Finally he came to a small cafe and knocked on the door.

"I know it's late," he said to the surprised proprietor. "But is there any chance you could cache a small Czech?"

THE OLDEST TRICK

In a small town in Texas, the local madam operated a telephone service. The police finally arrested her and seized her big black book in which her talent was listed. Each officer on the force was assigned a group of the names in it and told to check them out. After a week, the Chief called a meeting to get their reports. When it became the turn of Officer Ralph to tell what he had found, he said, "I'm sorry, chief, but I think I should disqualify myself. One of the ladies on whom I called is an eighty-four-year-old woman. She is so charming that I have to tell you that I have fallen in love with her." "I don't believe it!" exclaimed the Chief. "I'm sure surprised at you, Ralph. You've been a policeman almost all your life -- and here you are, falling for the oldest trick in the book!"

ANALOGIES AND METAPHORS FOUND IN HIGH SCHOOL ESSAYS

1. Her face was a perfect oval, like a circle that had its two sides gently compressed by a Thigh Master.
2. His thoughts tumbled in his head, making and breaking alliances like underpants in a dryer without Cling Free.
3. He spoke with the wisdom that can only come from experience, like a guy who went blind because he looked at a solar eclipse without one of those boxes with a pinhole in it and now goes around the country speaking at high schools about the dangers of looking at a solar eclipse without one of those boxes with a pinhole in it.
4. She grew on him like she was a colony of E. coli and he was room-temperature Canadian beef.
5. She had a deep, throaty, genuine laugh, like that sound a dog makes just before it throws up.
6. Her vocabulary was as bad as, like, whatever.
7. He was as tall as a six-foot-three-inch tree.
8. The revelation that his marriage of 30 years had disintegrated because of his wife's infidelity came as a rude shock, like a surcharge at a formerly surcharge-free ATM.
9. The little boat gently drifted across the pond exactly the way a bowling ball wouldn't.
10. McBride fell 12 stories, hitting the pavement like a Hefty bag filled with vegetable soup.
11. From the attic came an unearthly howl. The whole scene had an eerie, surreal quality, like when you're on vacation in another city and Jeopardy comes on at 7:00 p.m. instead of 7:30.
12. Her hair glistened in the rain like a nose hair after a sneeze.
13. The hailstones leaped from the pavement, just like maggots when you fry them in hot grease.

14. Long separated by cruel fate, the star-crossed lovers raced across the grassy field toward each other like two freight trains, one having left Cleveland at 6:36 p.m. traveling at 55 mph, the other from Topeka at 4:19 p.m. at a speed of 35 mph.

15. They lived in a typical suburban neighborhood with picket fences that resembled Nancy Kerrigan's teeth.

16. John and Mary had never met. They were like two hummingbirds who had also never met.

17. He fell for her like his heart was a mob informant and she was the East River.

18. Even in his last years, Grand pappy had a mind like a steel trap only one that had been left out so long, it had rusted shut.

19. Shots rang out, as shots are known to do.

20. The plan was simple, like my brother-in-law Phil. But unlike Phil, his plan just might work!

21. The young fighter had a hungry look, the kind you get from not eating for a while.

22. He was as lame as a duck. Not the metaphorical lame duck, either, but a real duck that was actually lame. Maybe from stepping on a land mine or something.

23. The ballerina rose gracefully en Pointe and extended one slender leg behind her, like a dog at a fire hydrant.

24. It was an American tradition, like fathers chasing kids around with power tools.

25. He was deeply in love. When she spoke, he thought he heard bells, as if she were a garbage truck backing up.

26. Her eyes were like limpid pools, only they had forgotten to put in any pH cleanser.

27. She walked into my office like a centipede with 98 missing legs.

28. It hurt the way your tongue hurts after you accidentally staple it to the wall.

BUDDHISM AND CHANGE

A Buddhist Zen master went up to a hot dog vendor at a baseball game and said, "Make me one with everything." When the Zen master paid with a twenty-dollar bill, the hot-dog vendor put the bill in the cash drawer. "Where's my change?" the Zen master asked. "Change must come from within," the hot-dog vendor replied.

VERBAL ONE-LINERS

- The snack bar next door to an atom smasher was called "The Fission Chips."
- On April Fools Day, a mother put a fire cracker under the pancakes. She blew her stack.
- A new chef from India was fired a week after starting the job. He keeps favoring curry.
- A couple of kids tried using pickles for a ping-pong game. They had the volley of the dills.
- The four food groups: Fast, Frozen, Instant and Chocolate.
- A friend got some vinegar in his ear, now he suffers from pickled hearing.
- Overweight is something that just sort of snacks up on you.
- Sign in restaurant window: "Eat now - Pay waiter."
- I thought that you were trying to get into shape? I am. The shape I've selected is a triangle
- Energizer Bunny arrested -- charged with battery.
- A pessimist's blood type is always b-negative.
- I was reading a book on "The History of Glue" and I couldn't put it down.
- Practice safe eating -- always use condiments.
- A Freudian slip is when you say one thing but mean your mother.
- Shotgun wedding: A case of wife or death.
- I used to work in a blanket factory, but it folded.
- If electricity comes from electrons... does that mean that morality comes from morons?

- A hangover is the wrath of grapes.
- Corduroy pillows are making headlines.
- Is a book on voyeurism a peeping tome?
- Dancing cheek-to-cheek is really a form of floor play.
- Banning the bra was a big flop.
- Sea captains don't like crew cuts.
- Does the name Pavlov ring a bell?
- When you dream in color, it's a pigment of your imagination.
- Reading whilst sunbathing makes you well-red.
- When two egotists meet, it's an I for an I.
- Alarms: What an octopus is.
- Dockyard: A physician's garden.
- Incongruous: Where bills are passed.
- Khakis: What you need to start the car in Boston.
- Judicious: Lox and Bagels and Matzo Ball Soup
- Oboe: An English tramp.
- Pasteurize: Too far to see.
- Propaganda: A gentlemanly goose.
- Toboggan: Why we go to an auction
- Police can do a search if it's warranted.
- I signed up for an Origami class, but it folded.
- If you pushed a pig down a hill would he be a sausage roll?
- He showed the apprentice how to lay cement by using a concrete example.
- I went to buy some property with a hill on it, but it was a little steep.

THE MARINA

It was a hot summer's day, and Luke was in the marina, having a few beers aboard his boat, patriotically named the "Fourth of July." He was waiting for his friend, Opie, to arrive so they could go for a cruise.

Opie was late, unfortunately, because he had to pick up his wife from her appointment with the obstetrician. Her examinations were cheap because the doctor, a fellow named Juan, was Opie's cousin.

Anyway, the appointment went over time, and Opie was late getting to the marina. Luke had been drinking all this time, and was feeling no pain. When he saw Opie finally walking down the pier, he jumped up, staggered to the side of the boat to wave to his friend, and nearly fell in!

Opie got there just in time to grab Luke.

Thus, it was that O. B. Juan's kin, Opie, saved Luke from falling to the dock side of the Fourth.

REASONS WHY THE ENGLISH LANGUAGE IS SO HARD TO LEARN

1) The bandage was wound around the wound.
2) The farm was used to produce produce.
3) The dump was so full that it had to refuse more refuse.
4) We must polish the Polish furniture.
5) He could lead if he would get the lead out.
6) The soldier decided to desert his dessert in the desert.
7) Since there is no time like the present, he thought it was time to present the present.
8) A bass was painted on the head of the bass drum.
9) When shot at, the dove dove into the bushes.
10) I did not object to the object.
11) The insurance was invalid for the invalid.
12) There was a row among the oarsmen about how to row.
13) They were too close to the door to close it.
14) The buck does funny things when the does are present.
15) A seamstress and a sewer fell down into a sewer line.
16) To help with planting, the farmer taught his sow to sow.
17) The wind was too strong to wind the sail.
18) After a number of injections my jaw got number.
19) Upon seeing the tear in the painting I shed a tear.
20) I had to subject the subject to a series of tests.
21) How can I intimate this to my most intimate friend?

THE TWINS

A woman has twins, and gives them up for adoption. One of them goes to a family in Egypt, and is named "Amal." The other goes to a family in Spain. They name him "Juan".

Years later, Juan sends a picture of himself to his mom. Upon receiving the picture, she tells her husband that she wishes she also had a picture of Amal. Her husband responds, "But they are twins - if you've seen Juan, you've seen Amal.

MISCELLANEOUS PUNS

Two vultures board an airplane, each carrying two dead raccoons. The stewardess looks at them and says, "I'm sorry, gentlemen, only one carrion allowed per passenger."

Did you hear that NASA recently put a bunch of Holsteins into low earth orbit? They called it the herd shot 'round the world.

Two boll weevils grew up in South Carolina. One went to Hollywood and became a famous actor. The other stayed behind in the cotton fields and never amounted to much. The second one, naturally, became known as the lesser of two weevils.

Two Eskimos sitting in a kayak were chilly, but when they lit a fire in the craft, it sank proving once again that you can't have your kayak and heat it too.

Bill and Dale built a skating rink in the middle of a pasture. One day a shepherd leading his flock decided to take a shortcut across the rink. The sheep, however, were afraid of the ice and wouldn't cross it. Desperate, the shepherd began tugging them to the other side. "Look at that," remarked Bill to Dale. "That guy is trying to pull the wool over our ice!"

A three legged dog walks into a saloon in the Old West. He slides up to the bar and announces: "I'm looking for the man who shot my paw."

Hans and Stein were playing in their yard in Zurich when one of the boys accidentally swallowed a coin and started choking. Hans ran inside to get help, yelling "Mom! Dad! Come quick! There's a franc in Stein!"

Did you hear about the Buddhist who refused Novocain during a root canal? He wanted to transcend dental medication.

A group of chess enthusiasts checked into a hotel and were standing in the lobby discussing their recent tournament victories. After about an hour, the manager came out of the office and asked them to disperse. "But why?" they asked, as they moved off. "Because," he said, "I can't stand chess nuts boasting in an open foyer."

These friars were behind on their belfry payments, so they opened up a small florist shop to raise funds. Since everyone liked to buy flowers from the men of God, a rival florist across town thought the competition was unfair. He asked the good fathers to close down, but they would not. He went back and begged the friars to close. They ignored him. So, the rival florist hired Hugh MacTaggart, the roughest and most vicious thug in town to "persuade" them to close. Hugh beat up the friars and trashed their store, saying he'd be back if they didn't close up shop. Terrified, they did so, thereby proving that: Only Hugh can prevent florist friars.

There was a guy who sent ten different puns to friends, in the hope that at least one of the puns would make them laugh. Unfortunately, no pun in ten did.

QUASIMODO'S REPLACEMENT

After Quasimodo's death, the bishop of the Cathedral of Notre Dame sent word through the streets of Paris that a new bell ringer was needed. The bishop decided that he would conduct the interviews personally and went up into the belfry to begin the screening process. After observing several applicants demonstrate their skills, he had decided to call it a day. Just then, an armless man approached him and announced that he was there to apply for the bell ringer's job. The bishop was incredulous. "You have no arms!"

"No matter," said the man. "Observe!" And he began striking the bells with his face, producing a beautiful melody on the carillon. The bishop listened in astonishment; convinced he had finally found a replacement for Quasimodo. But suddenly, rushing forward to strike a bell, the armless man tripped and plunged headlong out of the belfry window to his death in the street below.

The stunned bishop rushed to his side. When he reached the street, a crowd had gathered around the fallen figure, drawn by the beautiful music they had heard only moments before. As they silently parted to let the bishop through, one of them asked, "Bishop, who was this man?" I don't know his name," the bishop sadly replied, "but his face rings a bell."

QUASIMODO'S REPLACEMENT...CONTINUED

The following day, despite the sadness that weighed heavily on his heart due to the unfortunate death of the armless campanologist, the bishop continued his interviews for the bell ringer of Notre Dame. The first man to approach him said, "Your Excellency, I am the brother of the poor armless wretch that fell to his death from this very belfry yesterday. I pray that you honor his life by allowing me to replace him in this duty. "The bishop agreed to give the man an audition, and, as the armless man's brother stooped to pick up a mallet to strike the first bell, he groaned, clutched at his chest, twirled around and died on the spot.

Two monks, hearing the bishop's cries of grief at this second tragedy, rushed up the stairs to his side. "What has happened? Who is this man?" the first monk asked breathlessly.

"I don't know his name," sighed the distraught bishop, but...He's a dead ringer for his brother."

REAL ADS FROM NEWSPAPERS

- Mixing bowl set designed to please a cook with round bottom for efficient beating.
- Semi-Annual after-Christmas Sale.
- And now, the Superstore--unequaled in size, unmatched in variety, unrivaled inconvenience.
- We will oil your sewing machine and adjust tension in your home for $1.00.
- Girl wanted to assist magician in cutting-off-head illusion. Blue Cross and salary.
- For Sale. Three canaries of undermined sex.
- Get rid of aunts: Zap does the job in 24 hours.
- Christmas tag-sale. Handmade gifts for the hard-to-find person.

REAL LINES FROM HOLLYWOOD SQUARES
(PETER MARSHALL, HOST)

Q. Do female frogs croak?

A. Paul Lynde: If you hold their little heads under water long enough.

Q. If you're going to make a parachute jump, at least how high should you be?

A. Charley Weaver: Three days of steady drinking should do it.

Q. True or False, a pea can last as long as 5,000 years.

A. George Gobel: Boy, it sure seems that way sometimes.

Q. You've been having trouble going to sleep. Are you probably a man or a woman?

A. Don Knotts: That's what's been keeping me awake.

Q. According to Cosmopolitan, if you meet a stranger at a party and you think that he is attractive, is it okay to come out and ask him if he's married.

A. Rose Marie: No; wait until morning.

Q. Which of your five senses tends to diminish as you get older?

A. Charley Weaver: My sense of decency.

Q. In Hawaiian, does it take more than three words to say "I Love You"?

A. Vincent Price: No, you can say it with a pineapple and a twenty.

Q. What are "Do It," "I Can Help," and "I Can't Get Enough"?

A. George Gobel: I don't know, but it's coming from the next apartment.

Q. As you grow older, do you tend to gesture more or less with your hands while talking?

A. Rose Marie: You ask me one more growing old question Peter, and I'll give you a gesture you'll never forget.

Q. Paul, why do Hell's Angels wear leather?
A. Paul Lynde: Because chiffon wrinkles too easily.

Q. Charley, you've just decided to grow strawberries. Are you going to get any during the first year?
A. Charley Weaver: Of course not, I'm too busy growing strawberries.

Q. In bowling, what's a perfect score?
A. Rose Marie: Ralph, the pin boy.

Q. It is considered in bad taste to discuss two subjects at nudist camps. One is politics, what is the other?
A. Paul Lynde: Tape measures.

Q. During a tornado, are you safer in the bedroom or in the closet?
A. Rose Marie: Unfortunately Peter, I'm always safe in the bedroom.

Q. Can boys join the Camp Fire Girls?
A. Marty Allen: Only after lights out.

Q. When you pat a dog on its head he will wag his tail. What will a goose do?
A. Paul Lynde: Make him bark?

Q. If you were pregnant for two years, what would you give birth to?
A. Paul Lynde: Whatever it is, it would never be afraid of the dark.

Q. According to Ann Landers, is there anything wrong with getting into the habit of kissing a lot of people?
A. Charley Weaver: It got me out of the army.

Q. It is the most abused and neglected part of your body, what is it?
A. Paul Lynde: Mine may be abused, but it certainly isn't neglected.

Q. Back in the old days, when Great Grandpa put horseradish on his head, what was he trying to do?
A. George Gobel: Get it in his mouth.

Q. Who stays pregnant for a longer period of time, your wife or your elephant?
A. Paul Lynde: Who told you about my elephant?

Q. When couples have a baby, who is responsible for its sex?
A. Charley Weaver: I'll lend him the car, the rest is up to him.

Q. Jackie Gleason recently revealed that he firmly believes in them and has actually seen them on at least two occasions. What are they?
A. Charley Weaver: His feet.

Q. According to Ann Landers, what are two things you should never do in bed?
A. Paul Lynde: Point and laugh.

RIDDLES (FROM SKEGEL@SOCAL.RR.COM)

What did the farmer use to fix the rip in his pants? *A cabbage patch*
What would you call a grandfather clock? *An old timer.*
Why couldn't the chicken find her eggs *She mislaid them.*
How do trees get on the Internet? *They log in.*
Why do people dislike going to the dentist? *Because he is boring.*

APPROPRIATE ENGLISH

Maury is getting along in years and finds that he is unable to perform sexually. He finally goes to his doctor, who tries a few things, but nothing seems to work.

So the doctor refers him to an American Indian shaman. The shaman says, "I can cure this." That said, he throws a white powder in a flame, and there is a flash with billowing blue smoke. Then he says, "This is powerful medicine. You can use it only once a year. All you have to do is say '123'; it shall rise for as long as you wish!"

Maury then asks, "What happens when it's over, I don't want to continue?"

The shaman replies: "All you or your partner has to say is '1234' and it will go down. But be warned: it will not work again for another full year!"

Maury rushes home, eager to try out his new powers and prowess. That night he is ready to surprise Mrs. Maury. He showers, shaves, and puts on his most exotic shaving lotion. He gets into bed, and lying next to her, says, "123." He suddenly becomes more aroused than any time in his life...just as the medicine man had promised.

Mrs. Maury, who had been facing away, turns over and asks, "What did you say '123' for?"

And that, my friends, is why you should not end a sentence with a preposition.

About the Author

R. BRUCE BAUM, ED.D., CLL

PROFESSOR, BUFFALO STATE COLLEGE
1300 ELMWOOD AVE. BUFFALO, N.Y. 14222

HEAD HONCHO, HUMORCREATIVITY.COM
146 MARINER ST. BUFFALO, N.Y. 14201

880-6299 (MOBILE) (716) 878-4639 (WORK) 885-2045 (HOME)
EMAIL: BAUMRB@BUFFALOSTATE.EDU
HONCHO@HUMORCREATIVITY.COM
WEBSITE: HTTP://WWW.HUMORCREATIVITY.COM

Dr. R. Bruce Baum, a legend in his own mind, is a Professor in the Exceptional Education Department at Buffalo State College and the 'Head Honcho' of *HumorCreativity.Com*. He received degrees from the University of Cincinnati, and Indiana University. In addition to this book, Dr. Baum is author of *How to Motivate Audiences: 121 Warmups, Icebreakers and Activities for Promoting Creative Problem Soving, Teamwork and Laughter, 20 Magic Tricks for the Magically Impaired* (DVD) and *The MEGA Training CD.* He received the *President's Award for Excellence in Teaching* from Buffalo State College. He is a Colleague in the Creative Education Foundation, a leader in the Annual Creative Problem Solving Institute, a member of the International Brotherhood of Magicians, an Ambassador with the Center for Development of Human Services, a member of the Roswell Park Cancer Institute Humor Project, a Certified Laughter Leader and a member of the Association for Applied and Therapeutic Humor. He has traveled to South Africa, Cyprus, Costa Rica, and Singapore to help bring humor, laughter and creativity to those parts of the world. In his spare time, Dr. Baum is a Rocket Scientist, Bronco Rider, Taxidermist, Explorer, Brain Surgeon and Gourmet.

CPSIA information can be obtained
at www.ICGtesting.com
Printed in the USA
FFOW04n1936030717
37449FF